Beyond Her Sphere

BARBARA J. HARRIS

Beyond Her Sphere
WOMEN AND THE PROFESSIONS IN AMERICAN HISTORY

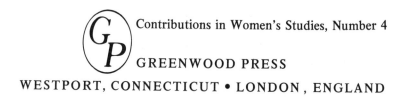

Contributions in Women's Studies, Number 4

GREENWOOD PRESS

WESTPORT, CONNECTICUT • LONDON, ENGLAND

Library of Congress Cataloging in Publication Data

Harris, Barbara, 1942-
 Beyond her sphere.

 (Contributions in women's studies; no. 4 ISSN 0147-
104X)
 Based on a series of lectures given at Pace University.
 Bibliography: p.
 Includes index.
 1. Women—United States—Addresses, essays, lectures.
2. Professions—United States—Addresses, essays,
lectures. 3. Women—Employment—United States—Addresses, essays, lectures. I. Title. II. Series.
HQ1410.H37   301.41'2'0973   78-4017
ISBN 0-313-20415-2

Library of Congress Catalog Card Number: 78–4017
ISBN: 0–313–20415–2
ISSN: 0147–104X

First published in 1978

Greenwood Press, Inc.
51 Riverside Avenue, Westport, Connecticut 06880

Printed in the United States of America

10 9 8 7 6 5 4 3 2 1

To Mildred Campbell and Evelyn A. Clark
of Vassar College, with deepest appreciation
for their inspiration, support, and friendship

Contents

Preface

In September 1974, Pace University inaugurated a Career Management Program for Women, generously funded by the Mellon Foundation. The program, designed for college graduates who had received the B.A. degree, combined the traditional M.B.A. with a six-month internship. Sandra Ekberg-Jordan, director of the program, asked me to deliver a series of lectures on the history of professional women in America to the first class. The audience received them most enthusiastically and encouraged me to revise them for publication. This book is the result.

The problem of the professional female in the United States is inextricably connected to the whole history of women in this country. The position of American women is in turn closely related to the history of women in European civilization. Therefore, these lectures provide a synthesis and general interpretation of the position and role of females in Western society, focusing particularly on those aspects of women's history that bear directly on the experience of females with professional and intellectual aspirations.

Although my subject has necessitated that I deal with an enormous range of topics through a very long period of time, it also excludes certain aspects of women's history. The great majority of professional females in this country are and have been middle-class and white.

Therefore, I am mostly concerned in this book with white, middle-class women and with those aspects of European and American social history intimately related to their lives. I pay little attention, for instance, to women in the trade unions because they are peripheral to my subject. I have tried, however, to be sensitive to issues of class and race and to show how the women with whom I am concerned fit into the larger and more complex society in which they live.

I wish to thank my husband, Joel B. Harris, who listened to the first version of these lectures, often in the wee hours of the morning, and offered both encouragement and criticism. I would also like to express my deepest appreciation to two colleagues and friends, Rosalind Rosenberg of Columbia University and Jean Yellin of Pace University, who read an earlier version of this book and spent hours discussing both subject matter and organization with me. I know how busy they both are and feel real gratitude for the time that they gave to my work. The staff of the Pace University Library assisted me in innumerable ways while I was preparing the final manuscript of this book. Thanks go especially to Janice Axton for her invaluable and willing help. Finally I wish to thank my typist, Barbara Egidi, for her competent and cheerful help in putting my manuscript into its final form. I assume full responsibility for all remaining errors and omissions.

Barbara J. Harris

Beyond Her Sphere

I

An Ideology of Inferiority: The Inheritance of Europe

From a historical point of view, the problem of the professional woman in the United States is one segment of the total problem of the position and role of the female in Western civilization. When American women first demanded equal access to the professions, well over a century ago, they confronted two widely held social prejudices. One was the belief that females were intellectually inferior to males and, therefore, rightfully kept in a subordinate position. They were excluded from the professions because they were unfit for any vocation that relied predominantly on mental abilities or on the capacity to make decisions and direct others. The second prejudice held that respectable women should not work outside the home, an idea central to the Victorian cult of domesticity.

The first of these attitudes is by far the older and more deeply rooted in our culture. It did not originate in this country, but goes back instead to the fusion of the classical, Christian, and Germanic traditions in the early Middle Ages that gave birth to Western European civilization. When the first settlers crossed the Atlantic, they carried with them, along with their theology, political ideas, and more material possessions, the conviction that women were inferior.

In medieval culture, the primary source of ideas proclaiming the inferiority, wickedness, and necessary subjection of women was Catho-

lic theology. [1] In the first centuries of the church's existence, Christian
thinkers had created a misogynous ideology out of the Judaic and
classical traditions that formed the basis of Catholic ideas on the
subject.

Saint Paul, the real founder of the church, was the first Christian
misogynist. Paul insisted relentlessly that God commanded woman to
be totally subject to man. This was her punishment for bringing sin
into the world and tempting Adam to eat of the forbidden fruit. He
proved her inferiority further by reference to the story of Creation:
Adam was created in God's image; Eve, only later, out of Adam's rib,
almost as an afterthought. "Wives, submit yourselves unto your own
husbands, as unto the Lord. For the husband is the head of the wife,
even as Christ is the head of the church. . . ."[2] "Let not a woman to
teach, nor to usurp authority over the man, but to be in silence. For
Adam was formed, then Eve. And Adam was not deceived, but the
woman being deceived was in the transgression."[3] In Saint Paul's
account, Adam's guilt was washed away as surely as if he had passed
through the purifying waters of the River Jordan, and Eve was left to
bear the responsibility for the Fall of Man alone. Furthermore, Paul
neatly glossed over the fact that the first book of Genesis contains two
different stories of the Creation. One is the version that he used to
support his doctrines about the subordination of women. The other
says that God created man and woman together in His image. In the
latter version Eve was not an afterthought or less godlike than Adam.

Following in Paul's footsteps, the early church fathers deepened
and broadened the misogynous current in Christian thought. In the
second century, Saint Clement proclaimed that every woman should
be overwhelmed with shame at the very thought that she was a
woman. In a treatise entitled *On the Apparel of Women*, Tertullian
said that women should dress in mourning to expiate Eve's sin and
should wear veils to avoid tempting men. All of the patristic writers
seemed to be obsessed with woman as the Eternal Seductress. They
had little confidence that men would be any more successful than
Adam in resisting her wiles. This emphasis stemmed from the strong
ascetic influence on the early church and the concomitant assertion
that chastity was the most perfect expression of the Christian life. The
fathers projected all their fears—that men could not, or would not,

live up to the celibate ideal—onto women, who, as the daughters of Eve, were destined to repeat forever the betrayal of mankind.

The high value placed on chastity inevitably redounded to the disadvantage of the institution of marriage. Both Saint Jerome and Saint Augustine placed it third along the scale of Christian purity: first came absolute virginity; second, incomplete and belated chastity after marriage or widowhood; and third, matrimony itself.[4] Here again the fathers took their cue from Saint Paul:

> Now concerning the things which you wrote unto me: It is good for a man not to touch a woman. Nevertheless, to avoid fornication, let every man have his own wife, and let every woman have her own husband. . . . For I would that all men were even as I myself. . . . I say therefore to the unmarried and widows, It is good for them if they abide even as I. But if they cannot contain, let them marry: for it is better to marry than burn.[5]

The evolution of attitudes toward marriage in Western society is itself a long and fascinating story that I can only touch on briefly here. Nonetheless, the negative impact of Christian thinking is worth mentioning, since it deprecates the central institution in most women's lives and was a direct outgrowth of hostility toward the female sex.

In the high Middle Ages, Catholic philosophers incorporated portions of ancient philosophy, particularly Aristotelianism, into Christian theology. Aristotle's doctrines on women reinforced the negative attitudes toward women that originated in the patristic period. In deceptively scientific terms, Aristotle stated as fact certain ideas that were embedded in Christian thought on theological grounds. The convergence of theology and philosophy, of revelation and science, made the ideas all that much more persuasive and increased their hold over the medieval mind. In *The Generation of Animals*, Aristotle explained the process of reproduction and carefully differentiated between the male and female roles. According to Aristotle, the mother's function is completely passive: she supplies the matter for the child's body and serves as an incubator until the time of birth. The father, on the other hand, plays an active role, initiating the process with his semen and giving the child his form or soul. Since all matter moves from incompleteness toward its form and since the human form comes from the male, all children should, logically speaking, be boys.

There are, however, cases of deviation or deformity, and woman is one of them, albeit one required by nature for the preservation of the species. Given this biological doctrine, it is not surprising that Aristotle regarded the domination of man over woman as part of the natural hierarchy or that he allotted her, in keeping with her lower position, a smaller portion of either reason or moral virtue.[6]

It was on these foundations that Western European culture built its conception of women. For a millennium or more these assumptions and judgments went virtually unchallenged. It would be tedious to follow the ramifications of these ideas in medieval thought in great detail, but it might be useful to see what Thomas Aquinas, the greatest medieval Catholic thinker, made of them. In discussing the creation of woman, Saint Thomas was caught between his reverent inclination to judge the whole creation, God's handiwork, as good and the Aristotelian idea that woman, part of that work, was a deformity, weaker than man in body and mind and more inclined to sin. One can feel the tension in his solution: from an individual point of view, the female was defective and misbegotten; but from that of the species, she was essential and desirable, since she helped man procreate and freed him for intellectual activities. Woman's only purpose was marriage and reproduction, while man was created for nobler purposes. The subjection of woman was the direct consequence of sin. Yet, even Eve's guilt in the Fall did not undermine Aquinas's conviction that her creation was both necessary and good. Without her there would have been no occasion for sin, and the universe would have been imperfect because incomplete.

On a less elevated philosophical plane, a story recounted by a fifteenth-century English mystic, Richard Rolle, illustrates the pervasive effect and demeaning implications of Christian attitudes toward women. Rolle told of a woman who spent her life enclosed in a tomb and had her food passed to her through a small hole so that no one could see or hear her. After many years someone asked her why she hid herself. She replied that her beauty once tempted a young man and injured his soul. She preferred to live in a tomb, rather than hurt anyone else created in God's image. Rolle's reaction was to exclaim, "Lo! so perfectly a woman lived."[7]

Some scholars maintain that the cult of the Virgin Mary and the literature of courtly love, both twelfth- and thirteenth-century developments, modified and counteracted the anti-feminism of medieval thought. This is certainly one of the themes of Henry Adams's brilliant work, *Mont St. Michel and Chartres*.[8] Nonetheless, despite Adam's persuasiveness and the superficial plausibility of this view, I think it quite misses the mark.

The cult of Mary was essentially a cult of virginity: Mary was pure because she was a virgin; she was a virgin because she was pure. She performed miracles to save the chastity of those who called on her and sought forgiveness for pentitents who had lost theirs. The problem is that the whole celibate ideal was connected from the beginning with hostility to and fear of women, although in theory it was equally pertinent to both sexes.[9] The church fathers consistently combined their praise of virgins with hatred of women in general.[10] Medieval literature was certainly filled with the tales of female saints and holy maidens who willingly faced disapproval, torture, and death to preserve their chastity. Nonetheless, a subtle difference between them and comparable male figures exists. The threat to the women came from Romans or pagans who wanted them to surrender their maidenhood as a sign of abjuring Christianity or from parents who wanted their daughters to marry. In the latter category, one thinks of Saint Clare secretly stealing from her home to join Saint Francis, and of Saint Catherine of Siena, whose family recognized her vocation only after a long, fruitless struggle to compel her to marry. The case of male saints and holy figures was often quite different. Temptation came to them not in the form of particular threats to their celibacy, such as the women faced, but as the more diffuse danger that came from living in a world inhabited by women, whose very existence bred sin and corruption. Saint Jerome, Saint Anthony, Saint Benedict, and the early hermits literally fled into the wilderness to avoid them. Origen castrated himself to escape danger.[11]

The medieval gloss on the stories of Jacob's daughter Dinah and of David and Bathsheba is illuminating in this respect. A Shechemite raped Dinah when she went out to see the countryside. In revenge her brothers slew all the males of the Shechemite city. To escape the wrath of other Canaanite peoples, Jacob and his family then fled. The *Ancren Riwle*, written in the twelfth century, blames Dinah for all these disasters, because she started the chain of events by allowing herself to be seen.[12] In the second story, David committed adultery with Bathsheba after spying on her in her bath. When Bathsheba became pregnant, he sent her husband Uriah to the front lines of battle so that he would be killed. Then he married Bathsheba himself. Again, medieval writers blamed Bathsheba for tempting David and cited the incident to illustrate the fact that women ruin men.[13] Interestingly, this was not the interpretation in the Old Testament, in which God blamed and punished David.[14]

The whole cult of celibacy and the Virgin was built on the fundamental Christian assumption that woman is the temptress, man the tempted. As the object of male temptation, woman came to be regarded as its cause.[15] This was one of the few instances in which medieval thought assigned man the more passive role. Mary, a woman, symbolized virginity, but that did not alter this reality. Indeed, since she was totally unique, the Mother of God, there was no logical reason why her cult should redound to the benefit of her sex.[16] The whole ideal of celibacy had to be discarded before the perception of females could change much for the better.[17]

The cult of the Virgin also raised problems more concrete than the rather conceptual ones that I have been discussing. Despite its emphasis on chastity as an ideal for men and women and its encouragement of the cult of Mary, the church made comparatively little effort to provide ways for women to pursue the ideal. The obvious place for females dedicated to celibacy was a convent. Yet, comparatively few convents existed, and they were rather small. In 1216, for example, England had 3,000 nuns in 140 convents, compared to 6,200 monks in 340 religious houses for men.[18] Ironically, the high Middle Ages, which saw the cult of Mary rise to its all-time height, also saw the disappearance of the influential abbesses characteristic of the early Middle Ages and the rapid spread of two orders, the Cluniac and Cistercian, which excluded women.[19] In any case, men with the vocation for celibacy did not have to become monks. They could also be priests, canons, or friars, all alternatives closed to females. Anyone living in the Middle Ages, therefore, saw many more men than women pursuing the highest form of Christian life, a confirmation of what everyone surely already knew about the relative worth of the two sexes.

The idea of courtly love was no more effective than the worship of the Virgin in significantly moderating the anti-feminism of medieval culture.[20] Historians do not agree on the function of courtly love in medieval culture or on the extent to which the lyric poetry and romances that have come down to us reflect social reality. [21] If nothing else, this literature certainly expresses the aspirations or anxieties of a segment of the feudal aristocracy. The essence of courtly love was a passionate, even obsessive, love between a man and woman who were not married to each other. [22] Courtly love could not exist between husband and wife because it depended on absolute freedom. Typically, the man in this relationship was a young, single knight, handsome, pious, courteous, and brave. The object of his passion was almost always a married woman and a member of a higher social class, thus doubly unattainable. The intensity, purity, and single-mindedness of the knight's love inspired him to great deeds—either to win the attention and affection of his lady or, once he had, to please her. To be consumed by such a passion was to be transformed and elevated. For once in the Middle Ages, love between the sexes was something to aspire to. In strict theory, this love existed primarily on the emotional plane, with the lady conferring few favors on her lover. Even in literature, however, the theory broke down, and sooner or later most of these passions became physical and adulterous. [23]

The ideals of courtly love conflicted sharply with traditional Christian standards by recommending an all-embracing passion besides the love of God, insisting that it be adulterous, and according the woman a much more active and dominant role in the relationship than medieval writers usually approved. Nonetheless, romance literature itself contained internal evidence that the ideals of courtly love did not transform or replace older cultural values. The great romance cycles all ended in tragedy and death. Guinevere's adultery with Lancelot led inexorably to the death of King Arthur and end of the Round Table. Tristan and Isolde were trapped in a hopeless passion after they mistakenly drank a love potion together, which Isolde's mother had prepared for her to share with King Mark on her wedding night. As the lovers foresaw, their passion resulted in sorrow, guilt, and death. [24]

Even more to the point, some of the literature itself used courtly love as a basis for launching further attacks on females. Andreas Capellanus's treatise entitled *The Art of Courtly Love* contained elaborate instructions for conducting a love affair. It ended with an extended diatribe against women, called "The Rejection of Love." In the second part of the *Roman de la Rose*, one of the most popular works of the later Middle Ages, Jean de Meung urged the lover to withdraw his allegiance from love, satirized marriage, and savagely attacked women. In her analysis of such literature Joan Ferrante has made some interesting observations about adultery in the romance cycle. She notes that in love triangles, when a man was caught between two women, he did not normally commit adultery, and a way might even be found for him to marry both. The two women usually represented different aspects of his aspirations. When a woman was caught between two men, however, she betrayed her husband and involved her lover in a conflict of loyalty. She represented destructive passion. Tristan was an ostensible exception because he married and, technically, also committed adultery. However, Ferrante maintains that the story treats only Isolde's adultery as such. [25] Whatever its impact on a small elite, the literature of courtly love was much too ambivalent in its attitude toward women to undermine the deeply rooted misogyny of medieval culture.

The first full-scale attack on this tradition came during the Renaissance. The humanists, who defined and spread the outlook of that period, challenged accepted notions about feminine intellectual inferiority. Whether their ideas stemmed from self-interest, from the fact that they found women in the upper class as receptive to their cultural program and pleas for patronage as men, or from more disinterested motives is not clear. What is clear is that for the first time in centuries an influential group of intellectuals maintained that women would benefit from approximately the same education as men and ought to have it. In a famous essay on women's education, Leonardo Bruni recommended that women study Latin and then read the early Christian writers and classical authors such as Cicero, Virgil, Livy, and Sallust. [26] They should have a modest proficiency in arithmetic, geometry, and astrology and be thoroughly grounded in history and poetry. The only subject in the humanist curriculum that Bruni considered inappropriate for women was rhetoric: it was "absolutely outside the province of woman." He felt, on the other hand, that religion and morals were particularly suitable for them. The two most famous humanist schools in Italy, Vittorino da Feltre's at Mantua and Guarino da Verona's at Ferrara, were open to both sexes. [27]

Humanist ideas about women gained acceptance during the Italian

Renaissance because they suited the life-style emerging among members of the economic and social elite. This aristocracy demonstrated its superior status through its intellectual and cultural activities and increasingly regarded an ill-educated wife or daughter as a sign of social inferiority. An unrefined or unlearned woman had no place in the atmosphere of self-conscious intellectualism and cultivation that flourished in aristocratic palaces and villas. The female's social success depended much too closely on her cultural and intellectual qualities for her father to neglect her education. In many families the wife actually played a more important role in artistic and literary patronage than her husband.

Still another factor facilitating the spread of humanist ideas about women was that their reevaluation of female intelligence and education did not lead them to redefine woman's role in society as a whole. The humanists expected the polished and erudite women that they educated to marry husbands chosen by their fathers and to be obedient wives. Thus, these women added luster to the courts of Renaissance Italy without challenging deeply engrained notions about the subjection of women. [28]

Within this conservative context the Italian humanists opened the debate about the nature and character of females, which has gone on intermittently ever since. Once women emerged as patrons and models of learning, the arguments used to support medieval ideas about the wickedness and inferiority of women came under attack. Females played an important and independent enough role in Renaissance culture to ensure that. Perhaps the most lucid, and certainly one of the most widely read, discussions of the subject appeared in Castiglione's *Book of the Courtier*.[29] The *Courtier* is a dialogue, set at the court of Urbino, one of the most famous in Renaissance Italy, in which the participants discussed the qualities found in the perfect courtier and court lady. In book three, which deals with women, Guiliano d'Medici and Gasparo Pallavicino argue about female nature. Castiglione showed d'Medici, who defended women, as having the better of the argument.

D'Medici asserted women's intellectual equality, and even superiority, to men. He totally rejected the Aristotelian notion of woman as an accident of nature, on the basis that she is essential to the preservation of the species. Although he recognized both physical and personality differences between the sexes, he regarded these differences as a sign of the female's perfect adaptation to her special function, motherhood, rather than as a sign of her inferiority. That she lived longer than men might even indicate her physical superiority. On a very novel ground he rejected the theological position that women; as descendants of Eve, are the source of evil and human misery: "Do you not know that this very transgression was repaired by a Woman, who brought us so much greater gain than the other had done us damage that the sin that was atoned by such merits is called most fortunate?" He asserted that for every admirable man whom Pallavicino cited he could show a woman of equal or greater merit. He also denied that women were more unchaste than men or more responsible for sexual sin: every woman who sinned needed an equally guilty man. Nor did he accept Pallavicino's defense of the double standard; men had invented it for their own convenience and pleasure. When Pallavicino claimed—as proof of female inferiority—that most women want to be men, d'Medici lightly turned the argument aside with the reply that this simply reflected their natural desire to escape the authority that men unilaterally exercised over them. Castiglione left very little of the medieval position on females intact. [30]

By the sixteenth century the Renaissance spread across the Alps, carrying with it humanist ideas about female education and Castiglione's *Book of the Courtier*. The ruling families of Northern Europe were soon producing learned and cultivated women in every way equal to their Italian counterparts, a group that included Catherine of Aragon, Marguerite of Navarre, Renée of Ferrara, Lady Jane Grey, and Elizabeth I of England. In the latter country the passion for learning extended somewhat down the social scale to women in the untitled, but well-to-do, classes. Here the most distinguished were the daughters of Sir Thomas More and Sir Anthony Cooke. [31] Indeed, living in More's household and becoming acquainted with his eldest daughter, Margaret, finally convinced Erasmus that women should have first-rate educations. In Lyons, France, women who belonged to the urban elite usually had a vernacular education, though very few of them were educated in Latin. Women from this class organized important literary salons in Paris, Lyons, and Poitiers. [32]

The English took up the debate over women with an enthusiasm that inspired an incredible amount of writing in the second half of the sixteenth century and the first decades of the seventeenth. With little effort I have collected the titles of fifty pamphlets, books, and plays that contributed to the controversy, as well as of twenty-four works on marriage and the duties of wives, which were related directly or peripherally to the debate. This bibliography, no doubt, is far from complete. The English controversialists never resolved the questions that they raised: Are females good or bad? Are they as intelligent as men? Nonetheless, their arguments ended the unanimity about these issues that characterized the Middle Ages.

It is difficult to come to any final conclusions about the impact of the Renaissance on traditional attitudes toward women. Certainly, misogynous ideas never held unchallenged sway in Europe again. From that time on, the debate about females broke out periodically. Those who defended them frequently cited the admirable women of the Renaissance elite to prove that females were both intelligent and virtuous.

In the seventeenth century, humanist ideas about educating women became much less influential. In both England and France the learned lady had difficulty in establishing herself.[33] The educational ideal of the précieuses, the women active in Parisian salons in the seventeenth century, was quite limited in its intellectual content. Yet these women and their supporters were the most vocal advocates of an active role for women.[34] In England fewer females studied Latin, although it was still the basis of education for males. Anne Clifford's father forbade her to study foreign languages, although he prescribed a serious curriculum including literature in translation, science, and history. Ralph Verney expressed horror when his goddaughter, Ann Denton, reported that she hoped to learn Latin, Greek, and Hebrew. He wrote to her immediately to squelch the idea. One of the most brilliant women in seventeenth-century England, Margaret Cavendish, Duchess of Newcastle, received the kind of training that one normally associates with a second-rate finishing school. Significantly, Margaret herself defended male superiority in print: "For nature has made man's body more able to endure labor, and man's brain more clear to understand and contrive than woman's, and as great a difference there is between them, as there is between the longest and strongest willow, compared to the strongest and largest oak."[35] The only English woman in the period whose education even approached humanist standards was Lucy Hutchinson. According to her own account, she received her outstanding training because a dream during pregnancy had convinced her mother that she was carrying a prodigy. She studied Latin and French thoroughly and knew some Greek and Hebrew. As a child, she read incessantly, which pleased her father, but worried her mother. Her mother complained that she neglected such feminine accomplishments as dancing, needlework, and music.

The declining emphasis on giving women a rigorous education aroused some protest toward the end of the seventeenth century. Daniel Defoe and Mary Astell recommended the foundation of a woman's college in England. In France, the Abbe Fénelon complained about the pervasive ignorance of women. Louis XIV's second wife, Madame de Maintenon, founded a school for girls at Saint-Cyr. That the curriculum was considered an improvement says a great deal about the state of female education. It consisted of reading, writing, arithmetic, geography, mythology, poetry, deportment, dancing, and needlework. There was no Latin, and all book learning took second place to building Christian character.

Blame for the deterioration of upper-class women's education in the seventeenth century is frequently placed on the Protestant Reformation, a movement that ran parallel to the Renaissance in the sixteenth century and was a major influence in that century and the next. Protestantism was a religion based on the Bible, its theology drawn particularly from Saint Paul. This led, so the argument runs, to a renewed emphasis on the inferiority, wickedness, and subjection of women.[36] Many Protestant pronouncements on females certainly sounded like direct descendants of those in the Bible and the writings of the church fathers and give credence to this theory. The difficulty with this explanation is that humanist ideas about education lost influence in Catholic as well as Protestant countries. In any case, Pauline theology, with its emphasis on the inferiority and subjection of women, was an integral part of Catholic theology both before and after the Reformation. Clearly, therefore, something other than Protestantism was responsible for the decline of the Renaissance ideal of the educated woman.

The general weakening of humanist cultural ideals in the century and a half after the outbreak of both the Catholic and the Protestant reform movements was certainly a major factor. Leaders in both camps increasingly denigrated secular learning and insisted that only religious knowledge was desirable or necessary. For many post-Reformation thinkers, questions relating to the salvation of the soul were as central and exclusive of all other concerns as they had been to their medieval predecessors. By the late sixteenth century—certainly by the beginning of the seventeenth—these currents influenced the intellectual and educational environment. In England, for example, the Puritans fulminated against the literature and music that are regarded as the glory of the Elizabethan and Jacobean periods.

An even more fundamental reason for the decline of Renaissance ideas about female intellectual ability and education was the disjunction between these ideas and the reality of women's lives. The fact that humanists did not advocate changing the role of women made it easier for their views to win initial acceptance. However, a society that continued to treat women as the property of their fathers and husbands found it difficult to think of them as intellectual equals. Social reality, which did not change during the Renaissance or for centuries afterwards, confined humanist ideas about educating women to a narrow elite from the beginning and, in the long run, made them untenable even there.

The impact of Protestant attitudes toward women is even more difficult to assess than that of humanist ideas. In the short run, the renewed reliance on Saint Paul perpetuated and gave new life to traditional misogyny. At the same time, Protestant clergymen advocated a minimal literacy for males and females because they insisted on the priesthood of all believers and the necessity of each individual's ability to interpret the Bible. Wallace Notestein maintains that there was an impressive increase in female literacy in England between 1580 and 1650.[37] Carol Lougee has noted that although women's literacy rose in the early modern period, their position vis-à-vis men actually deteriorated because men's literacy rose so much more. The gap between the sexes increased, and women's experience became increasingly different from men's.[38] Without exaggerating the immediate impact of this aspect of Protestantism, it should be clear that sooner or later this religious environment would produce women who used their biblical learning to attack the church's teaching on women.

The other central Protestant doctrine that had enormous implications for women was the total rejection of the celibate ideal, an ideal that was intimately connected to the fundamental misogyny of European culture. When they eliminated the monastery, Protestant theologians redefined the home as a school for character and as the place for cultivating the gentler Christian virtues formerly associated with members of religious orders.[39] Protestant theologians insisted on a positive duty to marry and form a godly household, which they viewed as the smallest unit in the Christian commonwealth. The family was a crucial institution in providing the discipline and instruction necessary to sanctify individuals and to prepare them for the conversion experience at the heart of early Protestantism. The Protestant—particularly the Calvinist—insistence on using institutions to discipline and control individuals is comparable to the process in early modern France that Philippe Ariès discusses in *Centuries of Childhood*. Ariès sees the emergence of the idea of childhood, the evolution of new authoritarian schools, and the changes in the structure of the family as part of a larger process in which a small elite of educators, churchmen, and royal bureaucrats struggled to impose order on the chaotic society inherited from the Middle Ages. What Ariès is saying in the largest sense is that modernization involved extending institutional control over individual behavior.[40] In this context, Protestant ideas about the family can be seen as another aspect of modernization.

Given their views about the family, Protestants considered matrimony a positive good, rather than a mere means to perpetuate the human race and provide an outlet for lust. Within marriage, the relationship between man and wife should be that of partners. Although it was a partnership between unequals and the woman was expected to obey her husband, the ideal marriage entailed mutual respect and sharing of responsibility.[41] This conception had the potential of generating the idea that the partners in matrimony were and ought to be equals. It was not inevitable that Protestant views of marriage would evolve in that direction, but they were more likely to do so than were attitudes framed in the context of Catholic theology.[42]

When the English colonists settled in North America, they brought with them both traditional ideas about the inferiority and subjection of women and newer Protestant attitudes toward literacy and marriage. During the seventeenth century, the older misogynous tradition was much in evidence. Ministers from Massachusetts to the Carolinas thundered the words of Saint Paul from the pulpit with depressing regularity. John Winthrop, first governor of the Massachusetts Bay Colony, made the following entry in his journal in 1645:

> Mr. Hopkins, the governor of Hartford upon Connecticut, came to Boston, and brought his wife with him, (a godly young woman, and of special parts,) who was fallen into a sad infirmity, the loss of her understanding and reason, which had been growing upon her divers years, by occasion of her giving herself wholly to reading and writing, and had written many books. Her husband, being very loving and tender of her, was loath to grieve her; but he saw his error, when it was too late. For if she had attended her household affairs, and such things as belong to women, and not gone out of her way and calling to meddle in such things as are proper for men, whose minds are stronger, etc., she had kept her wits. . . .[43]

The trial of Anne Hutchinson was equally revealing. Mrs. Hutchinson was accused both of heresy and of taking a more active role in religion than suited a woman. Early in her trial, Governor Winthrop accused her of being "a woman that hath had a great share in the promoting and divulging of those opinions that are causes of this trouble. . . . you have maintained a meeting and an assembly in your house that hath been condemned by the general assembly as a thing not tolerable nor comely in the sight of God nor fitting for your sex. . . .[44] This issue kept recurring throughout the proceedings. Hutchinson defended herself by referring to "a clear rule in Titus, that the elder women should instruct the younger and then I must have a time wherein I must do it." Winthrop countered, "But you must take it in this sense that elder women must instruct the younger about their business and to love their husbands and not to make them to clash." The official attitude toward females who held independent theological views was well expressed by the governor's ill-humored remark, "We do not mean to discourse with those of your sex. . . ."[45]

Not only did Anne Hutchinson step boldly out of the prescribed feminine role, but she also threatened the sexual order in family, church, and state by appealing to large numbers of women. Both Ben Barker-Benfield and Lyle Koehler have argued convincingly that women used antinomianism to express their discontent with their subordinate role and the restrictive definition of acceptable female behavior.[46] Unusually large numbers of women ran into trouble with the religious and secular authorities for deviant behavior, some of it criminal, during the years of crisis. [47]

Despite the Protestant doctrine that every believer should be able to read Scripture, educating girls was evidently a much lower priority than educating boys in early colonial society. Even when girls were taught to read, which allowed them to fulfill their religious obligations, they often did not learn to write. [48] In her study of women in the southern colonies, Julia Spruill focused on the total inadequacy of female education. She estimated that only a third of the women could sign their names, compared to 60 percent of the men. [49] In colonial New England, the gap between female and male literacy actually increased, because the public schools discriminated against girls. Among the first generation of settlers about half of the men and a third of the women could sign their names. By the end of the colonial period, the proportion of men reached 80 percent or more, while female literacy stagnated at the level of 40 to 45 percent. [50]

Colonial ideas about women and the family were less uncompromisingly misogynous than Winthrop's pronouncements at Anne Hutchinson's trial or the colonial record on educating women might lead one to expect. A recent survey of ministerial literature between 1668 and 1735 shows that some clergymen emphasized the spiritual equality of the sexes rather than Eve's guilt for original sin. They projected an androgynous vision of piety and virtue. This tendency was particularly pronounced after 1700, most notably in the sermons of Cotton Mather. [51]

Edmund Morgan's classic study, *The Puritan Family*, emphasizes that the Puritans thought of matrimony in terms of companionship, a remedy for human loneliness, and a partnership between husband and wife. [52] They considered love essential to matrimony, although they expected it to follow, rather than to precede, the wedding. The importance that they attached to marriage forced them to revise the traditional image of woman. John Cotton wrote,

Women are Creatures without which there is no comfortable Living for man; it is true of them what is wont to be said of Governments, *That bad ones are better than none*: They are a sort of Blasphemers then who despise and decry them, and call them *a necessary Evil*, for they are *a necessary Good*: such as it was not good that man should be without. [53]

At the same time, the Puritans insisted on upholding the patriarchal authority of the husband. They compared marriage to the covenant between God and His Elect, an apt analogy that contained the idea of mutual duties based on a contract between unequals.[54] In the last analysis, the Puritans expected and enjoined godly women to obey their husbands in the same spirit that they enjoined the saints to obey God.

In the southern colonies, Protestant doctrines about marriage were combined with even more conservative notions about the proper relationship between husband and wife. Julia Spruill suggests that there was an even greater insistence on traditional patriarchal authority in the South than in New England.[55] Men, particularly in the upper class, were more likely than their Puritan counterparts to treat their daughters and wives like property.

The emergence of a landed economy dominated by large plantations in the South meant that through their dowries and inheritances females had the same kind of material value that they had among the landed English aristocracy. In both cases this kind of economy encouraged men to view women as economic assets or liabilities. Such an attitude was much less appropriate to conditions in New England. Slavery strengthened these patterns of thought by making property in human beings one of the foundations of the society.

Seventeenth-century colonists were thus quite traditional in their attitudes toward women. Despite the evidence that Puritans developed Protestant doctrines about marriage in directions favorable to women, colonial family structure remained patriarchal in theory and practice. Men dominated church and state and cited Saint Paul to justify their position.

The fundamental patriarchal character of early colonial society and the persistence of female subordination need emphasis because so much of the discussion of the position of women before 1750 focuses on their crucial role in the economy. The basic economic unit was the family, whose viability depended as much on the contribution of the wife as on that of the husband. Furthermore, in the context of a critical labor shortage and a harsh subsistence economy, women without husbands were often forced to take on unaccustomed and atypical roles. Because women and men worked together to ensure the success of a common economic enterprise, historians have suggested that sexual stereotypes were weaker, male and female spheres less sharply defined, and women's abilities accorded more respect than in seventeenth-century England or nineteenth-century America. They see the history of American women as one of decline, with the crucial deterioration occurring in the late eighteenth and early nineteenth centuries as a by-product of industrialization.[56]

While there is some truth in this point of view, historians must beware of overemphasizing the contrast in the position of women before and after industrialization. The colonial woman always performed her economic role within a larger context of subordination. As Mary Ryan expresses it, "The coexistence of woman's central economic and social function with her constant subordination to the patriarchal male is aptly captured by the biblical symbol that heralded colonial femininity: 'Adam's Rib.'"[57] Within the household, husbands and wives did not share tasks indiscriminately. Functions were divided along sexual lines that reflected traditional European sex-role stereotypes.[58] Although historians such as Elisabeth Dexter, Gerda Lerner, and Julia Spruill have emphasized the existence and importance of colonial women who engaged in business or crafts outside the home, other scholars, such as Joan Wilson and Mary Beth Norton, have raised convincing questions about their significance in colonial society.[59] The fact that very few "she-merchants" or craftswomen had competent, healthy husbands strongly suggests that the social ideal and norm was the wife-mother who worked entirely within the domestic sphere. While colonial society accepted the activities and enterprise of women whom necessity forced into atypical roles, it was unquestionably organized around a sexual division of labor and the subjection of women. Joan Wilson has made the point cogently:

It is true . . . for most of the period up to 1750 that conditions *out of necessity* increased the functional independence and importance of all women. . . . much of the alleged freedom from sexism of colonial women was due to their initial numerical scarcity and the critical labor shortage in the New World throughout the seventeenth and eighteenth centuries. Such increased reproductive roles (economic as well as biological) reflected the logic of necessity and *not any fundamental change* in the sexist, patriarchal attitudes that had been transplanted from Europe.[60]

The fundamental traditionalism of early colonial attitudes toward women explains why there was so little resistance to the more inflexible, restrictive definition of the female role that asserted itself along the eastern seaboard after 1750 as the conditions of the frontier passed. In her study of the southern colonies, Julia Spruill noted that attitudes toward women were much more rigidly traditionalist in the eighteenth century than in the early days of the colonies, especially in the East. While seventeenth-century marriage manuals stressed the mutual duties of mates, eighteenth-century versions emphasized the duties of wives and deemphasized those of husbands. She suggests that the roles allotted to women, and even attitudes toward them, became somewhat more egalitarian than the European norm under the pressure of frontier conditions and emergencies. As society became more settled, however, traditional views reasserted themselves, particularly among the upper and middle classes.[61]

Recent scholarship indicates that this trend affected all the colonies. A new definition of femininity emerged in the late eighteenth century, particularly among the merchant and planter classes. This definition underscored the contrast between female and male characteristics. In place of the seventeenth-century model of the woman as helpmate, the eighteenth century pictured a submissive and dependent creature whose happiness depended on marriage and whose moral superiority gave her the duty to civilize and tame young men.[62] The spread of female seminaries after 1750 reflected and encouraged this development by institutionalizing a double standard of sex-stereotyped education. The seminaries concentrated on developing feminine virtues such as submissiveness, piety, and domesticity, rather than on teaching academic subjects.[63]

Even the enthusiastic educational reformers of the revolutionary era and the 1790s rejected the idea that women and men should receive the same education. They assigned women the weighty task of ensuring the safety and survival of the young republic by raising their sons to be virtuous citizens and by condemning and correcting any moral lapses in their husbands. Significantly, the success of the republican mother depended on her character rather than on her academic or technical skills. The role also provided women with a political function without removing them from the home. In this way it permitted even the most progressive thinkers to avoid considering seriously whether the political principles of the republic were consistent with excluding women from full citizenship and the vote. [64]

During the closing decades of the eighteenth century the idea that men and women existed in separate spheres suited to their respective characters—and the proper female sphere was the home—became more and more central to American ideas about women. A letter from Sarah Osborne to the Reverend Joseph Fish as early as 1767 raises serious question about the commonly held view that sex roles in the colonial period were less confining than after industrialization. In the letter Osborne felt it necessary to defend herself both for working as a teacher and for assuming leadership in the Newport revival of 1766-67. [65] Mary Beth Norton's work on loyalist women points in the same direction. With few exceptions, the 488 women in her sample engaged in business outside the home only if necessity forced them to. As a group they knew very little about their husbands' business or financial affairs, which apparently fell outside the accepted female sphere. Furthermore, both the behavior and the language of the loyalist women revealed that they consciously felt inferior because of their sex. [66]

Therefore, it is clear that the ideology of male superiority remained virtually unchallenged throughout the colonial period. Changes in the definition of femininity during the late eighteenth century pointed not in the direction of greater equality, but toward the Victorian definition of womanhood. Traditional misogynous ideas were thus part of the ideological inheritance of the new nation and constituted one of the major obstacles to females who openly expressed professional aspirations for themselves or their sex early in the nineteenth century.

Notes

1. Carolly Erickson, *The Medieval Vision* (New York: Oxford University Press, 1976), chap. 8. Katherine M. Rogers, *The Troublesome Helpmate: A History of Misogyny in Literature* (Seattle: University of Washington Press, 1966), chap. 1, secs. 1-4; chap. 2, secs. 3-4. Although I think this generalization is valid, I do not mean to imply that Catholic thought about women was monolithic and unchanging. There was always a certain tension between the images of woman as Eve and Mary. Eileen Power notes this ambivalence but agrees with my general point of view; "The Position of Women," in *The*

Legacy of the Middle Ages, ed. C. G. Crump and E. F. Jacob (Oxford: Clarendon Press, 1926), pp. 401-7. Joan Ferrante agrees that misogyny dominated
biblical and early Christian tradition; *Woman As Image in Medieval Literature, From the Twelfth Century to Dante* (New York: Columbia University
Press, 1975), chap. 1. David Herlihy stresses the ambivalence of Christian
tradition about women; *Women in Medieval Society,* Smith History Lecture
(Houston: University of St. Thomas, 1971), p. 4. Roland Bainton discusses the
ambivalence of early Christian literature on women, but sees the New
Testament as a major source of the disparagement of women; *Women in the
Reformation of Germany and Italy* (Boston: Beacon Press, 1971), pp. 12-13.
JoAnn McNamara and Suzanne Wemple put more emphasis than I do on the
doctrine of the spiritual equality of the sexes; "Sanctity and Power: The Dual
Pursuit of Medieval Women," in *Becoming Visible,* ed. Renate Bridenthal
and Claudia Koonz (Boston: Houghton Mifflin, 1977), pp. 90-118. The thesis
of JoAnn McNamara's article, "Sexual Equality and the Cult of the Virgin in
Early Christian Thought," *Feminist Studies* 3 (Spring-Summer 1976): 145-
58, is that feminist and anticlerical writers have overemphasized the misogynous element in early Christian thought. She states that patristic writers
were committed to the doctrine of the spiritual equality of men and women,
but that this equality must be understood as a celestial condition. The church
fathers' conservative views on women's roles and the subordination of wives
stemmed from their estimate of "her [temporal] condition not her nature" (p.
149). I question the historical significance or relevance of a doctrine of equality that has little, if any, impact in this world. Furthermore, McNamara argues that the praise of virginity did not result from hostility toward women or
sex per se. See pages 6-8 above for my reasons for disagreeing with her on this
point. Even McNamara recognizes the tendency of early Christian writers "to
equate 'masculine' with the higher attributes" and "to despise the nature of
women" (p. 152). I interpret the church fathers' praise of the "manliness" of
virgin martyrs as an example of the former tendency and reject McNamara's
explanation that "the manliness of the virgin woman was a transcendence of
the sexual nature itself" (p. 154).

    2. Eph. 5:22-3.

    3. 1 Tim. 2: 11-14.

    4. John Benton notes that despite the high value placed on the celibate
state, the expectation was that most people would marry; "Clio and Venus:
An Historical View of Medieval Love," in *The Meaning of Courtly Love,* ed. F.
X. Newman (Albany: State University of New York Press, 1968), p. 21.

    5. 1 Cor. 7: 1-2, 7-9.

    6. Maryanne Cline Horowitz, "Aristotle and Women," *Journal of the
History of Biology* 9 (Fall 1976): 183-213, for a complete scholarly discussion

of Aristotle's views on women.

7. Quoted in Rogers, *Troublesome Helpmate*, p. 68.

8. Emily James Putnam, *The Lady* (New York: G. P. Putnam's Sons, 1910), pp. 120, 127-57. Eileen Power, *Medieval Women*, ed. M. M. Postan (Cambridge: Cambridge University Press, 1975), introduces her discussion of the cult of the Virgin and of the cult of the lady by calling them both doctrines of the superiority of women (p. 19). However, her subsequent remarks qualify this judgment considerably, particularly in the case of the latter (pp. 19-28).

9. Erickson, *Medieval Vision*, pp. 189-190.

10. Ibid., pp. 189-94.

11. I disagree with Roland Bainton, who says that monasticism was a revolt not against sexuality or women, but against the secularization of Christianity through the influx of nominal Christians into the church after Constantine's revolution; *Women in Germany and Italy*, p. 12.

12. Rogers, *Troublesome Helpmate*, p. 71.

13. Ibid., pp. 5, 71. See also Sebastian Brandt, *Ship of Fools*, 2 vols. trans. Alexander Barclay (New York: AMS Press, 1966), 2: 163.

14. See Rogers, *Troublesome Helpmate*, p. 5. 2 Sam. 11-12.

15. Ferrante, *Woman in Medieval Literature*, p. 2.

16. Ibid., p. 20, makes an almost identical point.

17. Power, *Medieval Women*, makes a similar point: "Monasticism may have offered a refuge for some women; but the refuge merely sealed the degradation of women in general by confining full approbation to those who withdrew themselves from the world" (p. 16).

18. Dom David Knowles, *The Religious Orders in England*, 3 vols. (Cambridge: Cambridge University Press, 1957), 2: 256.

19. Putnam, *The Lady*, pp. 69-105. Herlihy, *Women in Medieval Society*, pp. 8-10. McNamara and Wemple, "Sanctity and Power," pp. 110-11. Susan Mosher Stuard, ed., *Women in Medieval Society* (Philadelphia: University of Pennsylvania Press, 1976), p. 8. Lina Eckenstein, *Woman Under Monasticism* (New York: Russell & Russell, 1963), pp. 185-201, 481. Bainton, *Women of Germany and Italy*, p. 13, states that the Georgian reform strengthened the strand of Christian thought that disparaged women and marriage.

20. See Benton, "Clio and Venus," p. 35, and Power, "Position of Women," p. 406, for similar interpretations. Putnam, *The Lady*, p. 127, is ambivalent about the impact of courtly love on the position of women. Joan Kelly-Gadol, "Did Women Have a Renaissance?" in *Becoming Visible*, ed. Bridenthal and Koonz, pp. 141-44, takes a completely different position. She sees the doctrines of courtly love as liberating for women because they expressed an ideal that freed female sexuality from the bonds of marriage and male control, whether or not courtly love was translated into actual practice among the aristocracy.

21. George Duby, "In Northwestern France: The 'Youth' in Twelfth-Century Aristocratic Society," in *Lordship and Community in Medieval Europe: Selected Readings*, ed. Frederic L. Cheyette, (New York: Holt, Rinehart and Winston, 1968), pp. 137-55, and Herbert Moller, "The Social Causation of the Courtly Love Complex," *Comparative Studies in Society and History* 1 (1958): 137-68, both discuss the social reality reflected in the literature of courtly love. Moller states explicitly that although the courtly love complex expressed the anxieties, strivings, and insecurities of the knightly class in the twelfth and thirteenth centuries, it did not reflect the courtship or marriage patterns of that class in reality. He asserts that men in this class would not tolerate adultery in their wives and that the poetry did not reflect real affairs between the troubadours and the wives of feudal noblemen. He makes the latter point even more strongly in "The Meaning of Courtly Love," *Journal of American Folklore* 73 (January-March 1960): 40. Benton, "Clio and Venus," pp. 24-28, denies that courtly love even advocated adulterous love. He says that adultery was taken extremely seriously by the feudal nobility, that adultery with the lord's wife was a form of treason, and that the tradition of private vengeance in cases of adultery was very strong. He claims that the troubadours would have been killed, had they advocated adultery in real life.

E. William Monter questions whether courtly love reflected social reality on the grounds that iconographical evidence of courtly love comes very late; that there was little improvement in women's legal position during the later Middle Ages, when the conventions of courtly love were most fashionable; and that the only didactic treatise by a late medieval nobleman, composed for his daughters, condemns courtly love vigorously; "Pedestal and Stake: Courtly Love and Witchcraft," in *Becoming Visible*, ed. Bridenthal and Koonz, pp. 125-26. J. Huizinga maintains that there was a real distinction between courtly love and real life. *The Waning of the Middle Ages* (Garden City, N.Y.: Doubleday, 1954), pp. 126-27.

Kelly-Gadol tries to bypass the question of whether courtly love existed in real life: "This is not to raise the fruitless question of whether such love relationships actually existed or if they were mere literary conventions. The real issue regarding ideology is, rather, what kind of society could posit *as a social ideal* a love relation outside of marriage, one that women freely entered and that, despite its reciprocity, made women the gift givers while men did the service" (Did Women Have a Renaissance?" p. 144). I do not see how a historian can possibly establish the function of an ideology in a society without knowing what the social reality was. Furthermore, despite this disavowal, Kelly-Gadol does make a number of assumptions about the relationship between social reality and courtly love. She maintains that as an ideal it reflected a society in which women had real political and social power and enjoyed a significant amount of sexual freedom after marriage. She sees adultery as functional in a world characterized by political marriage and notes the tolerance of illegitimacy in the Middle Ages (pp. 144-46). Recent work emphasizing the social and political power of medieval upper-class women, including the work by Herlihy that she cites, all refer to the early Middle Ages and emphasize that women suffered a real deterioration of status and power in the feudal age, the very period that gave birth to the literature of courtly love.

In this connection McNamara and Wemple are much more convincing in their suggestion that its development under the patronage of women reflected an effort on their part to carve out an area of cultural influence in a period when their position was deteriorating; "Sanctity and Power," p. 116. Medieval sources are filled with documents and references indicating a certain tolerance of illegitimacy, but it is the bastards of men—not women—and of husbands—not wives—who appear in the records. Moller and Benton are certainly correct on this point. Furthermore, this tolerance should not be exaggerated. To give an example, the English common law disinherited children born out of wedlock even if their parents subsequently married.

22. Benton denies that the love referred to in the literature of courtly love was a passionate, sexual attachment and says that it was a love of friendship; "Clio and Venus," pp. 30-33. This interpretation does not accord with my own reading of that literature or the interpretation of most of the scholars expert on the subject.

23. See note 21 above on the relationship of the theme of adultery in this literature to sexual mores in real life.

24. Ferrante argues along similar lines in *Woman in Medieval Literature*. In her analysis of Chrétien's *Chevalier de la Charette*, she points out that when Guinevere was absent, she functioned as Lancelot's inspiration and inspired him to do what no other knight in this world could. But when he was in her presence, her effect was always destructive. In the end Lancelot's love cut him off from his king and his world (pp. 81-83) In Tristan, love caused everyone who experienced it to suffer (p. 93). Ferrante concludes that the vulgate cycle of Arthurian romance ultimately condemned secular love between man and woman and exalted virginity and total devotion to God as the ideal for both sexes. At the beginning, the literature of chivalry presented women as the object of and inspiration for the noblest activity; but in the context of the quest for the Holy Grail, women became worldly attractions who prevented heroes from reaching their goals and saving their souls (pp. 117-22).

25. Ibid., pp. 92-93.

26. Leonardo Bruni d'Arezzo, "De Studiis et Literis," In *Vittorino da Feltre and Other Humanist Educators*, ed. William Harrison Woodward, Classics in Education, no. 18 (New York: Bureau of Publications, Teachers College, Columbia University, 1964), pp. 119-33.

27. Kelly-Gadol has a very different view of the impact of humanism on women's education. She thinks that it narrowed women's influence in courtly society because it put the education of both sexes under the control of men; "Did Women Have a Renaissance?" pp. 151-52. In my opinion, she overestimates the influence that feudal women had over the education of boys. The crucial training of males was military and was always in the hands of men. The rare medieval woman educated in the book learning of her society, like Héloïse, was of necessity educated by men. Renaissance humanists performed that function for the children of the upper classes, though they certainly educated more boys than girls. In comparing the situation in the Renaissance to that in the Middle Ages, Kelly-Gadol exaggerates the influence that women in the feudal aristocracy exerted on education and culture through the literature and manners of courtly love.

28. Most authors define the position of upper-class Renaissance women as a subordinate and restricted one. Lauro Martines, "A Way of Looking at Women in Renaissance Florence," *Journal of Medieval and Renaissance Studies* 4 (Spring 1974): 15-28. John Gage, *Life in Italy at the Time of the Medici* (New York: G. P. Putnam's Sons, 1968), pp. 179-90. Diana Hughes, "Urban Growth and Family Structure in Medieval Genoa," *Past and Present*, no. 66 (February 1975), pp. 1-28; Iris Origo, *The Merchant of Prato, Francesco Di Marco Datini* (New York: Alfred A. Knopf, 1957), pt. 2, chaps. 1-2. Within this general framework, women, particularly widows, often exerted considerable influence within the family and effectively managed large households and/or estates. David Herlihy, *The Family in Renaissance Italy*, Forums in History (St. Charles, Mo.: Forum Press, 1974), pp. 10-12. Stanley Chojnacki, "Dowries and Kinsmen in Early Renaissance Venice," *Journal of Interdisciplinary History* 5 (Spring 1975): 571-600. Stanley Chojnacki, "Patrician Women in Early Renaissance Venice," *Studies in the Renaissance* 21 (1974): 176-203. Also see Origo and Martines, cited above.

The question on which historians differ is whether the position of women in the Renaissance, particularly upper-class women, deteriorated from the preceding feudal age. Kelly-Gadol has made the most explicit and influential argument for a real contraction of women's influence and scope of action in the renaissance; "Did Women Have a Renaissance?" Stuard makes this argument more modestly in *Women in Medieval Society*, p. 5. Within limits there is merit to this point of view. The development of commercial capitalism created a new key sector of the economy that virtually excluded women, Political developments in the city-states, particularly the republics, created new constitutional and administrative forms that reduced the opportunities for women to participate in public affairs.

On the other hand, there is much more continuity between the feudal age and the Renaissance than Kelly-Gadol admits. In the hereditary states women in the ruling families had the same sorts of opportunities to exercise power and influence as their medieval predecessors—opportunities dependent on the absence of husbands or the succession of minor sons. In the economic sphere, there does not seem to me to have been an enormous qualitative difference between the activities of the lady of the castle who administered her husband's estates and household and those of Francesco Di Datini's wife, when administering his. There was certainly more continuity than change in the economic roles of women in the petit bourgeois and artisan classes. The crucial deterioration in the position of women occurred not in the transition from the feudal age to the Renaissance, but in the eleventh and twelfth centuries, as Western Europe emerged from the more chaotic early medieval period. David Herlihy, "Land, Family and Women in Continental Europe, 701-1200," in *Women in Medieval Society*, pp. 13-45. JoAnn McNamara and Suzanne Wemple, "The Power of Women Through the Family in Medieval Europe: 500-1100," in *Clio's Consciousness Raised*, ed. Mary S. Hartman and Lois Banner (New York: Harper Torchbooks, 1974), pp. 103-18. McNamara and Wemple, "Sanctity and Power," pp. 90-118. Dorothy M. Stenton, *The English Women in History* (London: George Allen & Unwin, 1957), chaps. 1-2. Putnam, *The Lady*, pp. 115-18.

29. Baldesar Castiglione, *The Book of the Courtier* (Garden City, N.Y.: Doubleday, 1959), pp. 205-82.

30. Gage thinks Castiglione left the debate inconclusive rather than favoring women, as I feel he did; *Life in Italy*, pp. 180-81. In "Did Women Have a Renaissance?" Kelly-Gadol says that Castiglione debated the question of women "much to their favor," but interprets his work as a sign of the greater subjection of Renaissance women because he "established in *The Courtier* a fateful bond between love and marriage." He broke with the courtly love tradition and replaced it with a Neoplatonic notion of spiritual love (p. 155). Kelly-Gadol has overdrawn the contrast between medieval and Renaissance versions of courtly love. Huizinga, *Waning of the Middle Ages*, pp. 107-8. The double standard existed in the Middle Ages and was not a creation of the Renaissance. I do not believe that in real life the feudal nobility tolerated adultery in their wives; see note 21 above.

31. More advocated a rigorous classical education for girls as well as practical training. Both boys and girls were educated in his household school. His most successful student was his daughter Margaret, who knew Latin well enough to impress Erasmus and Reginald Pole. See Elizabeth Rogers, ed., *St. Thomas More: Selected Letters* (New Haven: Yale University Press, 1961), pp. 103-7, 109-10, 147-152, 154-55. R. W. Chambers, *Thomas More* (Ann Arbor: University of Michigan Press, 1968), pp. 175-91.

32. Natalie Zemon Davis, *Society and Culture in Early Modern France*

(Stanford, Calif.: Stanford University Press, 1975), p. 72.
33. Ibid., p. 94.
34. Carolyn C. Lougee, *Le Paradis des Femmes: Women, Salons, and Social Stratification in Seventeenth-Century France* (Princeton, N.J.: Princeton University Press, 1976), pp. 29-30.
35. Quoted in Margaret Cavendish, Duchess of Newcastle, "From the World's Olio," in *By a Woman Writt: Literature from Six Centuries by and about Women*, ed. Joan Goulianos (Baltimore: Penguin Books, 1974), p. 56.
36. Rogers, *Troublesome Helpmate*, pp. 135-59.
37. Wallace Notestein, "The English Women, 1580-1650," in *Studies in Social History*, ed. J. H. Plumb (New York: Longmans, Green & Co., 1955), pp. 102-3. Bainton, *Women in Germany and Italy*, p. 14, makes a similar point about Protestantism.
38. Carolyn C. Lougee, "Modern European History," *Signs* 2 (Spring 1977): 632. The widening gap between male and female literacy has certainly been documented for Puritan New England; see Nancy F. Cott, *The Bonds of Womenhood: "Woman's Sphere" in New England, 1780-1835* (New Haven: Yale University Press, 1977), pp. 102-3.
39. Bainton, *Women in Germany and Italy*, pp. 9-10.
40. Philippe Ariès, *Centuries of Childhood: A Social History of Family Life* (New York: Vintage Books, 1962), pp. 405-15, for summary statement of these views. Michael Walzer, *The Revolution of the Saints* (Cambridge, Mass.: Harvard University Press, 1965), pp. 183-98.
41. Bainton, *Women in Germany and Italy*, pp. 9-10. Edmund S. Morgan, *The Puritan Family: Religion and Domestic Relations in Seventeenth-Century New England* (New York: Harper & Row, 1966), chap. 2. William Haller and Malleville Haller, "The Puritan Art of Love," *Huntingdon Library Quarterly* 5 (January 1942): 235-72. James Johnson, "The Covenant Idea and the Puritan View of Marriage," *Journal of the History of Ideas* 32 (January-March 1971): 107-18. Lawrence Stone, "The Rise of the Nuclear Family in Early Modern England: The Patriarchal Stage," in *The Family in History*, ed. Charles E. Rosenberg (Philadelphia: University of Pennsylvania Press, 1975), pp. 26-28.
42. For a sensitive and perceptive analysis of the impact of Protestantism —especially Calvinism—on women, see Davis, *Society and Culture in France*, pp. 65-69. Davis sees Protestantism as involving both gain and loss for women. She is, of course, specifically concerned with the impact of Calvinism on a French city, though many of the factors that she discusses were operative in English Protestantism as well.
43. John Winthrop, *Winthrop's Journal: "History of New England,"* *1630-1649*, 2 vols, (New York: Barnes & Noble, 1953), 2: 225.

44. "Examination of Mrs. Ann Hutchinson," in *Root of Bitterness: Documents of the Social History of American Women*, ed. Nancy F. Cott (New York: E. P. Dutton, 1972), p. 34.

45. Ibid., pp. 36-37.

46. Ben Barker-Benfield, "Anne Hutchinson and the Puritan Attitude Toward Women," *Feminist Studies* 1 (Fall 1972): 65-96. Lyle Koehler, "The Case of the American Jezebels: Anne Hutchinson and Female Agitation During the Years of Antinomian Turmoil, 1636-40," *William and Mary Quarterly* 31 (January 1974): 55-78.

47. Roger Thompson, *Women in Stuart England and America: A Comparative Study* (Boston: Routledge and Kegan Paul, 1974), p. 88.

48. Joan Hoff Wilson, "The Illusion of Change: Women and the American Revolution," in *The American Revolution, Explorations in the History of American Radicalism*, ed. Alfred F. Young (DeKalb: Northern Illinois University Press, 1976), p. 408.

49. Julia Spruill, *Women's Life and Work in the Southern Colonies* (New York: W. W. Norton, 1972), p. 187.

50. Cott, *Bonds of Womanhood*, pp. 102-3.

51. Laurel Thatcher Ulrich, "Vertuous Women Found: New England Ministerial Literature, 1668-1735," *American Quarterly* 28 (Spring 1976): 20-40.

52. Morgan, *The Puritan Family*, chap. 2. Johnson, "Covenant Idea and Puritan View of Marriage," pp. 107-18. William Haller and Malleville Haller, "The Puritan Art of Love," pp. 235-72. Natalie Davis notes that this view of marriage was not entirely peculiar to Protestants, having originated among Catholic humanists like Erasmus, *Society and Culture in France*, p. 90.

53. Quoted in Morgan, *The Puritan Family*, p. 29.

54. Johnson, "Covenant Idea and the Puritan View of Marriage," pp. 107-18.

55. Spruill, *Women's Life in the Southern Colonies*, pp. 43-44, 78-79, 163-64, and chaps. 7, 10.

56. Thompson, *Women in England and America*, chaps. 1, 3, 5. Gerda Lerner, "The Lady and the Mill Girl: Changes in the Status of Women in the Age of Jackson," in *Our American Sisters: Women in American Life and Thought*, 2d ed., ed. Jean E. Friedman and William G. Shade (Boston: Allyn and Bacon, 1976), pp. 120-32. Elisabeth A. Dexter, *Colonial Women of Affairs: Women in Business and Professions in America Before 1776*, 2d ed., rev. (Clifton, N.J.: Augustus Kelley Publishers, 1972), pp. 190-92. This is basically Mary P. Ryan's point of view, although her analysis of the colonial economy and its impact on women contains some contradictions; *Womanhood in America, From Colonial Times to the Present* (New York: New View-

points, 1975), pp. 21-45. She emphasizes throughout the crucial role that women played in the family economy. However, she says on p. 30 that a sexual division of labor existed within the home, on p. 44 that there was no "sharp dichotomy" between male and female roles. The whole thrust of her discussion is more supportive of the former proposition.

57. Ryan, *Womanhood in America*, p. 13.

58. Ibid., p. 13, but see n. 56 for her ambivalence on this point. Also Wilson, "Illusion of Change," p. 394.

59. Dexter, *Colonial Women of Affairs*, chaps. 1, 2, 3, Conclusion. Lerner, "Lady and the Mill Girl," p. 121. Spruill, *Women's Life in the Southern Colonies*, chaps. 11-14. J. Wilson, "Illusion of Change," pp. 395-96. Mary Beth Norton, "Eighteenth-Century American Women in Peace and War: The Case of the Loyalists," *William and Mary Quarterly* 33 (July 1976): 395-97.

60. J. Wilson, "Illusion of Change," p. 393.

61. Spruill, *Women's Life in the Southern Colonies*, pp. 163-64, 241-46, and chap. 10.

62. Ryan, *Womanhood in America*, pp. 107-13.

63. J. Wilson, "Illusion of Change," p. 412.

64. Linda K. Kerber, "The Republican Mother: Women and the Enlightenment—An American Perspective," *American Quarterly* 28 (Summer 1976): 187-205. Linda K. Kerber, "Daughters of Columbia: Educating Women for the Republic, 1787-1805," in *Our American Sisters*, ed. Friedman and Shade, pp. 87-89.

65. Quoted in Mary Beth Norton, "'My Resting Reaping Times': Sarah Osborne's Defense of Her 'Unfeminine' Activities, 1767," *Signs* 2 (Winter 1976): 515-29.

66. Norton, "Eighteenth-Century American Women," pp. 386-409.

II

The Cult of Domesticity

In England and the United States, the nineteenth-century cult of domesticity or true womanhood was superimposed on the older European tradition that proclaimed the inferiority of women. The cluster of ideas and standards of behavior subsumed under these labels powerfully reinforced the deep, preexisting cultural bias against females with intellectual and professional aspirations. The majority of women internalized these values. The few rebellious females who demanded opportunities to enter institutions of higher education and the professions found this model used over and over to justify rebuffing their claims. The cult of domesticity became such an integral part of American social ideology that its definition of women's role long survived the passing of the nineteenth century. For all these reasons, an exploration of its content, origins, and influence is crucial to understanding the history of women in the professions.

For purposes of analysis and exposition, historians tend to treat the cult of true womanhood as a relatively coherent, consistent set of cultural norms. Although this technique has its uses, particularly at the introductory level, the complexity of Victorian ideas about females and the distortion inherent in abstracting a simple ideal type from reality must be recognized. In addition, the class nature of the cult of domesticity as a behavioral model must be underscored. In the United

States, the life-style that this ideal prescribed was accessible only to white, middle- and upper-class women in more settled areas of the country. Its code of behavior took no account of the problems and harsh necessities of poor women, women on the frontier, and slave women. Indeed, one could argue that a privileged elite was able to translate the model of true womanhood into social reality solely because a large number of less fortunate females existed to be exploited sexually, and as domestic servants. Only by keeping these complexities in mind is it possible to analyze the character and origins of the cult of domesticity without losing all sense of historical reality.[1]

The cult of true womanhood was a compound of four ideas: a sharp dichotomy between the home and the economic world outside that paralleled a sharp contrast between female and male natures, the designation of the home as the female's only proper sphere, the moral superiority of woman, and the idealization of her function as mother. In the Victorian mind these conceptions were loosely connected with the older tradition of the female's intellectual inferiority. By the mid-nineteenth century, this cluster of ideas designated the values and code of behavior that predominated among the middle classes and all others who aspired to respectability.

At the heart of the cult of domesticity were a rigid conceptual distinction between the home and the economy and a determination to preserve that separation as desirable. The world outside the home, the man's sphere, was the scene of the economic struggles and intellectual endeavors that allowed men to expend their abundant energies and employ their natural talents. The highly competitive character of this economy drove men to exhausting efforts and encouraged them to resort to less than Christian methods to increase their profits. The world outside the home was, in short, the brutal environment of untrammeled capitalism in the early days of the Industrial Revolution.

From this world, man retreated to the home, the woman's sphere, for physical and spiritual refreshment. Here he found shelter from the anxieties of modern society and a sanctuary for moral and spiritual values that could not survive outside the domestic circle. Presiding over this veritable temple was woman. Her mission was to ensure that her mate found an orderly, tranquil environment when he returned from his economic struggles. Even more important, life in the home had to express the highest moral and Christian values. The woman had to guard against any outside influences that might breed corruption or scandal. Family prayers, family Bible reading, and regular family attendance at church on Sunday mornings all testified to the Victorian tendency to direct their religious energy toward the home. In an influential lecture, "Of Queens' Gardens," John Ruskin expressed these ideas in their most exalted form.

The man's power is active, progressive, defensive. He is eminently the doer, the creator, the discoverer, the defender. His intellect is for speculation and invention; his energy for adventure, for war, and for conquest. . . . But the woman's power is for rule, not for battle,—and her intellect is not for invention or creation, but for sweet ordering, arrangement, and decision. . . . By her office, and place, she is protected from all danger and temptation. The man, in his rough work in open world, must encounter all peril and trial:—to him, therefore, the failure, the offence, the inevitable error: often he must be wounded, or subdued, often misled, and *always* hardened. But he guards the woman from all this; within his house, as ruled by her, unless she herself has sought it, need enter no danger, no temptation, no cause of error or offence. This is the true nature of home—it is the place of Peace; the shelter, not only from all injury, but from all terror, doubt, and division. . . . This, then, I believe to be,—will you not admit it to be,—the woman's true place and power? But do not you see that to fulfill this, she must—as far as one can use such terms of a human creature—be incapable of error? So far as she rules, all must be right, or nothing is. She must be enduringly, incorruptibly good; instinctively, infallibly wise—wise, not for self-development, but for self-renunciation: wise, not that she may see herself above her husband, but that she may never fail from his side: wise, not with the narrowness of insolent and loveless pride, but with the passionate gentleness of an infinitely variable, because infinitely applicable, modesty of service. [2]

As Ruskin's comments make clear, the wife's dominion in the home existed in the context of continued subordination. The essence of her role lay in sacrificing herself in the service of her husband, children, and other relatives. The woman who approached the ideal obliterated her sense of self and virtually existed only in relation to others. The advice literature and popular fiction of the period endlessly recommended the most extreme self-abnegation as the female ideal. Two examples from the works of popular authors come to mind as illustrations of this point. In Louisa May Alcott's *Little Women* the idealized mother figure, Marmee, tells Jo, "You think your temper is the worst in the world, but mine used to be just like it. . . . I've been trying to cure it for forty years, and have only succeeded in controlling it. I am angry nearly every day of my life, Jo, but I have learned not to show it; and I still hope to learn not to feel it, though it may take me another forty years to do so."[3] The saintly spinster aunt described by Harriet Beecher Stowe in "The Cathedral" told a friend "of what she had suffered from the strength of her personal antipathies. 'I thank God,' she said, 'that I believe at last I have overcome all that too, and that there has not been, for some years, any human being toward whom I have felt a movement of dislike.'"[4] The mark of spiritual progress for woman was the complete repression of her feelings. Socialized to deny her desires for self-assertion and power, the model nineteenth-century woman accepted that her husband's authority was sanctioned by God, nature, and tradition. Thus, even though the cult of domesticity frequently proclaimed the equality of the male and female spheres, in fact—and even in theory—the home over which the wife presided was always seen as ultimately subordinate to male authority.

Although the Victorians believed that the cult of domesticity represented eternal values, the sharp separation of the woman's sphere in the home from the man's outside was actually of very recent origin. In the Middle Ages, females participated in almost every area of the economy, although within each sector there was a sexual division of labor. The determining factor was that the home and the place of work were one and the same. In the feudal classes women supervised huge establishments that included a wide variety of domestic industries, ranging from baking, brewing, and tanning to making cloth, candles, and soap. When their husbands were away, they also ran the family estates. Children in this class were often sent to live with the most important noble and royal families to be educated, in which case the lady of the house was responsible for teaching them reading and writing, etiquette, and chess. Finally, she acted as the doctor for her family, servants, and everyone else in the neighborhood.

In the towns, bourgeois women played an active role in the trade and craft industries that were the mainstay of the medieval urban economy. Although individual enterprises were controlled by the guilds and the husband was normally the guild member, the whole family worked with him to keep the business going. The fact that most town dwellers lived behind or above their workshops facilitated this pattern. Men expected their wives to be able to manage without difficulty in their absence. A fascinating essay on medieval Genoa by Diàne Hughes shows how the artisan wife's contribution to the domestic economy increased her power and status within the family.[5]

In some cases females could join guilds on their own, and there were numerous instances of medieval women who functioned as independent traders. According to Eileen Power, women were rarely admitted to English craft guilds as full members. Furthermore, guilds did not exist in trades, such as the silk industry, that were exclusively in their hands. They were members of social and religious guilds and participated in the social and religious activities of the craft organizations.[6] A survey of English guilds in 1389 indicates that seventy-two of eighty-five allowed females to join on an equal basis with males, while only nine excluded them completely. Four admitted the widows of deceased members.[7] These guilds included some with economic functions, though the majority were social and religious in character. Women were full members of the barbers', furriers', and carpenters', and saddlers' guilds in Norwich; of the fullers', tailors', and tylers' in Lincoln; and of the joiners' and carpenters' in Worcester. Even guilds that did not admit independent female traders made some provision for the widows of members. They were usually allowed to continue their husbands' businesses for a limited period or on condition that they married another guild member.[8]

As in any primitive agrarian economy, peasant women played an essential part in medieval agriculture. They kept house; made candles, cloth, linen, and sheepskin bags for domestic consumption; worked in the fields, especially at busy seasons; tended the poultry; sheared the sheep; and often brewed beer. Many peasant women held land in their own right, subject to the same obligations and enjoying the same privileges as their male counterparts.

Finally, medieval women played a central role in what Eileen Power calls "bye industries," which were carried on in home, town, and country. Most of these were connected with the production or sale of food, drink, and textiles. Many women participated in two or three of these bye industries. Power thinks that apart from homemaking, they constituted women's most important contribution to the economy. They controlled all the spinning and silk making, some of the weaving, and a good deal of the brewing in medieval England. Interestingly, bread making, largely a town craft, was mostly in the hands of men.[9]

The first break in the medieval economic pattern occurred when trade and finance became too large-scale and complicated to be contained in the traditional domestic setting, with the development, in short, of what economic historians call commercial capitalism. Women took no part in the precocious development of Italian banking, long-distance trade, and manufacturing that took place in the twelfth, thirteenth, fourteenth, and fifteenth centuries. Raymond de Roover's exhaustive study of the Medici bank scarcely mentions a female.[10] Italian Renaissance social theory proclaimed that a woman should leave home for only three reasons: to marry, to enter a convent, or to go into domestic service (among the lower classes). The practice was not quite so restrictive. Although wives were generally confined to family and household tasks, the wives of merchants and public officials often devoted much of their time to nondomestic matters because their husbands were away for long periods.[11] In the sixteenth century, when England was undergoing the kind of expansion that Italy had experienced centuries earlier, the development had a similar effect on women. Both the great London livery companies and the newer joint-stock companies formed to trade and colonize were strictly male enterprises. The crucial fact was the changing character of participation as the economy developed. In the earlier medieval period, participation entailed work in a shop attached to the home, something obviously possible for both sexes. In the newer enterprises of commercial capitalism, participation meant long-distance travel or investment of capital. Since under English law women could control only wealth vested in trusts, which normally restricted its use, they could not share in these newer economic activities.

In *Working Life of Women in the Seventeenth Century*, Alice Clark argues that the position of women in trades and crafts, in which they were traditionally important, deteriorated in the seventeenth century.[12] She blames this adverse trend on the development of capitalism and particularly on the fact that crafts and trades were moving out of the home, leaving behind economically dependent, unproductive women. As capitalist entrepreneurs became wealthier and expanded their operations, their wives became less and less involved in their businesses and led increasingly frivolous, economically useless lives. Actually, Alice Clark antedated considerably a development that did not begin until the end of the seventeenth century and was not completed until well into the eighteenth.[13] The most important shift in production in the seventeenth century took place in the textile industry, which moved from the towns to the countryside, where it utilized the putting-out system. In this form of production, the capitalist invested in raw materials, which he then took to the homes of individual workers to process. Sometimes they worked on their own looms and spinning wheels, sometimes on his. In a period of low agricultural wages this system enabled rural families to supplement the income from their meager holdings and wages as day laborers. It involved the women in the family as much, if not more, than the men and, if anything, increased their financial importance.[14]

By and large, bourgeois women withdrew from business and productive enterprises in the eighteenth century, not the seventeenth.[15] Daniel Defoe attributed the process to their desire to imitate their social superiors; but whatever the reason, it undermined the mutual economic dependence of husband and wife long characteristic of this class. The Industrial Revolution, beginning around 1760 and continuing well into the nineteenth century, destroyed the traditional crafts and transferred more and more kinds of production from the home to factory. This development further reduced married women's productive role. Finally, as a result of industrialization, British trade reached such heights that it put the achievements of all previous centuries in the shade. Middle-class women were excluded from this sector of the economy because of its increasing distance from the home and their inability to control capital. Furthermore, as the commercial and industrial classes became wealthier, more and more of its members adopted genteel life-styles that precluded working wives.

On this side of the Atlantic, the colonial economy was characterized by the kind of small-scale agriculture and business typical of pre-industrial society. This situation encouraged economic cooperation between husbands and wives, allowed women to carry on after their husbands' deaths, and even permitted them to act as independent traders and entrepreneurs. Elisabeth Dexter and Julia Spruill show colonial women participating in every sort of economic activity.[16] They learned crafts, from printing to carpentry, from their fathers and husbands. Many were an integral part of their husbands' businesses and were quite capable of continuing in the event that they became widows. In addition, many women started and ran their own businesses. These relatively favorable economic conditions were much more characteristic of the early colonial period than the later. Roger Thompson attributes them primarily to the extreme labor shortage and secondarily to the relative prosperity, compared to England. [17] Even so, it is important not to exaggerate the opportunities open to colonial women nor to overestimate their position in the economy. Within family businesses functions were usually divided along traditional sexual lines. From the earliest years of settlement, women were considered adjunct and secondary to men in the economy, despite the labor shortage. Consequently, they were paid much less than men for performing the same jobs. [18] Despite the attention given by historians to independent "she-merchants" and craftswomen, most of them were widows, which strongly suggests that women emerged from the domestic sphere only when necessity forced them to. [19] Spruill feels that middle-class and upper-class southern women were less likely to go into business on their own in the eighteenth century than in the seventeenth. Higher standards of living, a yearning for gentility, and a desire to conform to English standards encouraged those who could afford it to embrace the model of the idle lady. [20]

In *Career Women of America, 1776-1840*, Dexter observes that although more women worked after the Revolution than before, there was more criticism of the employed female than earlier. [21] She traces this to the growing influence of the ideal of the lady living in ornamental idleness, an explanation that parallels Spruill's analysis of the contrast between the seventeenth and eighteenth centuries in the southern colonies. Dexter also points out the declining numbers of female doctors and midwives. [22]

In more recent work, both John Demos and Gerda Lerner describe the early nineteenth century as a period in which employment opportunities for middle-class women decreased and in which the climate of opinion was increasingly hostile to women of this class who worked. [23] At the same time, industrialization, particularly in New England's textile mills, dramatically expanded jobs for working-class women and drew many young, single females off the farms and out of their homes for the first time. As Gerda Lerner emphasizes, trends in

employment in the nineteenth century were quite different for work-
ing- and middle-class women. [24]

Furthermore, occupational opportunities for women varied considerably from region to region because of the progressive opening and
settlement of the frontier. Conditions reminiscent of the early colonial
period persisted on the frontier and in sparsely populated rural areas
long after they disappeared on the East Coast and in more settled
parts of the Midwest. Throughout the nineteenth century, the cult of
domesticity was completely incompatible with the condition of the
economy in certain parts of the United States. Finally, in the antebellum South, where the ideal of the lady reached its most extravagant
heights, scant attention was paid to the femininity of black women,
whether free or slave. [25] Thus, class, region, and race limited the
spread of this ideal, although in general its influence grew throughout
the late eighteenth and early nineteenth centuries.

While the growing exclusion of females from the economy deprived
them of many of their traditional functions, the cult of domesticity
assigned them new moral and religious duties that it considered
equally important. The creators and disseminators of this new cultural ideal transformed the female from sinful Eve into the conscience
of her age without explicitly acknowledging their departure from
Christian tradition. Household work and child rearing remained, as
they had always been, the heart of married women's work, but now
these functions were given a new ethical and spiritual significance.

This vision of women's social mission was dependent on a complex
view of femininity that associated it with nature, the emotions, and the
soul and saw it as completely opposed to reason and intellect. Victorian Americans believed that women's reproductive organs determined the state of their physical and emotional health, while their
behavior and character in turn affected the health of their reproductive systems. This dependence on biological forces combined with
women's acutely sensitive nerves to make them more affectionate and
emotional than men, as well as more inclined to physical and mental
illness. The great crises in the female life cycle—menstruation, pregnancy, childbirth, and menopause—all derived from women's reproductive function. To surmount these crises successfully, they had to
devote themselves to ordinary domestic routines and avoid rigorously

any shocks to their nervous systems, unfeminine activities, and, above all, intellectual pursuits that robbed their uteri of adequate supplies of blood and energy. Defining female nature in this way obviously reinforced the social identification of women with motherhood. Indeed, it was widely believed that women who did not have children were particularly prone to cancer, degenerative diseases, and insanity.

The virtual equation of females with their reproductive organs coexisted with the widely held conviction that their rational faculties were much less developed than men's. The discovery by physical anthropologists that men's brains were much larger than women's seemed to confirm this belief. Doctors and scientists concluded that women were inherently unfit for intellectual endeavors. They should devote themselves to maternity, for which they were clearly designed, and surrender their unnatural, self-destructive ambitions to enter colleges and the learned professions. [26]

Although the constant emphasis on women's subordination to these biological forces associated them with the natural and the physical, the Victorians also maintained, somewhat inconsistently, that women were more spiritual, more otherworldly, and more moral than men. This assertion flowed from the nineteenth-century view of male and female virtue and sexuality. [27] Like traditional Christian thinkers, the Victorians tended to equate sin with sexual offenses and to see lust as a major cause of human misery and wrongdoing. Unlike them, however, the Victorians associated passion with men rather than women. They believed that females had little, if any, sexual drive, while males were prey to almost uncontrollable sexual impulses. While marriage manuals recognized that women might enjoy sex, they generally assumed that they could tolerate abstinence with relative equanimity. [28] The nineteenth century distinguished sharply between the sexual and maternal instincts. Since sexuality was part of humanity's animal nature, men were closer to beasts than women and more prone to sin. Women's asexuality elevated them in the hierarchy of nature and identified them with moral purity.

In conformity with these conceptions, the Victorians assumed that men took the active role in sexual relations, while women were entirely passive. They submitted to their husbands because it was their duty to bear children and to allow their mates to use their bodies as an outlet for male lust. Whatever they felt, respectable ladies did not admit to enjoying sex: to do so would have raised questions about their character and virtue. [29]

The notion that men took the sexual initiative because they could not repress their shameful impulses encouraged the idea that female purity was constantly endangered by male lust. This belief was a major theme in the thought of female moral reformers who wanted to end prostitution. In line with their understanding of sexuality, they regarded prostitutes as the hapless victims of masculine passion rather than as archetypes of evil. They hoped to eliminate brothels by forcing men to control their instincts and to conform to a "higher" feminine ethic. [30]

In a recent article Carl Degler has challenged this interpretation of Victorian attitudes toward female sexuality. [31] He asks specifically whether doctors and other experts uniformly assumed that women experienced little sexual desire or pleasure and whether middle-class behavior conformed to such preconceptions, answering both questions in the negative. Degler certainly proves that some doctors and women recognized and accepted female sexuality in the last third of the century (his earliest source dates from 1869). While he does not succeed in refuting the interpretation of the cult of true womanhood presented here, he eliminates the possibility of assuming that all nineteenth-century Americans subscribed to its doctrines about women's sexual nature. He has not, however, solved the problem of deciding how much relative importance to attach to ideas that recognized female passion. In fact, the attitudes associated with the cult of domesticity represented the beliefs of many more middle-class Victorian Americans than the ideas on which Degler focuses. [32] His statement that "the so-called Victorian conception of women's sexuality was more that of an ideology trying to be established than the prevalent views" goes too far in the direction of revisionism. [33]

In the second part of the article, Degler switches his attention from medical and advice literature (thus circumventing the question of whether it was prescriptive or descriptive) to an actual survey of female sexual behavior and attitudes. The study of forty-five women was conducted by Dr. Clelia Mosher (1863-1940) of Stanford University between the early 1890s and 1920. Of the questionnaires that could be dated, seventeen were completed before 1900, fourteen between 1913 and 1917, and five in 1920. Thirty-three of the respondents were born before 1870. Degler offers their answers as evidence that nineteenth-century women both desired and enjoyed sexual relations. For all its interest, the Mosher survey cannot sustain that claim. The size of the sample was far too small to support any generalization about middle-class women. Even more important, the respondents were atypical members of their class because they were far better educated, a fact that may well have influenced their attitudes toward sex. Furthermore, it is unclear whether answers given to a survey done between 1892 and 1920 can be taken to represent nineteenth-century opinion, even if most of the respondents were born before 1870. During the thirty-year period when the survey was carried out, attacks on Victorian conceptions of sex by such people as Havelock Ellis, Ellen Key, and Edward Carpenter influenced educated opinion and initiated the process that Paul Robinson has called "the modernization of sex." James McGovern dates the first sexual revolution from these years.[34] Since there is no way of knowing whether the respondents were influenced by these ideas or not, great caution needs to be exercised in drawing conclusions from their answers.

Although the absolute prohibition on sexual relations outside of marriage theoretically applied to both sexes, in practice the full force of social disapproval for any breaches of the code fell on women.[35] Any middle-class female guilty of premarital or extramarital relations was immediately and forever a social outcast. George Eliot's letters show her full awareness that ostracism was the price she would have to pay for her illicit liaison with George Lewes.

The first major problem at Queen Victoria's court occurred when one of her mother's ladies-in-waiting, Lady Flora Hastings, became ill and suffered physical changes that made her look pregnant. Although she denied the charge, Lady Flora eventually submitted to a humiliating examination by two court doctors. They pronounced her a virgin and stated that she was not and never had been pregnant. Since Victoria detested her mother and everyone connected with her household, she cut Lady Flora in the most brutal manner while she was under suspicion. Even after her exoneration, the queen refused to apologize for her behavior, but simply readmitted her to the royal presence. Lady Flora's relatives continued to feel injured, especially because one of the examining physicians perpetuated suspicion by observing, "though she is a virgin still . . . it might be possible and one could not tell if such things could not happen . . . there was an enlargement in the womb like a child." Victoria persisted in referring to Lady Flora as that "nasty woman." Five months later the unfortunate female died in great pain. According to her family, the cruel and unjust treatment meted out to her by the queen had increased her suffering immeasurably. [36]

In a society so intolerant of any woman suspected of breaching its sexual code, the appearance of virtue was almost as important as virtue itself. Since ignorance and embarrassment were taken as signs of innocence, the most elementary facts of life were carefully hidden from unmarried girls. Sex, childbirth, and the body in general were all forbidden subjects. When Emma Willard opened her female seminary in Troy, New York, in 1821, she shocked her contemporaries by including physiology in the curriculum. To maintain decorum, heavy paper was pasted over the illustrations of the human body. [37] On another level, Victorian clothing served the same purpose by concealing the lower half of the female body. It was, indeed, considered the grossest impropriety to mention in mixed company that women had legs. The nineteenth century even excluded women from their age-old role as midwives on the ground that the presence of females at childbirth endangered their modesty and character. [38] This sort of protective concern inevitably extended to books: Shakespeare, for example, was considered as much too lewd for women to read in any but carefully expurgated editions. Despite these efforts to protect their innocence, it is doubtful that American girls were as ignorant of life as they seemed, according to Barbara Welter. [39]

Both before and after marriage, prudent women protected their reputations by carefully avoiding any compromising situation, If, in spite of all precautions, an improper remark or mention of sex reached their ears, ladies displayed their embarrassment and virtue by lowering their eyes, pretending not to understand, blushing, expressing shock, or, in extreme cases, fainting. Fanny Kemble, an English actress who married an American plantation owner, thought that American society was even more restrictive in some respects than English. When she traveled from Philadelphia to Georgia, she noted in her diary, "The separation of men and women . . . so rigidly observed by all travelling Americans took place . . . a most peculiar and amusing custom."[40] Frances Trollope commented on the social segregation of the two sexes.[41] In the same period, Tocqueville noted the extraordinary constraints placed on American wives, although he also observed that before marriage American women were much freer than their peers in France.[42]

One of the most perplexing interpretative problems connected with the cult of domesticity is that of the origins of its view of women, which stood in such direct opposition to the stereotypes most deeply rooted in Christian civilization. In *The Victorian Frame of Mind*, Walter Houghton attributes it to romanticism and to the need "to counteract the debasing influence on religion as well as morals of a masculine life preoccupied with worldly goods and worldly ambitions."[43] The latter observation begs the question, which is precisely why the nineteenth century turned to woman, hitherto conceived as Eve, as a remedy for its moral problems. Houghton's reference to romanticism is not much more helpful.

Romanticism is a particularly uninformative label because of the richness and complexity of the movement that it is meant to describe. Furthermore, many of the central impulses conventionally described as romantic undermine, rather than encourage, the ethos expressed in the cult of domesticity. The insistence on the unity of flesh and spirit, the glorification of the physical and the emotional, the acceptance of man and all his drives as good, and the rejection of fixed social rules—all emphasize the physical side of human nature, male and female, and legitimize sexuality without any reference to marriage.

The real source of the cult of true womanhood was the attitude toward love, marriage, and women that was emerging in the middle classes in the eighteenth century. The basis of their outlook was, in turn, a secularized version of Protestant doctrines about matrimony.[44] In England and America, the most authentic advocates of Protestant views on the subject were the Puritans. Contrary to their reputation, the Puritans did not deny the sexual impulse or underestimate the importance of physical relations in marriage. Indeed, they condemned couples who did not cohabit, even if it were by mutual agreement. Because of their realism in this respect, they unequivocally asserted that love was the key to successful marriage. Although love came after the wedding, a long enough courtship was necessary to ensure that there was no natural repugnance between the betrothed. Puritan preachers exhorted parents not to interfere with the promptings of their children's hearts. In short, for the first time in English culture, marriage was explicitly connected to love.[45]

Unlike traditional Catholic thinkers, the Puritans valued matrimony as the highest form of Christian life. The home and family that it created were the smallest unit in the godly commonwealth. Domestic prayer, Bible reading, and moral discipline were necessary to sanctify those who struggled to do God's will on earth. So strong was the prejudice against the unmarried in early New England that towns often compelled bachelors to live with married men and their families.[46]

Because they valued matrimony so highly and recognized the importance of the sexual element to its success, the Puritans took premarital and extramarital relations even more seriously than most of their contemporaries.[47] They tried to enforce standards that were often honored more in the breach than in the observance, particularly in aristocratic circles. In seventeenth-century New England, the penalty for adultery was death, although the law was rarely enforced. Morgan attributed this leniency to the frequency of offenses of this type.[48]

During the Restoration, a reaction against the Puritan view of marriage and insistence on sexual fidelity set in. The upper classes particularly turned against the serious moralism characterizing the Puritan approach to life. The development of the London Season, which centered on Charles II's promiscuous court, created an artificial world in which men and women openly spent much of their time in sexual intrigue. Since among the aristocracy marriage functioned primarily as a social and economic liaison unrelated to love, granting sexual freedom to both parties was often the only way to make their unions palatable. Such adjustments involved a relatively equal acceptance of male and female sexuality, and Restoration comedy provides evidence that this milieu did recognize women as lusty creatures.

Despite this, advocates of the much older double standard also survived. George Saville, Marquis of Halifax, was probably the most widely read.[49] Keith Thomas attributes the double standard to "the desire of men for absolute property in women, a desire which cannot be satisfied if the man has reason to believe that the woman has once been possessed by another man."[50] Although he points out the particular strength of this attitude among the upper classes, he does not explain *why* the prevalence of the double standard should vary from one class to another. The reason, in my opinion, is that in the aristocracy women actually functioned as property. Through their dowries and inheritances, they conveyed property from their fathers to their husbands. Aristocratic men rightly associated their wives and daughters with wealth and counted them as economic assets. In such circumstances they easily fell into the habit of regarding women themselves—and, hence, their chastity—among their property. Females did not have quite this significance among poorer economic groups.

Whatever their attitude toward women of their own class, aristocratic men rarely felt any compunction about pursuing middle- and lower-class women, particularly domestic servants. There was some parallel to this pattern in the southern colonies among men in the planter class, who made a fetish of their wives' and daughters' chastity while they openly exploited their female slaves.

Because of the persistence of nonconformity or dissent, the terms used to describe English Puritanism after the Restoration, no corresponding shift in values among the middle classes occurred. The Puritan conception of matrimony as a partnership remained attractive in a class in which wives still often functioned as their husbands' helpmates in business. In an increasingly secular context, therefore, the bourgeoisie inherited and retained a view of marriage that connected it with love and insisted on permarital chastity and marital fidelity. Since sexual passion was the major threat to their marital ideal, they expressed increasingly negative attitudes toward it. They particularly associated destructive lust with men, since the prevalence of the double standard ensured that males were the more obvious sexual offenders. That aristocratic men pursued the wives and daughters of the middle and lower classes almost as a birthright only accentuated the feeling that women were the helpless victims of male passion.

In the eighteenth century, the idea had already appeared that marriage was a form of social discipline for unregenerate men, while women were more or less exempt from sexual feeling. To a certain extent, females accepted suitors not to secure joint satisfaction, but to elevate them morally. The economic security that women sought in marriage was a fair trade for the ethical benefits that they conferred.

One of the reasons that the eighteenth century considered it shocking for a woman to marry beneath her station was that it showed she had surrendered to sexual passion. [51] Dr. Johnson's widowed friend, Mrs. Thrale, caused shock and dismay when she admitted to choosing her second husband, an Italian musician, for love.

All that was needed to turn the chaste, morally superior women of eighteenth-century bourgeois culture into the ideal of true womanhood, in fact, was to heighten and poeticize the ideas of feminine asexuality and of the female's mission to elevate the more passionate male. The evangelical revival contributed to this process in the final years of the eighteenth century and early decades of the nineteenth. In conjunction with the French Revolution, which was perceived as a moral threat, evangelicalism spread the cult of sexual purity and induced at least a portion of the upper class to accept codes of behavior that originated in the bourgeoisie. [52]

The triumph of this middle-class ethos was connected to the fact that these decades saw the triumph of the Industrial Revolution in England and the rise of the bourgeoisie to a position of economic and political power that it had never held before. The contrast between male and female nature was extended to include sins flowing from materialism, greed, and unlimited economic competition, a logical extension in an economy that excluded women. Males were aggressive, selfish, tough, and lusty; females were passive, altruistic, soft, and sexless. Since the very survival of individual and social virtue depended on women, their natural purity had to be carefully protected in the home. Thus, in the late eighteenth and early nineteenth centuries, economic and ideological movements converged to produce the image of females central to the cult of true womanhood.

In the colonies, where there was no aristocracy in the European sense, Protestant attitudes toward love and marriage faced little competition from an opposing set of values and code of behavior. As in England, the double standard encouraged both sexes to regard men as more passionate than women and to idealize females as the guardians of sexual virtue. [53] The double standard was particularly evident in the South, where the emphasis on the white woman's chastity paralleled the shameless sexual exploitation of female slaves. Since England supplied eighteenth-century Americans with most of their reading material, opinion on this side of the Atlantic was influenced by English novels, conduct books, and marriage manuals, which espoused the view that women were less sexually driven than men.[54]

Finally, and probably of crucial importance, the first decades of the nineteenth century saw both the Second Great Awakening and what Barbara Welter calls the "feminization of religion."[55] As men were swept up in the restless westward search for land, the first stages of industrialization, and the tumultuous politics of the Jacksonian era, they increasingly left the churches and the care of their souls to women. This association of religion with the feminine sphere enabled women, who suffered from status anxiety as more and more functions were removed from the home, to define themselves and to achieve a sense of belonging to a community. The groups and organizations attached to the churches also provided them with a chance to use the full range of their moral, intellectual, and physical powers. Finally, as Nancy Cott has perceptively pointed out, the evangelical churches required a religious choice—submission to God—that reflected the proper relationship of women to authority figures, but at the same time permitted them to assert themselves privately and publicly against the male power structure by appealing to a higher authority. The inclusion of religion in the female sphere seemed natural in a society that regarded women as the purer sex.[56] Conversely, the association of women, religion, and the church reinforced the ideas that they were ethically superior to men and acted as the guardians of community morality. Ministers, who depended increasingly on female congregations, united with them in the struggle against male sin.[57] Since moral righteousness meant completely avoiding illicit sexuality, the woman's new religious function strengthened the belief that she was less tempted by strong instinctual drives. The connection between the evangelical revival and the woman idealized by the cult of true womanhood was particularly explicit in the thought of the female moral reformers.

As I have emphasized, the image of woman central to the cult of domesticity originated, and was most influential, among the middle classes. Recent scholarship has produced evidence that sexual practices and attitudes among the lower classes varied considerably from middle-class norms. According to Keith Thomas, the insistence on female chastity was much less intense among the English lower

classes than among the aristocracy or the bourgeoisie.[58] His suggestion conforms to P. E. H. Hair's findings of considerable illegitimacy
and bridal pregnancy among the peasantry as far back as the sixteenth century.[59] Even more significant in underscoring the contrast
between middle- and lower-class mores is Hair's findings that illegitimacy rates increased dramatically in the eighteenth century and remained at those higher levels through the nineteenth, the very period
when middle-class sexual mores were becoming more repressive.

Historians do not agree on the significance of these higher illegitimacy rates. Edward Shorter dates a sexual revolution among the
European lower classes from the era of the French Revolution.[60] He
interprets higher illegitimacy rates as evidence of increased premarital and extramarital sex. Joan Scott and Louise Tilly take a very different view.[61] They believe that premarital sex was common among the
peasantry in the preindustrial era. Women entered such relations in
the expectation that marriage would follow. In the context of cohesive
rural communities their expectations were fulfilled, particularly in
the event of pregnancy, so illegitimacy rates remained low. When they
moved to cities, females of peasant origin continued traditional sexual
practices, but with very different results. The expectation of marriage
was not fulfilled, and illegitimacy rates soared. Scott and Tilly attribute the new consequences of customary mores to the greater mobility
of men in an urban setting, to poverty, especially the female's lack of a
dowry or money for a proper wedding, and to the absence of the kind
of community pressure to marry that came from family, church, and
neighbors in a rural village.

The movement of illegitimacy rates was somewhat different on this
side of the Atlantic. As in Europe, rates soared in the eighteenth century. Here, however, they declined markedly in the early nineteenth
century, while European rates remained high. In their analysis of the
American pattern, Daniel Smith and Michael Hindus agree with
Scott and Tilly in connecting high illegitimacy rates with the disintegration of community control over young adults. However, whereas
Scott and Tilly find this erosion to be dependent on fundamental economic change, Smith and Hindus trace it to a revolt of the young
against the authority of the family. Smith and Hindus also differ from
Scott and Tilly in their description of sexual mores in communities
with low illegitimacy rates. As indicated above, Scott and Tilly main-

tain that in traditional Europe low illegitimacy rates coexisted with relatively permissive norms of sexual behavior. Smith and Hindus find, in contrast, that in America the successful enforcement of repressive sexual ideologies accounted for the low incidence of illegitimacy and premarital pregnancy in both the seventeenth and the nineteenth centuries. The difference between the two periods was that the Puritans relied on external controls to confine sex to marriage, the Victorians on self-repression.[62] Whatever the reason for rising illegitimacy rates, their appearance at the very time when middle-class sexual mores were becoming more restrictive underscores the class character of the cult of true womanhood. Charles Rosenberg even suggests that one reason that the middle classes expressed so much hostility to their servants was envy and fear of their greater sexual freedom.[63]

Within the safe island of her home, the woman's most important function was bearing and raising children. Indeed, the definition of the woman as mother was a more and more accurate description of reality as fewer and fewer economic functions were performed in the home. In the Victorian period motherhood came to have the emotional and semisacred connotations that tempt one to write it with a capital *M*. The mother's task was to see to the physical well-being of her offspring, to preserve their moral innocence, to protect them from evil influences, and to inspire them to pursue the highest spiritual values. If woman failed in this duty, she jeopardized the whole progress of civilization—an awesome responsibility, indeed. The literature of female moral reformers reflected these beliefs about motherhood, calling on mothers to destroy male sinfulness by indoctrinating their sons into a higher feminine morality.

The glorification of motherhood and exaggeration of its responsibilities were as new an element in Anglo-American culture as the opinion that women were particularly virtuous. Indeed, the two ideas evolved together and reinforced one another in eighteenth-century thought.

The central thesis of Philippe Aries's seminal work, *Centuries of Childhood*, is that new attitudes toward childhood and motherhood emerged in Western Europe in the seventeenth and eighteenth centuries.[64] Until well into the seventeenth century, motherhood was not considered one of women's major functions nor surrounded with awesome moral responsibilities. Because relatively little importance or prestige was attached to child rearing, women who could afford them used wet nurses. In some cases, the infant was even sent to live with the nurse. Since using wet nurses made women much more available to their husbands, upper-class men benefited from, and probably advocated, these arrangements. Affluent women who nursed their children were considered examples of extraordinary maternal devotion. [65]

Whatever arrangements were made for the infant, childhood ended much earlier than today, and youngsters entered the adult world long before puberty. Those destined for trade or a craft were apprenticed at the age of seven or eight and sent to live with their masters. [66] Parents in the lower classes placed their children in domestic service as soon as some menial job could be found for them. In *The World We Have Lost*, Peter Laslett observes that few children of the poor lived at home. [67]

In England, even parents free from financial necessity sent their offspring to live with others. [68] This custom originated in the Middle Ages, when placing a child in the home of someone of higher rank to be educated was a primary form of social climbing. [69] By the sixteenth century the English often attributed it to their fear that they would be too indulgent of their children's faults and spoil them. [70] In the 1570s, for example, Sir Robert Sidney wrote to his wife, Barbara, about placing their two daughters:

You know wel enough, whoe hath bin desirous to have them, and where they should bee as wel looked unto, as they can be in your own House, and more to their Good, and less to my charges. I meene for the Girls with my Lady of Huntington, and my Lady of Warwick, with whom also you told me you were willing to leave them. They are not so yong now, but that they may wel bee from their mother. Mary is almost ten, and Kate almost eight; and though I cannot find fault hether unto, with their Bringing Up, yet I know every Day more and more, it wil bee fit for them to bee owt of their Father's Hows. For heer they cannot learne, what they may do in other Places; and yet, perhaps, take such Humors, which may be hurtful for them heerafter. [71]

Sabine Johnson, wife of a successful mid-sixteenth-century English merchant, spent much of her childhood in the home of an aunt and uncle, while she and her husband, in turn, helped to raise one of their nieces. [72] Ralph Josselin, a clergyman and yeoman farmer, sent all his children from home before they were fifteen-and-a-half. He apprenticed his two sons in London, placed two of his daughters in domestic service, and sent the other girls to school. [73] The Puritans frequently "put out" their children, a custom that they carried with them to the colonies. [74] Even if children remained at home, however, their mothers rarely had sole responsibility for their care much beyond the age of seven, particularly in the case of boys. In Renaissance Italy boys entered the communal day schools when they were seven, at the latest. Between the ages of ten and twelve they left home entirely to enter grammar school or to assume an apprenticeship that required them to live with their masters. [75] In his study of French families in the seventeenth and eighteenth centuries, David Hunt notes that in the earlier period strong emotional ties between mother and child were discouraged. Children belonged to their father, who made all the crucial decisions about their education, careers, and marriage. At about seven, boys were taken "out of the hands of women." [76] According to Levin Schüking, mothers in seventeenth-century Puritan families had little to do that was considered important in the process of child rearing except for teaching their offspring the catechism. Children had little respect for their mothers because they observed that they were less well educated and less cultivated than their mates and occupied an obviously subordinate place in the home. [77]

According to Ariès, in the seventeenth and eighteenth centuries, these attitudes and practices began to change. Ever since the late medieval period, influential educators and churchmen had viewed childhood as a separate stage of life in which the child should be segregated from the adult world and subjected to a special discipline. They advocated educational reforms based on these ideas and ultimately created the authoritarian boarding school of seventeenth-century France. Ariès sees their efforts as part of a larger process in which a small elite struggled to impose order, hierarchy, and discipline on the chaotic, turbulent world of the Middle Ages. In every area, institutional control over individual behavior increased. The triumph of absolutism and the spread of these new attitudes toward children were, therefore, parallel developments. Natalie Davis's work on sixteenth- and seventeenth-century France supports Ariès's thesis. She claims that both Protestant and Catholic political and religious authorities wanted to increase their control over the young in order to ensure that they would grow up with the right attitudes. [78]

By the eighteenth century educational and clerical reformers had succeeded in spreading their view of childhood into the upper and middle classes. The result was a change in the character of the family among these groups. They attached a new importance to the parent-child relationship and especially to the role of the family in the youngster's moral training. Parents were particularly concerned to protect their children from sexual knowledge and experience, which continued to be regarded as the major source of temptation and sin. In England and the American colonies, Puritan attitudes toward the family reflected the same process of modernization. [79] Since these changes coincided with the emergence of the view that women were free from lust and morally superior to men, the mother was especially suitable to assume the new ethical responsibilities vested in the home and family. The increasing emphasis on the woman's role as mother was a central element in the cult of domesticity and contributed to its development and appeal.

The family that this cult idealized was a large one. What is surprising to the twentieth century is how many middle-class nineteenth-century families included four, five, six, and seven children. Even in an unlikely group such as the early feminists, family size tended to be large. A survey of twenty-one of the leaders of the movement revealed that sixteen married, and nine of these had four or more children. [80] (So much for the stereotype of feminists as bitter old maids.)

Despite the impression that these large families create and the social approval accorded to them, the birth rate in the United States fell dramatically in the nineteenth century. The average number of children born to a white woman surviving to menopause fell from 7.04 in 1800 to 6.14 in 1840, to 4.24 in 1880, and finally to 3.56 in 1900. [81] Historians agree that conscious family limitation was responsible for this trend, but they disagree on the motives for it.

In their study of falling birth rates among middle-class English families in the last three decades of the nineteenth century, J. A. and Olive Banks attribute family limitation to the initiative of husbands, who sought to protect their comfortable standard of living in an era of economic depression and uncertainty by limiting the number of their children. [82] The Banks argue against the thesis that feminism contributed to the falling birth rate, because family planning was not one of the demands of English feminists, who were primarily concerned with single women, whether spinsters, widows, or females whose marriages had broken down. They also doubt that feminism had enough influence in the period to account for the significant decline in the birth rate. Furthermore, since relatively few married women worked outside the home before World War I, the Banks feel that they lacked a sufficient motive to limit the number of their children. Finally, dominant Victorian attitudes toward sexuality encouraged feminists to oppose, rather than support, contraception. With the prevalent association of sex, men, and bestiality, nineteenth-century woman wanted to extend female standards of virtue and chastity to men, not to separate sex from conception nor to free lust from its consequences. They considered contraception a means to subordinate women further to male lust, rather than to liberate them.

Recent research on family limitation in nineteenth-century America casts doubt on whether the Banks study can be applied to this country, even if it is accurate for England. [83] Daniel Smith argues that although the cult of domesticity did confine the vast majority of middle-class, respectable women to the home, it enabled them to increase their power vis-à-vis their husbands within this sphere. Conscious birth control resulted from their increased influence within the family. [84] Opposition to mechanical contraception, rooted in nineteenth-century views of sexuality, did not prevent conscious birth control, since the most popular methods were abstinence and *coitus interruptus*.

In a fascinating discussion of voluntary motherhood, Linda Gordon links three groups of feminists—proponents of free love, suffragists, and moral reformers—to propaganda for birth control through permanent or periodic abstinence. [85] All of these women idealized sexual self-control, rejected the necessity or desirability of frequent sexual intercourse, considered the wife's right to refuse her husband's sexual demands to be necessary for her personal integrity, and supported voluntary motherhood as part of their broad commitment to women's rights. Gordon and Smith, therefore, differ from the Bankses on two fundamental points: they do not equate contraception and birth control, nor do they equate confinement to the domestic sphere and powerlessness within the family. Finally, Gordon demonstrates that many public nineteenth-century feminists did openly advocate family limitation.

The cult of domesticity was thus a compound of ideas—the restriction of the woman's proper sphere to the home, her moral superiority, and the idealization of her function as mother—that were relatively new elements in English and American culture. These ideas joined with the older traditions of female subordination and intellectual inferiority to shape nineteenth-century attitudes toward women. Little attention was paid to the obvious conflict between idealizing women's maternal and moral nature and simultaneously advocating male superiority. Opponents of higher education for women and of their entrance into the professions drew indifferently on both sets of assumptions to bolster their case.

Nonetheless, it was the cult of domesticity, not the older tradition of female inferiority and subordination, that was most characteristic of nineteenth-century ideas about women and that appeared most frequently in the flood of fiction and nonfiction designed to define the female role and tell women how to behave. Many Victorian Americans who rejected, or at least equivocated about, ideas of female subordination and inferiority still advocated an exceedingly restricted role for women, because they accepted fully the assumptions of the cult of true womanhood.

The appeal of this ideal, even to women like Catharine Beecher and Sarah Hale who regarded themselves as champions of their sex, derived from its apparent success in compensating women for the real loss in economic and political status and function that they suffered from 1800 to 1850.[86] Industrialization and urbanization had removed and were continuing to remove many economic functions from the home. In a society that put a high premium on profit making, the transformation of females from producers to consumers invariably reduced their stature. In the same period, the development of public schools, the professionalization of medicine, and the increasing interest in organized philanthropy also diminished the importance of the domestic sphere. As long as women, particularly middle-class women, were confined to the home, they really did have fewer things to do that were highly valued by their culture. Yet, public opinion was less and less tolerant of females who sought roles outside the home. This loss of function, and of the self-esteem that went with it, occurred at the same time as a relative loss in the political domain. While the expansion of the franchise in the 1830s and 1840s gave the vote to virtually all white men, native females were left humiliated, as recent immigrants, whom they considered their inferiors, went to the polls. The cult of domesticity reflected these developments by drawing much sharper distinctions between male and female functions than had previously existed in American culture. Even more important, it made confinement to the home acceptable by assuring women that their presence as wives and mothers was necessary to preserve individual and social morality and to save the nation from sin.

Besides defining a new role for women as their traditional functions evaporated or rapidly changed character, the cult of domesticity established a new basis for social morality and stability in a culture that felt itself to be increasingly adrift in both these areas. In the early nineteenth century the most compelling tasks facing American men were conquering the land and making their fortunes. Since women were excluded from these activities, it was natural and practical to assign them the job of tending to the ethical and religious concerns for which their male relatives had no time. This division of function enabled the society to quiet its anxiety about the fundamental amorality of its commitment to materialism without changing its basic direction, It also preserved the sexual hierarchy in an era when almost every other form of social classification was crumbling in the face of extraordinary pressure toward egalitarianism. Finally, the inclusion of all females in the role defined by the cult of true womanhood underscored the absence of class divisions in the United States and the retention of only "natural" distinctions such as race and sex. [87]

From the 1860s on, Darwinism powerfully reinforced the influence of the cult of domesticity by justifying it in biological terms that were accepted as scientific truth. [88] In the late nineteenth century, science replaced religion as the ultimate arbiter of truth in almost every area of human thought. Consequently, the persistence of the cult of true womanhood was closely connected to the fact that most Americans believed it to be based on a scientific view of feminine nature. Darwinism did not alter prevalent views about women; it gave them a new up-to-date sanction.

Darwin asserted that evolution resulted from the survival of the more fit members of a species. The process of natural selection, as he called it, depended on chance variations within a species, which gave certain individuals a competitive advantage over others. Differences between the sexes developed in the same way. Men have a higher metabolic rate than women, which generated more variations among males and more aggressiveness than occurs among females. Since natural selection depended on choice among different characteristics, the greater variation among men meant that they have evolved more successfully into stronger and more intelligent beings than women. The specific mechanism that favored the survival of superior males was sexual selection. The female passively selected her mate by choosing the more handsome or stronger male. Over generations this produced offspring bearing the advantageous characteristics of the successful suitors.

Motherhood increased women's disadvantage because it made them dependent on men. This dependence removed them to a certain extent from the progressive process of natural selection by linking their survival to the success or failure of their mates, rather than to their own qualities in comparison with other women.

Since all sex-linked characteristics passed to the child from the parent of the same sex, boys inherited from their fathers the physical and mental advantages that resulted from the males' higher metabolic rate and greater influence of natural selection, while the girls of each generation started out further and further behind. According to Darwin, each parent transmitted non-sex-linked traits to children of both sexes. However, all characteristics acquired after puberty were sex-linked and could be passed only to offspring of the same sex. Males inherited all sex-linked characteristics from their fathers, females from their mothers.

Women had less developed brains for the same reasons that they were less fit in all areas. A hierarchy of mental functions moved in descending order, from reason to imagination to imitation to intuition to instinct. The more highly evolved male mind performed more efficiently at the higher range of this scale, the simpler female brain at the lower. The discovery by anthropologists that women's brains were smaller and less convoluted than men's seemed to confirm Darwin's theories.

For sixty years or more after publication of *The Origin of Species* in 1859, social scientists concerned with differences between the sexes thought almost exclusively in Darwinian terms. Many of them went even further than Darwin had in explaining human potential and behavior patterns by reference to instincts produced by evolution and operating independently of the social environment. One of the principal works on the subject, *The Evolution of Sex* by Patrick Geddes and J. Arthur Thomson, eliminated all social influences from its analysis of sex differences.

In spite of the dominance of the values and code of behavior embodied in the cult of domesticity, the role that it prescribed for women never met the needs of energetic and intelligent females. Nor did it really accord them high status despite the effusions of writers like Ruskin. One of the most influential women in nineteenth-century America, Catharine Beecher, recognized the problem in her own life and tried to solve it without challenging the basic definition of woman's sphere.[89] Beecher believed that the female's essential obligation was domestic and that raising a family was a sacred function. Nonetheless, she never married nor maintained a permanent home, and she fought to establish her position and achievements as an independent woman. She believed that women's power stemmed from their role as the saviors of society and from their dedication to the Christlike qualities of humility and self-sacrifice. She hoped to increase the female's status by turning household management into domestic science and expanding it to absorb women's intellectual and administrative capacities. She advocated teaching, which she considered a natural extension of the maternal function, as a proper career for single or needy females.[90]

Domestic science, motherhood, and teaching all required education, albeit one particularly designed to train women for their proper roles. In line with this belief Beecher established two secondary schools for women, the Hartford Female Seminary and the Western Female Institute in Cincinnati. She also founded the American Women's Educational Association, which inspired the establishment of schools in Milwaukee, Wisconsin; Dubuque, Iowa; and Quincy, Illinois. Thus, within a conservative frame of reference, Beecher became an advocate of women's education.

The founders of two other early institutions of higher education for women also developed their ideas without directly challenging the cult of domesticity. Emma Willard established her female seminary in Troy, New York, to educate girls for the roles and duties appropriate to their sex. She had, however, fairly broad ideas about the learning necessary to accomplish this end, so the education that she provided was actually on quite a high level.

Mary Lyon founded Mount Holyoke Female Seminary specifically to train teachers. Like Catharine Beecher, she considered that profession to be a natural adjunct to women's maternal function and had a high estimate of the necessary qualifications. With this in mind, she tried to offer the equivalent of a college education. To show that Mount Holyoke was not subversive in intent, as well as to save money, she required her students to perform all the housekeeping tasks necessary to keep the school running.

Although the cult of domesticity was really relevant only to the married middle-class woman, the standards that it set affected numerous females who did not fit into this category, especially the middle-class spinster without an adequate inheritance or a relative with whom to live. Faced by the necessity of maintaining her respectability while supporting herself, she had very few options.[91] Governess, teacher, author—there was little else she could do without losing status. Catharine Beecher's success in incorporating teaching into the cult of domesticity was therefore especially pertinent to the single woman's needs. By a happy coincidence, her achievement came at a time when the public school system was expanding rapidly and the need for teachers growing. Since education was one of the main items in a town's budget, the taxpayers were anxious to keep the cost of the schools low. One of the best ways was to hire females, since they normally received only 30 to 50 percent of the salary paid a man with comparable qualifications and duties.[92]

No other professions were open to the needy middle-class spinster. The two most important in this country were the ministry and the law. The first feminists attacked both for excluding females, but the situation did not even begin to change until after the Civil War. As long as colleges were closed to women, they obviously could not teach at that level. Even if they had had the requisite education, respectable females could not assume public roles at male institutions.

The situation in medicine was no better, but for different reasons.[93] During the nineteenth century, doctors first began to achieve professional status in this country, a complex process that involved establishing medical schools and a system of licensing to ensure that only graduates could legally practice. Medical schools did not, as a matter of policy, admit women. Gradually, as techniques developed that required training, particularly the use of the forceps, the doctors even drew midwifery into their spheres. In any case, Victorian notions about modesty and propriety excluded respectable women from any active role in assisting the process of childbirth. In 1818 a Boston physician wrote,

It is obvious that we cannot instruct women as we do men in the science of medicine; we cannot carry them into the dissecting room and the hospital. . . . I venture to say, that a female could scarce pass through the course of education, requisite to prepare her as she ought to be prepared, for the practice of midwifery without destroying those moral qualities of character, which are essential to the office.[94]

The experience of one of the first successful female doctors in this country, Harriot Hunt, is instructive.[95] Harriot and her sister Sarah studied medicine with an English couple named Mott, who had arrived in Boston, advertised as physicians, and cured Sarah of a prolonged and hitherto incurable illness. In 1835 the sisters went out on their own. Gradually they built up a successful practice, mostly among women and children, specializing in cases given up by other doctors as incurable. They relied heavily on good nursing, diet, bathing, exercise, and sanitation, In 1847, Harriot, practicing alone since her sister had married, applied for permission to attend lectures at Harvard Medical College. Although the dean was inclined to try the experiment, the governing board overruled him. Three years later they reversed their decision, but Harriot withdrew when the medical students rioted. In 1853 the Female Medical College of Philadelphia awarded her an honorary degree as Doctor of Medicine.

Although the cult of domesticity was particularly relevant to the middle class, it also affected women in the lower classes. Regardless of the ideal, many of them, whether single or married, had to work outside the home at jobs that failed to meet the standards of respectability. In the most prosperous segments of the working class, however, there was a conscious effort to imitate the bourgeois style of life, and wives tended to stay at home as soon as it was economically feasible. By the end of the nineteenth century, the British working class had absorbed many middle-class attitudes toward women. Except in the textile towns, wives were not supposed to work outside the home. The few who did were real exceptions to the rule. [96] A recent study of the laboring poor in Victorian England describes as the norm the family in which the wife did not work outside the home. In such households the husband lived on a significantly higher standard of living than either his wife or children, particularly in terms of food and medical care. By staying at home, these working-class women sacrificed both the power that contributing to the family income would have given them and the badly needed money that they might have earned. [97]

In the United States most of the workers in the early textile industry were young, single women attracted from the farms in the surrounding countryside. When they married, they left the mills, as one would expect in the nineteenth-century context. Even when immigrants replaced natives in factories, fewer wives worked on a regular basis than is often thought. [98]

Any estimate of the ideological dominance and behavioral influence of the cult of true womanhood must, therefore, always be balanced against the class, racial, and regional limitations on its applicability, the economic and psychic hardship suffered by middle-class spinsters and working-class women who struggled to conform to it, and the dissatisfaction of many of the middle-class wives for whom it was particularly intended. The contradictions and conflicts that the cult of domesticity inevitably engendered when an effort was made to translate it into reality inspired opposition to it at the very moment when it seemed to triumph.

Notes

1. The best study of the cult of domesticity is Nancy F. Cott, *The Bonds of Womanhood: "Woman's Sphere" in New England, 1780-1835* (New Haven: Yale University Press, 1977). Also highly recommended are Barbara Welter, *Dimity Convictions: The American Woman in the Nineteenth Century* (Athens: Ohio University Press, 1976), and Ann Douglas, *The Feminization of American Culture* (New York: Alfred A. Knopf, 1977). For an introduction to source material on the subject, see Nancy F. Cott, ed., *Root of Bitterness:*

Documents of the Social History of American Women (New York: E. P. Dutton, 1972). Everyone interested in the cult of true womanhood ought to read (or reread) Louisa May Alcott's *Little Women*, which depicts the socialization of four very different girls into conformity with the female model extolled by the cult of domesticity.

2. John Ruskin, "Of Queens' Gardens," in his *Sesame and Lilies* (New York: Thomas Y. Crowell & Co., n.d.), pp. 115-17.

3. Louisa May Alcott, *Little Women* (New York: Collier Books, 1962), p. 95.

4. Harriet Beecher Stowe, "The Cathedral," in *The Oven Birds: American Women on Womanhood, 1820-1920*, ed. Gail Parker (Garden City, N.Y.: Doubleday, 1972), p. 213.

5. Diane Hughes, "Domestic Ideals and Social Behavior: Evidence from Medieval Genoa," in *The Family in History*, ed. Charles E. Rosenberg (Philadelphia: University of Pennsylvania Press, 1975), pp. 124-43.

6. Eileen Power, *Medieval Women*, ed. M. M. Postan (Cambridge: Cambridge University Press, 1975), pp. 60-61. In France women were better integrated into the guild structure; ibid., pp. 62, 65.

7. Mary R. Beard, *Woman as Force in History* (New York: Collier Books, 1962), pp. 234-35.

8. Barbara Winchester, *Tudor Family Portrait* (London: Jonathan Cape, 1955), pp. 84-85, for examples of female merchants in England and the Low Countries.

9. Power, *Medieval Women*, pp. 62-67.

10. Raymond de Roover, *The Rise and Decline of the Medici Bank*, 1397-1494 (New York: W. W. Norton, 1966).

11. Lauro Martines, "A Way of Looking at Women in Renaissance Florence," *Journal of Medieval and Renaissance Studies* 4 (Spring 1974): 15-28. Iris Origo, *The Merchant of Prato: Francesco Di Marco Datini* (New York: Alfred A. Knopf, 1957), pt. 2, chaps. 1-2.

12. Alice Clark, *Working Life of Women in the Seventeenth Century* (New York: Augustus M. Kelley, 1968). Clark's thesis is stated clearly in the introduction, pp. 1-13. Natalie Zemon Davis, *Society and Culture in Early Modern France* (Stanford, Calif.: Stanford University Press, 1975), p. 94, sees a decline in the position of French women in middle-level commerce and farm work in roughly the same period.

13. Margaret George, "From 'Goodwife' to 'Mistress': The Transformation of the Female in Bourgeois Culture," *Science and Society* 37 (Summer 1973): 157-59.

14. Clark's book has had an enormous influence on all subsequent interpretations of the position of women in preindustrial, capitalist economies.

The most serious flaw in her thesis has been discussed in the text. However, there are many other problems with her work that need to be recognized because of its impact on contemporary scholarship. Clark's thesis of decline requires her to compare the situation of working women at the beginning of the seventeenth century with their situation at its end. Yet one of the obvious characteristics of her book is its loose sense of chronology. Clark puts evidence from different parts of the century together to make various points, without realizing that in so doing she undermines her contention that a basic trend significantly changed women's position between 1600 and 1700. The exploitation and suffering of women in the textile industries and of female agricultural laborers was due to chronic unemployment and underemployment, disorganized foreign and domestic markets, restrictions on labor mobility, and wage discrimination, rather than on the development of capitalism per se or the nonexistent movement of work out of the home. Indeed, many of these conditions were just as common in the Middle Ages as in the seventeenth century. As a matter of fact, the increasingly capitalistic orientation of agriculture and the textile industries created desperately needed jobs because they were both labor intensive.

Although Clark states that fewer women traded independently in the seventeenth century than earlier, she presents no convincing evidence for this statement, which can hardly be sustained by impressions based on the scattered examples that she cites. Her contention that the position of women in the fields of medicine and midwifery was deteriorating was more convincing than most of the generalizations, but to attribute the development in a vague way to capitalism is hardly satisfactory. The real problem was that improvements in technique and professionalization were beginning in an environment that already regarded women as inferior, assigned them subordinate social and economic roles, and routinely discriminated against them. Finally, Clark's whole book is based on an unrealistically rosy picture of women's place in the medieval economy, particularly in crafts and trades. See pages 35-37 above on that point.

15. George, "From 'Goodwife' to 'Mistress,'" pp. 157-59.

16. Elisabeth Dexter, *Colonial Women of Affairs: Women in Business and the Professions in America Before 1776*, 2d ed, rev. (Clifton, N.J.: Augustus Kelley Publishers, 1972). Julia Spruill, *Women's Life and Work in the Southern Colonies* (New York: W. W. Norton, 1972), chaps. 11-14.

17. Roger Thompson, *Women in Stuart England and America: A Comparative Study* (Boston: Routledge and Kegan Paul, 1974), pp. 60-77.

18. Cott, *Bonds of Womanhood*, pp. 20-22.

19. See above, pages 19-20, and Mary Roth Walsh, *"Doctors Wanted: No Women Need Apply": Sexual Barriers in the Medical Profession, 1835-1975*

(New Haven: Yale University Press, 1977), pp. 2-18.

20. Spruill, *Women's Life in the Southern Colonies*, pp. 241-42.

21. Elisabeth Dexter, *Career Women of America, 1776-1840* (Francetown, N.H.: Marshall Jones Company, 1950), pp. 219-27.

22. Ibid., pp. 225-26. Dexter is one of the influential historians writing on women who emphasizes the importance of female physicians and midwives in the colonial period; *Colonial Women of Affairs*, chap. 4 and pp. 189-94. Gerda Lerner takes this position in "The Lady and the Mill Girl: Changes in the Status of Women in the Age of Jackson," in *Our American Sisters: Women in American Life and Thought*, 2nd ed., ed. Jean E. Friedman and William G. Shade (Boston: Allyn and Bacon, 1976), pp. 122-24. For Mary Walsh's criticism of this view, see *Doctors Wanted*, pp. 2-18.

23. John Demos, "The American Family in Past Time," *American Scholar* 43 (Summer 1974): 433-35. Lerner, "Lady and the Mill Girl," pp. 120-32.

24. Lerner, "Lady and the Mill Girl," pp. 127-30.

25. Nancy Cott has noted correctly that the southern image of the lady belonged to an aristocratic tradition contrasting in important ways with the bourgeois cult of true womanhood that originated in New England. This is true despite many apparent similarities between them; *Bonds of Womanhood*, p. 11, n. 7.

26. For the material discussed in the last two paragraphs, see Welter, *Dimity Convictions*, chaps. 4-5; Carroll Smith-Rosenberg, "Puberty to Menopause: The Cycle of Femininity in Nineteenth-Century America," in *Clio's Consciousness Raised*, ed. Mary S. Hartman and Lois Banner (New York: Harper Torchbooks, 1974), pp. 23-37; Carroll Smith-Rosenberg, "The Hysterical Woman: Sex, Roles and Role Conflict in Nineteenth-Century America," *Social Research* 39 (Winter 1972): 652-78; Carroll Smith-Rosenberg and Charles E. Rosenberg, "The Female Animal: Medical and Biological Views of Woman and Her Role in Nineteenth-Century America," *The Journal of American History* 60 (September 1973): 332-56.

27. Recent works that support the interpretation of Victorian attitudes toward sexuality presented here include Ronald G. Walters, *Primers for Prudery: Sexual Advice to Victorian America* (Englewood Cliffs, N.J.: Prentice-Hall, 1974); Welter, *Dimity Convictions*, pp. 23-27; Michael Gordon, "From an Unfortunate Necessity to a Cult of Mutual Orgasm: Sex in American Marital Education Literature, 1830-1940," in *Studies in the Sociology of Sex*, ed. James M. Henslin (New York: Appleton-Century-Crofts, 1971), pp. 53-77; John Haller and Robin Haller, *The Physician and Sexuality in Victorian America* (Urbana: University of Illinois Press, 1974), chap, 3; Charles E. Rosenberg, "Sexuality, Class and Role in Nineteenth-Century America," *American Quarterly* 25 (May 1973): 131-53; Carroll Smith-Rosen-

berg, "Beauty, the Beast and the Militant Woman: A Case Study in Sex Roles and Social Stress in Jacksonian America," *American Quarterly* 23 (October 1971): 562-84; and Linda Gordon, "Voluntary Motherhood: The Beginnings of Feminist Birth Control Ideas in the United States," in *Clio's Consciousness Raised*, pp. 54-71.

28. M. Gordon, "An Unfortunate Necessity," p. 58.

29. Nancy F. Cott, "Eighteenth-Century Family Life and Social Life Revealed in Massachusetts Divorce Records," *Journal of Social History* 10 (Fall 1976): 27, 29, suggests that greater sexual openness was characteristic of colonial society.

30. Smith-Rosenberg, "Beauty, the Beast and the Militant Woman," pp. 570-75.

31. Carl N. Degler, "What Ought to Be and What Was: Women's Sexuality in the Nineteenth Century," *American Historical Review* 79 (December 1974): 1467-90.

32. Recent writers who agree with me without ignoring the existence of other attitudes toward sexuality are M. Gordon, "An Unfortunate Necessity," pp. 53-77; C. Rosenberg, "Sexuality, Class and Role," pp. 131-53; and Haller and Haller, *Physician in Victorian America*, chap. 3.

33. Degler, "What Ought to Be and What Was," p. 1471.

34. Paul Robinson, *The Modernization of Sex: Havelock Ellis, Alfred Kinsey, William Masters and Virginia Johnson* (New York: Harper & Row, 1976). James R. McGovern, "The American Woman's Pre-World War I Freedom in Manners and Morals," in *Our American Sisters*, ed. Friedman and Shade, pp. 345-65.

35. Haller and Haller, *Physician in Victorian America*, pp. 237-38, 270.

36. Elizabeth Longford, *Queen Victoria: Born to Succeed* (New York: Pyramid Books, 1966), pp. 94-107, 120-24. Sir Charles Clarke's comment is on p. 99; Victoria's, on p. 104.

37. Eleanor Flexner, *Century of Struggle: The Woman's Rights Movement in the United States* (New York: Atheneum, 1971), p. 26.

38. See, for example, the quotation on page 61.

39. Welter, *Dimity Convictions*, p. 13.

40. Frances Anne Kemble, *Journal of a Residence on a Georgian Plantation in 1838-1839* (New York: Alfred A. Knopf, 1961), pp. 14, 21.

41. Frances Trollope, *Domestic Manners of the Americans* (London: Folio Society, 1974), pp. 120-22.

42. Alexis de Tocqueville, *Democracy in America*, 2 vols. (New York: Vintage Books, 1945), vol. 2, book 3, chaps. 9-10.

43. Walter Houghton, *The Victorian Frame of Mind* (New Haven: Yale University Press, 1957), chap. 13, pt. 2, esp. pp. 350-51 (p. 351 quoted).

44. Ian Watt, *Rise of the Novel* (Berkeley and Los Angeles: University of California Press, 1957), pp. 154-64. Christopher Hill, "Clarissa Harlowe and Her Times," in his *Puritanism and Revolution* (London: Mercury Books, 1962), chap. 14. Marlene Legates, "The Cult of True Womanhood in Eighteenth-Century Thought," *Eighteenth-Century Studies* 10 (Fall 1976): 21-39. Levin L. Schücking, *The Puritan Family* (New York: Schocken Books, 1970), chaps. 1, 5.

45. Michael Walzer, *The Revolution of the Saints* (Cambridge, Mass,: Harvard University Press, 1965), pp. 193-95. Edmund S. Morgan, *The Puritan Family: Religion and Domestic Relations in Seventeenth-Century New England* (New York: Harper & Row, 1966), chap. 2. Schücking, *The Puritan Family*, sec. 1. Edmund S. Morgan, "The Puritans and Sex," in *American Family in Social-Historical Perspective*, ed. Michael Gordon (New York : St. Martin's Press, 1973), pp. 282-95. William Haller, "Hail Wedded Love," *ELH: A Journal of English Literary History* 13 (1946): 79-97. William Haller and Malleville Haller, "The Puritan Art of Love," *Huntingdon Library Quarterly* 5 (January 1942): 235-72. Roland Bainton says that the Reformation contributed to the decline of arranged marriages in general because it emphasized the couple's spiritual relationship; *Women of the Reformation in France and England* (Boston: Beacon Press, 1973), p. 8. For examples of romantic marriages in Puritan circles, see Winchester, *Tudor Family Portrait*, chap. 3, and Lucy Hutchinson, *Memoirs of the Life of Colonel Hutchinson with the Fragment of an Autobiography of Mrs. Hutchinson* (New York: Oxford University Press, 1973), pp. 29-33. On the recognition of romantic love in the making of actual colonial marriages, see Thompson, *Women in England and America*, pp. 121-31; J. William Frost, *The Quaker Family in Colonial America* (New York: St. Martin's Press, 1973), pp. 162-66; and Herman R. Lantz et al., "Pre-Industrial Patterns in the Colonial Family in America: A Content Analysis of Colonial Magazines," *American Sociological Review* 33 (June 1968): 420-21.

46. Morgan, *The Puritan Family*, chap. 2. James Johnson, "The Covenant Idea and the Puritan View of Marriage," *Journal of the History of Ideas* 32 (January-March 1971): 107-18, esp. 113. Lawrence Stone, "The Rise of the Nuclear Family in Early Modern England: The Patriarchal Stage." in *The Family in History*, ed. C. Rosenberg, pp. 26-32. Walzer, *Revolution of the Saints*, pp. 183-98.

47. Morgan, "Puritans and Sex," p. 284.

48. Ibid., pp. 285-86. Also Emil Oberholzer, Jr., *Delinquent Saints* (New York: Columbia University Press, 1956), pp. 127-51.

49. George Saville, Marquis of Halifax, "The Lady's New Year's Gifts; or, Advice to a Daughter," in his *Complete Works*, ed. J. P. Kenyon (Baltimore:

Pelican Classics, 1969), pp. 279-80, 295-300.

50. Keith Thomas, "The Double Standard," *Journal of the History of Ideas* 20 (April 1959): 216.

51. Watt, *Rise of the Novel*, pp. 160, 164.

52. Houghton, *Victorian Frame of Mind*, chap. 13. Eric Trudgill, *Madonnas and Magdalens: The Origins and Development of Victorian Sexual Attitudes* (New York: Holmes and Meier, 1976), pp. 19-37.

53. Cott, "Eighteenth-Century Family Life," p. 31. Lantz et al., "Pre-Industrial Patterns in America," pp. 422-24.

54. Spruill, *Women's Life in the Southern Colonies*, chap. 10.

55. Barbara Welter, "The Feminization of American Religion," in her *Dimity Convictions*, pp. 83-102.

56. Cott, *Bonds of Womanhood*, pp. 135-46. Nancy F. Cott, "Young Women in the Second Great Awakening in New England," *Feminist Studies* 3 (Fall 1975): 15-29.

57. Ann Douglas sees the feminization of religion as part of a larger cultural process that she calls the feminization of American culture. She traces it to the deteriorating position of two groups in the early nineteenth century, ministers and women, who joined forces to create a new area of cultural importance that they could control; *Feminization of American Culture*.

58. Thomas, "The Double Standard," pp. 204-6.

59. P. E. H. Hair, "Bridal Pregnancy in Earlier Rural England Further Examined," *Population Studies* 24 (March-November 1970): 59-70. Peter Laslett, *The World We Have Lost* (New York: Charles Scribner's Sons, 1965), chap. 6, finds much lower rates of bridal pregnancy in sixteenth- and seventeenth-century England. Pierre Goubert takes the same view for late seventeenth-century France; "Recent Theories and Research in French Population Between 1500 and 1700," in *Population in History*, ed. D. V. Glass and D. E. C. Eversley (Chicago: Aldine, 1965), p. 468.

60. Edward Shorter, "Illegitimacy, Sexual Revolution and Social Change in Modern Europe," in *American Family in Social-Historical Perspective*, ed. M. Gordon, pp. 296-304, for statement of thesis. Barbara J. Harris, "Recent Work on the History of the Family: A Review Article," *Feminist Studies* 3 (Spring-Summer 1976): 166-67.

61. Joan W. Scott and Louise A. Tilly, "Women's Work and the Family in Nineteenth Century Europe," in *The Family in History*, ed. C. Rosenberg, pp. 167-70. Louise A. Tilly, Joan W. Scott, and Miriam Cohen, "Women's Work and European Fertility Patterns," *Journal of Interdisciplinary History* 6 (Winter 1976): 447-76.

62. Daniel Scott Smith and Michael S. Hindus, "Premarital pregnancy in America, 1640-1971: An Overview and Interpretation," *Journal of Inter-*

disciplinary *History* 5 (Spring 1975): 537-70.

63. C. Rosenberg, "Sexuality, Class and Religion," pp. 143-44.

64. Philippe Ariès, *Centuries of Childhood: A Social History of Family Life* (New York: Vintage Books, 1962). Support for his thesis can be found in Sue Sheridan Walker, "Widow and Ward: The Feudal Law of Child Custody in Medieval England," *Feminist Studies* 3 (Spring-Summer 1976): 104-16; Origo, *Merchant of Prato*' pt. 2. chaps. 1-2; James Bruce Ross, "The Middle-Class Child in Urban Italy, Fourteenth to Early Sixteenth Century," in *The History of Childhood*, ed. Lloyd de Mause (New York: Harper Torchbooks, 1974), pp. 183-228; Winchester, *Tudor Family Portrait*, chaps. 1-3; Natalie Zemon Davis, "Ghosts, Kin, and Progeny: Some Features of Family Life in Early Modern France," *Daedalus* 106 (Spring 1977): 87-114; Lawrence Stone, *Crisis of the Aristocracy, 1558-1641* (Oxford: Clarendon Press, 1965), pp. 589-671; and Walzer, *Revolution of the Saints*, pp. 183-98. Richard Goldthwaite argues that the kind of changes in the family that Ariès associates with the sixteenth through eighteenth centuries occurred in Florence in the early Renaissance; "The Florentine Palace as Domestic Architecture," *American Historical Review* 77 (October 1972): 977-1012. For a critique of his views, see Harris, "Recent Work on the History of the Family," pp. 161-62.

65. Hughes, "Domestic Ideals and Social Behavior," pp. 131-32. Ross, "Middle-Class Child in Urban Italy," pp. 184-96. Origo, *Merchant of Prato*, pp. 199-201. Winchester, *Tudor Family Portrait*, p. 106. Stone, *Crisis of the Aristocracy*, pp. 592-93. David Hunt, *Parents and Children in History: The Psychology of Family Life in Early Modern France* (New York: Harper Torchbooks, 1972), pp. 100-9. Walzer, *Revolution of the Saints*, p. 192, notes that the Puritans disapproved of using wet nurses, which is interesting since they are the first group in England associated with the transition to more modern forms of family life. Two examples of Puritan families in which mothers did nurse their own children are given by Hutchinson, *Memoirs*, p. 287, and Alan Macfarlane, *The Family Life of Ralph Josselin, a Seventeenth Century Clergyman* (Cambridge: Cambridge University Press, 1970), pp. 83, 86.

66. Winchester, *Tudor Family Portrait*, pp. 24-25; Hughes, "Domestic Ideals and Behavior," p. 132-133.

67. Laslett, *World We Have Lost*, pp. 45-46, 69-70. Macfarlane, *Family Life of Ralph Josselin*, pp. 208-10.

68. Macfarlane, *Family Life of Ralph Josselin*, pp. 205-8. Winchester, *Tudor Family Portrait*, pp. 24-25.

69. Winchester, *Tudor Family Portrait*, pp. 24-25. Walker, "Widow and Ward," pp. 104-10.

70. Macfarlane, *Family Life of Ralph Josselin*, pp. 205-6.

71. Quoted in Violet A. Wilson, *Society Women of Shakespeare's Time*

(Port Washington, N.Y.: Kennikat Press, 1970), p. 66.

72. Winchester, *Tudor Family Portrait*, pp. 63, 85.

73. Macfarlane, *Family Life of Ralph Josselin*, pp. 92-93.

74. Morgan, *The Puritan Family*, pp. 75-78. Frost, *The Quaker Family*, pp. 74, 143-47. John Demos, *A Little Commonwealth: Family Life in Plymouth Colony* (New York: Oxford University Press, 1970), pp. 71-81.

75. Ross, "Middle-Class Child in Urban Italy," pp. 211-15.

76. D. Hunt, *Parents and Children*, pp. 171-73, 180-86.

77. Schücking, *The Puritan Family*, pp. 85-88.

78. Davis, "Ghosts, Kin, and Progeny," pp. 105-8. For a psychological interpretation of this aspect of family life in early modern France, see D. Hunt, *Parents and Children*, pp. 133-58.

79. Walzer, *Revolution of the Saints*, pp. 190-93. Frost, *The Quaker Family*, pp. 74-79. Morgan, *The Puritan Family*, chaps. 1, 3, 4, 6. Stone, "Rise of the Nuclear Family," pp. 34-49.

80. Edward T. James, ed., *Notable American Women, 1607-1950*, 3 vols. (Cambridge, Mass.: Belknap Press, Harvard University Press, 1971). The twenty-one women were Susan B. Anthony, Elizabeth Cady Stanton, Lucy Stone, Lucretia Mott, Ernestine Rose, Angelina Grimké, Sarah Grimké, Amelia Bloomer, Lydia Child, Abby Kelley Foster, Pauline W. Davis, Antoinette Brown Blackwell, Elizabeth O. Smith, Frances D. Gage, Clarina Nichols, Matilda Gage, Josephine Griffing, Amanda Way, Caroline Severance, Hannah T. Cutler, and Mary U. Ferrin. The average number of their children was 3.09. In the population as a whole, the average number of children born to a white woman surviving to menopause was 6.14 in 1840 and 4.24 in 1880; Daniel Scott Smith, "Family Limitation, Sexual Control, and Domestic Feminism in Victorian America," in *Clio's Consciousness Raised*, ed. Hartman and Banner, p. 123.

81. Smith, "Family Limitation in Victorian America," p. 123.

82. J. A. Banks and Olive Banks, *Feminism and Family Planning in Victorian England* (New York: Schocken Books, 1964).

83. Patricia Branca, *Silent Sisterhood: Middle-Class Women in the Victorian Home* (Pittsburgh: Carnegie-Mellon University Press, 1975), pp. 114-42, argues about birth control in England along the same lines as Daniel Smith does for the United States.

84. Smith, "Family Limitation in Victorian America," pp. 119-20, for statement of thesis.

85. Linda Gordon, "Voluntary Motherhood," pp. 54-71. Haller and Haller, *Physician in Victorian America*, pp. 124-31, and M. Gordon, "An Unfortunate Necessity," pp. 63-64, both emphasize that continence was the most acceptable form of birth control in nineteenth-century America.

86. Douglas, *Feminization of American Culture*, chap. 2, is a brilliant exposition and elaboration of this point.

87. Cott, *Bonds of Womanhood*, pp. 97-100.

88. Rosalind Navin Rosenberg, "The Dissent from Darwin, 1890-1930: The New View of Woman among American Social Scientists" (Ph.D. diss., Stanford University, 1974), chap. 1, esp. pp. 7-18. The ideas attributed to Darwin come from *The Descent of Man* and are not the work of later Darwinists; *The Descent of Man* (Orig. pub. 1871; New York: Random House Modern Library Edition, n.d.), pp. 415, 446-47, 579-84, 899, 903. Rosalind Rosenberg, "In Search of Woman's Nature, 1850-1920," *Feminist Studies* 3 (Fall 1975): 141-54. Jill K. Conway, "Stereotypes of Femininity in a Theory of Sexual Evolution," in *Suffer and Be Still: Women in the Victorian Age*, ed. Martha Vicinus (Bloomington: Indiana University Press, 1973), pp. 140-54.

89. A recent and brilliant study of Beecher is Kathryn Kish Sklar, *Catharine Beecher: A Study in American Domesticity* (New Haven: Yale University Press, 1973). Sklar interprets Beecher's career as a complex response to her recognition that early nineteenth-century women were increasingly excluded from the mainstream of American life and to her apprehension that the cultural hegemony of the old New England elite to which she belonged was threatened. Sklar believes that women gained power and influence from the roles prescribed for them by the cult of domesticity as Beecher defined and propagated it.

90. Very late in her life Catharine Beecher became an advocate of professions for women without reference to the values and constraints of the cult of domesticity; ibid., pp. 265-70.

91. For a chilling description of the self-sacrifice and repression demanded of the respectable middle-class spinster, see Stowe, "The Cathedral," pp. 203-16. "Susan Miller," in Cott, *Root of Bitterness*, pp. 130-40, shows the transformation of a young woman into a spinster of this type.

92. Gerda Lerner, *The Woman in American History* (Menlo Park, Calif.: Addison-Wesley, 1971), p. 44.

93. Walsh, *Doctors Wanted*, chaps. 1-3.

94. Dexter, *Career Women of America*, p. 45.

95. Harriot Hunt, *Glances and Glimpses* (New York: Sourcebook Press, 1970). Walsh, *Doctors Wanted*, pp. 20-34.

96. Peter Stearns, "Working-Class Women in Britain, 1890-1914," in *Suffer and Be Still*, ed. Vicinus, pp. 113-5.

97. Laura Oren, "The Welfare of Women in Laboring Families: England, 1860-1950," in *Clio's Consciousness Raised*, ed. Hartman and Banner, pp. 226-44.

98. Virginia Yans McLaughlin, "Patterns of Work and Family Organiza-

tion: Buffalo's Italians," in *The Family in History*, ed. Theodore K. Rabb and Robert I. Rotberg (New York: Harper Torchbooks, 1971), pp. 111-26. Thomas Dublin, "Women, Work, and the Family: Female Operatives in the Lowell Mills, 1830-1860," *Feminist Studies* 3 (Fall 1975): 30-39.

III

Women in Rebellion

When, in the course of human events, it becomes necessary for one portion of the family of man to assume among the people of the earth a position different from that which they have hitherto occupied, but one to which the laws of nature and of nature's God entitle them, a decent respect to the opinions of mankind requires that they should declare the causes that impel them to such a course.

We hold these truths to be self-evident: that all men and women are created equal; that they are endowed by their Creator with certain inalienable rights; that among these are life, liberty, and the pursuit of happiness; that to secure these rights governments are instituted, deriving their just powers from the consent of the governed. Whenever any form of government becomes destructive of these ends, it is the right of those who suffer from it to refuse allegiance to it, and to insist upon the institution of a new government. . . . when a long train of abuses and usurpations, pursuing invariably the same object, evinces a design to reduce them under absolute despotism, it is their duty to throw off such government, and to provide new

guards for their future security. Such has been the patient
sufferance of the women under this government, and such
is now the necessity which constrains them to demand the
equal station to which they are entitled.

The history of mankind is a history of repeated injuries
and usurpations on the part of man toward woman,
having in direct object the establishment of an absolute
tyranny over her.[1]

These stirring words opened the Declaration of Sentiments, signed by
sixty-eight women and thirty-two men at the conclusion of the First
Woman's Rights Convention held in America, at Seneca Falls, New
York, in July 1848. Twelve resolutions followed, three of which were
particularly relevant to the barriers faced by women with professional aspirations.

Resolved, That woman is man's equal—was intended to be so by the Creator, and the highest good of the race demands that she be recognized as such.

Resolved, That woman has too long rested satisfied in the circumscribed
limits which corrupt customs and a perverted application of the Scriptures
have marked out for her, and that it is time she should move in the enlarged
sphere which her great Creator has assigned her.

Resolved, That the speedy success of our cause depends upon the zealous
and untiring efforts of both men and women, for the overthrow of the
monopoly of the pulpit, and for the securing to woman an equal participation with men in the various trades, professions, and commerce.[2]

The Seneca Falls convention inaugurated the first phase of the
woman's rights movement in the United States. The first American
feminists attacked belief in the inferiority of women and the cult of
domesticity, the two clusters of ideas that functioned as the major
ideological obstacles to nineteenth-century women dissatisfied with
their role. In the twelve years between 1848 and the outbreak of the
Civil War, scarcely a year passed without the meeting of a woman's
rights convention. In addition, feminists petitioned state legislatures
to grant married women legal rights. Hitherto, wives suffered "civil

death" upon marriage and had no legal existence or rights apart from their husbands. In these early years the movement's major achievement was to bring the woman's issue before the public and to convince growing, though still small, numbers of the necessity of organizing to achieve equal rights with men. By 1860, feminists also secured legislation in most states to improve the position of married women. A law passed in New York in that year, for example, gave them the right to own property, control their own earnings, and sue or be sued.[3]

Given the weight of tradition in Western society against granting women the kind of equality demanded at Seneca Falls, historians are faced with the problem of explaining why a feminist movement was born and took root in this country in the 1840s and 1850s. One of the traditional answers is to ascribe it to the Industrial Revolution.[4] According to this argument, industrialization had different, but important, effects on both lower- and middle-class women. It drew the former out of their homes into factories, where for the first time they enjoyed some sense of financial independence and escaped the influence and control of their families. They also met wage discrimination, barriers to upward mobility in the factory hierarchy, and other conditions that generated a feminist consciousness and made them responsive to the early woman's movement. Middle-class women, on the other hand, were stranded in the home with little to do as industrialization moved more and more of their functions outside it. Boredom with their shrinking and increasingly meaningless sphere undermined their acquiescence in the Victorian definition of their role and turned a small minority into active feminists. This minority founded and led the woman's movement.

There are a number of difficulties with this thesis. For one thing, industrialization was not far advanced in the United States in this period. Its use as an explanation is, on these grounds alone, somewhat questionable. In the autobiographies and accounts of the first generation of feminists, there is little evidence that new methods of production had reduced domestic work.[5] Whether they were of comfortable middle-class families or from poorer backgrounds, their complaint was not of idleness in the home, but of too much exhausting, unrewarding work. Elizabeth Cady Stanton's account of her decision to call the convention at Seneca Falls dwells at length on the continuous responsibility and lack of intellectual stimulus involved in her household duties.

[I now fully understood the practical difficulties most women had to contend with in the isolated household, and the impossibility of woman's best development if in contact, the chief part of her life, with servants and children. . . . The general discontent I felt with woman's portion as wife, mother, housekeeper, physician, and spiritual guide, the chaotic conditions into which everything fell without her constant supervision, and the wearied, anxious look of the majority of women impressed me with a strong feeling that some active measures should be taken to remedy the wrongs of society in general, and of women in particular. My experience at the World's Anti-Slavery Convention, all I had read of the legal status of women, and the oppression I saw everywhere, together swept across my soul, intensified now by many personal experiences.6]

When Lucy Stone was born, her mother sighed, "Oh dear! I am sorry it is a girl. A woman's life is so hard." 7 Abigail Scott Duniway reacted similarly to life in the Far West in the early days of her married life.

It was a hospitable neighborhood composed chiefly of bachelors, who found comfort in mobilizing at meal times at the homes of the few married men of the township, and seemed especially fond of congregating at the hospitable cabin home of my good husband, who was never quite so much in his glory as when entertaining them at his fireside, while I, if not washing, scrubbing, churning, or nursing the baby, was preparing their meals in our lean-to kitchen. To bear two children in two and a half years from my marriage day, to make thousands of pounds of butter every year for market, not including what was used in our free hotel at home; to sew and cook, and wash and iron; to bake and clean and stew and fry; to be, in short, a general pioneer drudge, with never a penny of my own, was not pleasant business.8]

Middle-class women who escaped from the home were able to do so only because they employed other females to perform the tasks that they scorned. Elizabeth Cady Stanton, the mother of five, said quite frankly that she owed much of the time that she dedicated to women's rights to the loyal service of Amelia Willard. Even Elizabeth Blackwell, who never married, used her adopted daughter Kitty as domestic help.9

If the small numbers of females who worked in factories in the 1830s and 1840s organized at all, they focused on their grievances as underpaid, overworked laborers, not on their general status as women. The early feminists did not come from their ranks.10

In *Everyone Was Brave*, William O'Neill explains the birth of feminism in completely different terms. He describes the early woman's movement as "one reaction to the great pressures that accompanied the emergence of the nuclear family."[11] His view is based, in turn, on Philippe Ariès's theory that the modern conjugal family, with its emphasis on privacy, domesticity, and child rearing, developed in the late seventeenth and the eighteenth centuries. Victorians confined their wives in this family and bestowed on them the moral and pedagogic responsibilities dictated by the cult of true womanhood. If, as Ariès claims, this family emerged in the eighteenth century and was reaching its fullest development only in the nineteenth century, then it is not, according to O'Neill, hard to understand the birth of feminism. Burdened with new and confining moral responsibilities as wives and mothers, women revolted.

In the precise form just stated, however, O'Neill's thesis is incorrect, since it rests on Philippe Ariès's conclusions about the evolution of the family in Western society. The work of demographic historians studying England, France, and colonial America has shown that the nuclear family was common at least as far back as 1600.[12] What was new in the early nineteenth century was not the nuclear family per se, but its connection with the Victorian ethos and the particular role that it assigned to women. The relatively recent origin of the cult of domesticity deprived the constraints and burdens that it imposed on women of the sanctions of time and sharpened the sense of grievance of those females dissatisfied with the nineteenth-century definition of their role. It is not surprising that the very generation that saw the appearance of the Victorian ethos in its full-blown form also saw the first revolt against it.

If industrialization contributed at all to the birth of feminism, it was indirectly, by contributing to the development of the cult of true womanhood. The Industrial Revolution created the physical gulf, exalted by this ideal, between the home and the new economic world. It also deprived women of important economic functions and made them receptive to an ideology that assigned them other crucial social functions. Finally, it increased the social influence of the middle classes, the group most wedded to the new views of female nature and the importance of motherhood.

The core of the feminist complaint against the cult of true womanhood was that it socialized women to accept the loss of function and status that occurred in early nineteenth-century America. The women and men who signed the declaration at Seneca Falls rejected the increasing divergence between the male and female spheres. Essentially, they demanded that women be allowed to follow men out of the home as fewer and fewer crucial economic and social functions were performed within it. As John Demos has aptly stated, the woman's movement "was not, at first, primarily about the vote; it was much more centrally about the right of women to work outside the home. The early feminists despised all the adoring rhetoric on woman-in-the-home; they sought to expose this myth of domesticity for what it really was. . . . Thus the initial stages of feminism are best seen . . . as a cry of protest against intolerable confinement."13

American women rebelling against Victorianism were fortunate in having at hand a ready-made ideology with which to attack nineteenth-century notions about separate male and female spheres: the philosophy of the Enlightenment, with its assertion of the equality and inalienable natural rights of each individual.14 Since Americans already accepted Enlightenment theory, the feminists had only to demonstrate that it was illogical and unjust to exclude women from the rights and privileges guaranteed to every human being. When Elizabeth Cady Stanton paraphrased the Declaration of Independence in the manifesto adopted at Seneca Falls, she was consciously linking the woman's rights movement to the American revolutionary tradition. She counted on this association to arouse women and to convince men of the justice of her claims.

Some historians attach so much importance to the influence of the Enlightenment—and its expression in the American Revolution—on the early feminists that they attribute the birth of the movement to those events.15 The difficulty with this explanation is that over half a century separated the Seneca Falls convention from the American Revolution. The historian is still left trying to explain why the response to the revolutionary example came when it did. The largest claim that can realistically be made for the Enlightenment is that it sharpened the sense of grievance that the first American feminists felt by giving them a widely accepted yardstick with which to measure reality.

Although in the largest sense it is accurate to ascribe the birth of the woman's rights movement to a revolt against the rapidly crystallizing Victorian ethos, particular conditions in the United States in the 1830s and 1840s increased women's dissatisfaction with the status quo and may be regarded as the immediate causes of the movement. Most important, in my opinion, were developments in the realm of education and the rise of abolitionism.[16] Between 1820 and 1850, public school systems throughout the United States expanded dramatically. Although most town governments were primarily interested in educating boys, they made some provision for girls, particularly at the elementary level. The Protestant insistence on the ability to read the Bible and the unwillingness of the fathers of daughters to support schools that excluded their offspring probably account for the initial steps in opening schools to girls. The first public high school for girls opened in Worcester, Massachusetts, in 1824. New York City and Boston followed two years later. In the same period, large numbers of private female academies and seminaries, which claimed to provide some sort of secondary education, opened. The best, like Emma Willard's school in Troy, New York, and Mount Holyoke, came close to providing the equivalent of a college education; the worst were little better than finishing schools.[17]

No college admitted women until Oberlin opened its doors to them in 1837. Even there the attitude toward female students was ambivalent. On one hand, the college established a Ladies' Department, which created a special "literary course" for women, supervised their conduct and morals, and administered a system of manual labor training that required female students to wash and sew for their male peers. On the other, it opened the regular liberal arts program to women who rejected the idea of a special course for their sex. By 1867, one-fifth of the female students had received regular degrees.

James Harris Fairchild, chief spokesman for the college and defender of coeducation, argued that society had an obligation to educate women as fully human beings and that they had the physical and mental capacity for higher education. Nevertheless, he considered educating women as secondary to Oberlin's primary function of training evangelical ministers and partly justified their presence through its contribution to that higher end. He believed that female students would exert a civilizing influence on the young men and teach them the social graces necessary to succeed in congregations made up largely of women. Fairchild also felt that coeducation would eliminate the autoerotic activities and sexual tensions characteristic of all-male colleges. Finally, he regarded the female students as a pool from which male graduates could choose useful, pious wives. Ministers should marry immediately after graduation, he felt, because single clergymen were a dangerous temptation to women in their churches.[18]

Many girls received enough schooling to develop a passion for learning, only to find that the best institutions of higher learning and many disciplines were closed to them. Emma Willard lost interest in math when she learned that women were not allowed to study higher mathematics because their brains were considered unequal to the strain.[19] Elizabeth Cady Stanton experienced "vexation and mortification" when she could not go to Union College with the boys with whom she had studied at the Johnstown Academy until the age of sixteen.[20] When Lucy Stone said she wanted to go to college, her father pronounced her crazy and her mother feared for her soul. At the age of sixteen, she began to teach school and save her money to pay for college. Nine years later she entered Oberlin. Even there she was thwarted by prevailing notions of propriety. Although she intended to devote her life to lecturing on behalf of abolitionism and woman's rights, the administration forbade her to debate with male students. She refused to write the address for her commencement because she could not read it herself. When she graduated in 1845, she was the first female from the state of Massachusetts to receive a college degree.[21]

The growth of public school systems opened the profession of teaching to women. Since female teachers were paid one-quarter to one-half of the salaries that men received, many towns preferred to employ them to keep the school budget low. This inequity in salaries humiliated and enraged Lucy Stone, Lucretia Mott, and Susan B. Anthony and constituted one of the experiences that turned them into feminists.[22]

Even more important than the development of education was the abolitionist movement.[23] Abolitionism appealed to two powerful currents in American culture—the egalitarian philosophy of the Enlightenment and the evangelical Christian revival. A movement with strong ethical and religious overtones inevitably attracted females. Trained to guard the moral purity of the home, they responded to the challenge of a moral crusade to cleanse America's soul. In the Victorian context, they particularly reacted to the separation of slave mothers from their children and to the sexual exploitation of female slaves. Emphasis on the appeal of the abolitionist movement to women who accepted dominant social and cultural values is not meant to deny the genuine radicalism of those who became outspoken abolitionists. Uncompromising abolitionism was always radical and never respectable. But it was the kind of radical movement likely to interest females whose consciences were formed in the particular atmosphere of early nineteenth-century America.

Abolitionism pushed women toward open feminism for many reasons. Constant appeal to the doctrines of natural rights and the equality of all human beings increased the influence of the American revolutionary tradition on them. More important, women who took an active role in the movement were attacked over and over for violating nineteenth-century views about female roles and propriety. Male abolitionists split over the issue of female participation, since many of them were reluctant to endanger their crusade for the slaves by connecting it to the issue of women. Sensing the vulnerability of the movement at this point, opponents assaulted female abolitionists with particular viciousness and exploited the opportunity to picture their efforts as particularly subversive of morality. "Why are all the old hens abolitionists? Because not being able to obtain husbands they think they may stand some chance for a negro if they can only make amalgamation fashionable." [24] Finally, the parallel between their situation and that of Black slaves increasingly impressed female abolitionists and sharpened their sense of grievance.

Two sisters from South Carolina, Sarah and Angelina Grimké were the first women to speak publicly against slavery. [25] In the 1820s they converted to Quakerism and then, filled with abhorrence of the whole slave system, left their family to live in Philadelphia. Gradually, they became disillusioned with orthodox Quakerism because of its racism and narrow conception of proper female behavior. In 1836, Angelina published *An Appeal to the Christian Women of the South* and Sarah produced *Epistle to the Clergy of the Southern States*. On the invitation of Theodore Weld, a leading figure in the New York City-based American Anti-Slavery Society, Angelina and Sarah began their careers as abolitionist speakers during the winter of 1836-37. At first they spoke in private homes to small groups of women, but they were so successful that they soon began lecturing in churches. Before long, their audiences included members of both sexes. In May, they helped to organize the Anti-Slavery Convention of American Women. Already Angelina was connecting the cause of females and slaves:

Women ought to feel a peculiar sympathy in the colored man's wrong, for, like him, she has been accused of mental inferiority, and denied the privileges of a liberal education. . . . if we have no right to act, then may *we* well be termed "the white slaves of the North," for like our brethran in bonds, we must seal our lips in silence and despair. [26]

During the following summer, the sisters began an extended speaking tour in New England, during which Angelina engaged in the first public debate between members of opposite sexes.

The activities of the Grimké sisters led the public to associate abolitionism and woman's rights. Even before their New England tour, Catharine Beecher published *An Essay on Slavery and Abolitionism with Reference to the Duty of American Females*, addressed to Angelina Grimké. [27] Earlier Beecher had advocated the expansion of female education and the employment of women as teachers without challenging the basic assumptions and dictates of the Victorian ethos. In this work, she opposed abolitionism and advocated gradualism and colonization instead. She maintained that divine law subjected women to men and forbade the organizing of female abolitionist societies and their petitioning Congress. Feminine efforts should be confined to the domestic circle.

Angelina replied in a series of letters to Catharine Beecher published in the *Emancipator* and the *Liberator* and later reprinted in book form. She defended abolitionist theory and tactics and especially attacked the idea of colonization on the ground that free Negroes were vehemently against it. In two of the ten letters she employed a full-fledged feminist argument to defend women's right to act as citizens.

Now, I believe it is woman's right to have a voice in all the laws and regulations by which she is to be *governed*, whether in Church or State: and that the present arrangements of society, on these points, are *a violation of human rights, a rank usurpation of power,* a violent seizure and confiscation of what is sacredly and inalienably hers. . . . *If* Ecclesiastical and Civil governments are ordained to God, *then* I contend that woman has just as much right to sit in solemn counsel in Conventions, Conferences, Associations and General Assemblies, as man—just as much right to sit upon the throne of England, or in the Presidential Chair of the United States. [28]

In the same period Sarah began a series, *Letters on the Equality of the Sexes,* which appeared in the *New England Spectator* and the *Liberator.* She rejected the biblical argument for the subjection of women on the ground that it simply reflected the patriarchal society in which Scripture was written She demanded equal educational opportunities and denounced training specifically designed to prepare women for marriage and domestic chores. She claimed legal equality and equal pay for equal work and rejected the whole notion of separate male and female spheres. "Whatever is *right* for a man to do, is *right* for a woman." [29] She exhorted her sisters to stop acquiescing to the status quo and assured men, "I ask no favors for my sex. . . . All I ask our bretheran is, that they will take their feet from off our necks, and permit us to stand upright on that ground which God designed us to occupy." [30]

While Sarah's letters were appearing, the Congregationalist ministers of Massachusetts circulated their infamous Pastoral Letter attacking the Grimké sisters. Following a general denunciation of the use of churches for abolitionist meetings and lectures, the letter called attention to "the dangers which at present seem to threaten the female character with wide-spread and permanent damage." It urged women to confine themselves to the sphere outlined for them in the New Testament and especially reprimanded those "who so far forget themselves as to itinerate in the character of public lecturers and teachers." [31] Despite the Pastoral Letter and unexpected opposition from Theodore Weld, who was alarmed at the intrusion of the woman's issue into the cause of abolitionism, Sarah continued to publish the letters, and the sisters continued their tour.

Although the Grimké sisters defied Victorian notions about woman's sphere in their abolitionist activities and broke a number of barriers about public speaking for the first time, they were not the only women active in the movement in the late 1830s. During this period, small groups founded female anti-slavery organizations in Philadelphia, Boston, and New York City. These organizations played a major role in circulating the anti-slavery petitions regularly submitted to Congress. As early as 1834, Representative Howard of Maryland questioned the right and propriety of women's active role in the petitioning movement. John Quincy Adams defended them in a series of speeches delivered from June 26 to June 30. In answer to Howard's argument that women had no right to petition because they could not vote, Adams asked rhetorically, "Is it so clear that they have no such right as the last?"[32] During this period, women such as Lucretia Mott, Abigail Kelley Foster, Maria Chapman, and Lydia Maria Child assumed increasingly prominent positions in the struggle against slavery and joined the Grimkés in drawing a connection between abolitionism and woman's rights.

In 1840 the issue of woman's rights became intertwined with a major split in the abolitionist movement. Although many serious disagreements were involved, the crisis was precipitated when, at a New York meeting of the American Anti-Slavery Society, a member of the more radical Boston group associated with William Lloyd Garrison appointed Abby Kelley to the business committee. The more conservative, pragmatic, politically oriented New York faction seceded to form the American and Foreign Anti-Slavery Society, which specifically limited membership to men. The Garrison group took over what was left of the original organization and elected females to the permanent executive committee.

During the same year the Garrison group sent representatives, including Lucretia Mott, to the World Anti-Slavery Convention in London. The Americans also included Henry Stanton, on his honeymoon trip with his young wife, Elizabeth. Despite the objections of some of the American leaders, the convention refused to seat the female delegates. They were forced to sit in the gallery behind a screen and could not join in the proceedings. To their credit, William Garrison and a number of others sat with them in protest. Lucretia Mott and Elizabeth Cady Stanton met for the first time on this occasion. During the hours that they sat together in the gallery or walked the streets after the sessions closed, Lucretia, twenty years Elizabeth's senior, converted her to the cause of woman's rights. Although they discussed calling a meeting on the subject, their plan was not fulfilled until eight years later, when a chance encounter led them to call the historic Seneca Falls convention.

[To summarize my view of the origins of the woman's rights movement, early feminism was a conscious revolt against both the Victorian ethos and the far older belief in female inferiority. It appeared first among educated, middle-class women who became involved in the abolitionist movement and then found their participation threatened by current ideas about the appropriate female role. Except in the indirect sense that it was one of the reasons for the rise of the cult of domesticity, industrialization does not seem to me to have played a major role in stimulating the birth of the woman's movement.]

Recent work on women's roles in nineteenth-century America has emphasized the great expansion of their sphere that occurred without challenging the cult of domesticity. This is the theme of Kathryn Kish Sklar's recent biography of Catharine Beecher. [33] Daniel Smith feels the trend was pronounced enough to refer to it as "domestic feminism." [34] The pioneers in women's education, who probably did more than anyone else in this period to effect change in the female sphere, advocated education for women and their entrance into the teaching profession on the basis of the values proclaimed by the cult of true womanhood. [35] In a similar way, females defended their careers as authors and their involvement in charitable, religious, temperance, and moral reform societies. [36]

Nonetheless, there was a real, if not irreconcilable, gap between women who advocated expanding the female role without challenging the domestic ideal and the founders of the woman's rights movement, who appealed to the egalitarian ideology of the Enlightenment and aggressively assumed roles normally restricted to males. The former certainly understood the genuine radicalism of the latter. Logically enough, Catharine Beecher opposed radical abolitionism, female participation in the anti-slavery movement, and the feminist movement launched at Seneca Falls. [37] For all their incipient feminism, the leaders of the Female Moral Reform Society drew back from endorsing Sarah Grimke's views on woman's rights. [38]

The most sensitive estimate of the effect of the cult of domesticity on the position of nineteenth-century women occurs in Nancy Cott's *Bonds of Womanhood*. She recognizes that the doctrine of women's sphere opened new areas of influence to women in the home, family, and religion and created a new sense of sexual solidarity without minimizing the fact that "in opening certain avenues to women because of their sex, it barricaded all others." [39] I completely agree with her final statement on the relationship between the cult of domesticity and feminism: "Proponents of woman's sphere largely agreed with feminists' desires to develop women's self-esteem and to free them from obeisance to men's whims, and the two views concurred on the need to advance educational opportunities and encourage women to be useful members of society. On the other hand, it oversimplifies to call woman's sphere ideology 'protofeminist' or to give both principles the same lineage." [40]

The split between domestic and public feminism continued until the closing decades of the nineteenth century. The advocates of woman's rights remained a small minority of American women, which is one reason for their limited success. In the last decade or two of the century the two currents merged, and for the first time acceptance of even part of the program of the woman's rights movement became a possibility. This process involved the transformation of the woman's rights movement into a single-minded drive for the vote, which sacrificed the broad program of the Seneca Falls Declaration. Characteristically, Elizabeth Cady Stanton never approved of the reduction of feminism to a single goal. At the same time the suffrage movement discarded the strategy of demanding the vote on the ground that women were equal to men. Instead, suffragists appealed to reasons that grew out of the cult of domesticity. They argued that women should be given the vote because they were different and would bring into the political arena their special talents as moral guardians of civilization and mothers of the race. [41]

Although the woman's rights movement reduced itself to a demand for the vote by 1900, in the pre-Civil War period its program was much broader. The Seneca Fall Declaration protested against the exclusion of women from the professions and trades and demanded equality in this area. John Demos feels that in the early years the right to work outside the home was a much more central concern than the right to vote. [42] Furthermore, from the beginning there was a close connection between organized feminism and the victories of women trying to open the professions to themselves and their sex. In an excellent recent study of women in the medical profession, Mary Walsh has written, "To view feminism as a struggle for woman's rights and the vote is to ignore the support and companionship it offered those women who had broken with their prescribed roles. It is clear that a female physician could not have functioned autonomously in nineteenth-century America." Elsewhere she observes, "the nineteenth-century feminist movement provided the major impetus for women physicians."[43] Her point should be generalized to include women's entrance into all the professions, not just medicine.

Indeed, one of the few areas in which the public feminists had any success in the antebellum period was gaining token entrance into professions hitherto closed to them. Lucy Stone entered Oberlin in 1843 and earned her degree four years later. She specifically sought education to prepare for a career speaking against slavery and in favor of woman's rights. Shortly after graduation, she became a paid lecturer for the American Anti-Slavery Society. Since she considered the abolitionist and woman's rights causes to be inextricably intertwined, she spoke for both from the platform. When the anti-slavery society, anxious to keep the two issues apart, reminded her that she was paid to speak only about the former, she replied firmly, "I was a woman before I was an abolitionist. I must speak for the women."[44] A compromise permitted her to give anti-slavery lectures on weekends and speeches on woman's rights during the week at her own expense. She arranged the latter on her own and passed the hat to cover costs. Later she charged an admission fee.

The year Lucy Stone graduated from Oberlin, another woman, Antoinette Brown, received her literary degree. To the horror of her parents and teachers, she then applied for admission to the theological course and announced her intention of becoming a minister. The faculty was clearly ambivalent in its attitude toward her. On one hand, they admitted her to the program and even published her exegesis of Saint Paul's antifeminist statements in the *Oberlin Quarterly Review*. On the other, they would not give her a student's license to preach, although they allowed her to keep any pulpit engagements that she made on her own. When she finished the course in 1850, the college refused to grant her a degree. For two years, Brown lectured on woman's rights, temperance, and anti-slavery. Occasionally, progressive Unitarian ministers invited her to preach in their churches. On

September 15, 1853, she was ordained as the minister of the First Congregational Church in Butler and Savannah, New York. She was the first ordained female minister in any recognized denomination in the United States. Dissatisfaction with Calvinist theology led her to resign her post a little over a year later. Eventually, she became a Unitarian. After her marriage to Samuel Blackwell in 1856, she managed a large household that included five children and devoted herself to philosophical study and writing. In the 1880s she returned to a somewhat more active role in the woman's movement.

Antoinette Brown Blackwell inspired another of the early female ministers, Olympia Brown. While Olympia was a student at the newly founded Antioch College in the 1850s, she heard Antoinette preach and decided to follow in her footsteps. In 1860 she entered the Saint Lawrence Theological School at Canton, New York. When she graduated two years later, she was ordained as a Universalist minister. During her lifetime, Olympia Brown filled pastorates in Weymouth, Massachusetts; Bridgeport, Connecticut; and Racine, Wisconsin. She was always active in the suffrage movement, particularly after her move to Wisconsin. In 1887, when she was over fifty years old, she resigned her ministry to devote herself to the woman's rights movement.

During the same period that Antoinette Brown Blackwell and Olympia Brown succeeded in entering America's most prestigious profession, the first successful attack on male domination of medicine took place. The assailant was Elizabeth Blackwell, Antoinette's sister-in-law. Elizabeth discovered her vocation in the 1840s, long before Antoinette had even met her brother Samuel. She studied privately with two physicians to prepare herself for entrance to medical school. Harvard, Yale, Bowdoin, and every school in Philadelphia and New York turned her down, but she continued to persevere. In 1847 she entered Geneva (later Syracuse), Medical College. After her graduation in 1849, she continued her studies in England and Paris. When she returned to New York City to start a medical practice in 1851, she was barred from the city's hospitals and dispensaries and was snubbed by her colleagues. Since no one would rent her rooms to use as an office, she bought a house that she could ill afford. She was so lonely that she adopted a seven-year-old orphan, Katherine Barry. Kitty, as she was called, grew up to be Dr. Blackwell's friend, housekeeper, secretary, and companion.[45] Finding it difficult to attract patients, Blackwell broke the ice by giving successful lectures on the principles of hygiene. In 1853 she opened a part-time dispensary for poor women. After several years of fund raising, she turned it into a full-fledged hospital, the New York Infirmary for Women and Children. By 1857 the loneliest and most difficult years of her career were over. Two women whom she had encouraged and aided to become physicians, her younger sister, Emily, and Maria Zakrzewska, joined her in New York. A number of prominent male doctors served as consultants to the infirmary, and Horace Greeley, a member of the board of trustees, supported it in the *New York Tribune*. Although her active career extended over another two decades, the worst struggles were behind her.

Mary Walsh thinks that Marie Zakrzewska was even more important than Elizabeth Blackwell in opening medical careers to women. She emigrated from Germany in 1853 on the mistaken belief that the United States provided great opportunities for women physicians. She became a doctor thanks to the untiring and generous support of the woman's movement: Elizabeth Blackwell secured her admission to the Cleveland Medical College, while Harriot Hunt and Caroline Severance raised the funds to pay for her education. After graduation, she returned to New York to open a private practice and work as resident physician and general manager of Blackwell's New York Infirmary for Women and Children. In 1859 she moved to Boston to become professor of obstetrics and resident physician in Samuel Gregory's New England Female Medical College. Unfortunately, the education at the college was poor, and Gregory resisted all of Zakrzewska's efforts to improve it. In 1862 she resigned to found the New England Hospital for Women and Children, a new training hospital for female doctors. The relatively large, well-organized Boston feminist community provided her with funds and moral support. Lucy Stone's militant *Woman's Journal*, founded in 1870, championed the cause of women physicians, challenged the right of society to erect barriers in their way, and gave the hospital and its doctors a good deal of free publicity. By 1872, Zakrzewska's hospital was one of the largest in Boston. Although it specialized in gynecology and obstetrics, it never experienced the epidemics of puerperal fever that raged periodically through Boston Lying-In Hospital. New England Hospital also provided female doctors with practical training. The large number of influential women physicians educated there are the best testimony to its success. By its twenty-fifth anniversary in 1887, Zakrzewska had achieved her goal of establishing a hospital run by women for women. It was indeed a "feminist showplace." Nonetheless, it is important to realize that Zakrzewska always saw separatism as a means to the end of integrating women into the mainstream of the medical profession. Her ultimate goal was to prove the ability of women doctors and secure their admission to the two pillars of the Boston medical community, the Massachusetts Medical Society and Harvard Medical School.[46]

Antoinette Brown Blackwell, Olympia Brown, Elizabeth and Emily Blackwell, and Marie Zakrzewska were all pioneers. All of them fought bitterly against prejudice and discrimination to enter the professions of their choice. When the Civil War broke out in 1860, closing the first period of the American woman's movement, there were still few females who dared to follow in their path. However, the first important steps had been taken.

Notes

1. First Woman's Rights Convention, "Declaration of Sentiments and Resolutions," in *Up from the Pedestal*, ed. Aileen S. Kraditor (Chicago: Quadrangle Books, 1968), p. 184.
2. Ibid., pp. 187-88.
3. Eleanor Flexner, *Century of Struggle: The Woman's Rights Movement in the United States* (New York: Atheneum, 1971), p. 88.
4. William L. O'Neill, *The Woman Movement: Feminism in the United States and England* (Chicago: Quadrangle Books, 1971), p. 16. Glenda Riley McIntosh, *The Origins of the Feminist Movement in America*, Forums in History (St. Charles, Mo.: Forum Press, 1973), pp. 3-4. Ray Strachey, *"The Cause": A Short History of the Women's Movement in Great Britain* (Port Washington, N.Y.: Kennikat Press, 1969), p. 12.
5. Ruth Schwartz Cowan, "A Case Study of Technological and Social Change: The Washing Machine and the Working Wife," in *Clio's Consciousness Raised*, ed. Mary Hartman and Lois Banner (New York: Harper Torchbooks, 1974), pp 245-53. In this essay, Cowan questions whether industrialization relieved women of domestic chores at all in the period before 1919.
6. Elizabeth Cady Stanton, *Eighty Years and More, Reminiscences 1815-1897* (New York: Schocken Books, 1971), pp. 147-48.

7. Quoted in Flexner, *Century of Struggle*, p. 69.
8. Abigail Scott Duniway, *Pathbreaking* (New York: Schocken Books, 1971), pp. 9-10. When one of Duniway's younger sisters was born, her mother remarked, "Poor Baby! She'll be a woman someday! Poor baby! A woman's lot is so hard"; ibid., p. 8. Her words echoed those of Lucy Stone's mother.
9. Stanton, *Eighty Years and More*, pp. 204-5. Alice S. Rossi, ed., *The Feminist Papers: From Adams to de Beauvoir* (New York: Bantam Books, 1974), p. 336.
10. There was a sense of sisterhood and type of feminist consciousness a-mong the Lowell mill girls in the 1830s and 1840s. Nonetheless, Harriet Robinson, who had worked at Lowell and became a woman's rights advocate, was an exception. Significantly, the Lowell girls organized to pursue trade union objectives. Flexner, *Century of Struggle*, pp. 55-61. Edward T. James, ed. *Notable American Women, 1607-1950*, 3 vols. (Cambridge, Mass.: Belknap Press, Harvard University Press, 1971), 3: 181-82. Thomas Dublin, "Women, Work, and the Family: Female Operatives in the Lowell Mills, 1830-1860," *Feminist Studies* 3 (Fall 1975): 30-39.
11. See William L. O'Neill, *Everyone Was Brave: A History of Feminism in America* (Chicago: Quadrangle Books, 1971), pp. 3-9, for statement of thesis. Quotation from p. 5.
12. Peter Laslett, *The World We Have Lost* (New York: Charles Scribner's Sons, 1965). Peter Laslett, "The Comparative History of Household and Family," in *American Family in Social-Historical Perspective*, ed. Michael Gordon (New York: St. Martin's Press, 1973), pp. 19-33. John Demos, *A Little Commonwealth: Family Life in Plymouth Colony* (New York: Oxford University Press, 1970), chap. 4.
Other recent work has suggested that Laslett may have insisted too rigidly on the universality of the nuclear family model since the sixteenth century. Lutz K. Berkner, "The Stem Family and the Developmental Cycle of the Peasant Household: An Eighteenth-Century Austrian Example," in *American Family in Social-Historical Perspective*, ed. M. Gordon, pp. 34-58. Philip Greven, *Four Generations: Population, Land, and Family in Colonial Andover, Massachusetts* (Ithaca, N.Y.: Cornell University Press, 1970). Robert Wheaton, "Family and Kinship in Western Europe: The Problem of the Joint Family Household," *Journal of Interdisciplinary History* 5 (Spring 1975): 601-28. Nonetheless, it is clear that there was no major shift in family structure in the seventeenth and eighteenth centuries such as Ariès suggests and that large numbers of Europeans and colonial Americans have lived in nuclear families since the seventeenth century.
13. John Demos, "The American Family in Past Time," *American Scholar* 43 (Summer 1974): 435. O'Neill, *Everyone Was Brave*, pp. 5-9, basically a-

grees with this interpretation, although he incorrectly connects the development of the cult of domesticity with a recent transition to the nuclear family. See Nancy Cott, *The Bonds of Womanhood: "Woman's Sphere" in New England, 1780-1835* (New Haven: Yale University Press, 1977), pp. 201-4.

14. Although the early feminists made good use of the philosophy and rhetoric of the Enlightenment as it was embodied in the American revolutionary tradition, Enlightenment thought was actually anti-feminist. Carolyn C. Lougee, "Modern European History," *Signs* 2 (Spring 1977): 643-45. Marlene Legates, "The Cult of True Womanhood in Eighteenth-Century Thought," *Eighteenth-Century Studies* 10 (Fall 1976): 21-39. Linda Kerber, "The Republican Mother: Women and the Enlightenment—An American Perspective," *American Quarterly* 28 (Summer 1976): 187-205.

15. O'Neill, *Woman Movement*, p. 16.

16. Most recent work on the expansion of women's education has emphasized the essential conservatism of the whole movement. See pages 59-60 above. McIntosh, *Origins of the Feminist Movement*, pp. 6-9. Susan M. Hartman, *The Paradox of Women's Progress, 1820-1920*, Forums in History (St. Charles, Mo.: Forum Press, 1974), pp. 4-8. Keith Melder, "Mask of Oppression: The Female Seminary Movement in the United States," *New York History* 55 (July 1974): 260-79. Ann Douglas, *The Feminization of American Culture* (New York: Alfred A. Knopf, 1977), p. 76. Louise Boas, *Woman's Education Begins: The Rise of the Women's Colleges* (New York: Arno Press, 1971), reveals the conservatism of the seminary movement despite her claim that the seminaries were equivalent to men's colleges.

17. Flexner, *Century of Struggle*, chap. 2.

18. Ronald W. Hogeland, "Co-education of the Sexes at Oberlin College: A Study of Social Ideas in Mid-Nineteenth Century America," *Journal of Social History* 6 (Fall 1972-Summer 1973): 160-76.

19. Flexner, *Century of Struggle*, p. 25.

20. Stanton, *Eighty Years and More*, p. 33.

21. James, *Notable American Women*, 3: 387-88. Constance B. Burnett, *Five for Freedom* (New York: Greenwood Press, 1968), chap. 3.

22. Flexner, *Century of Struggle*, p. 72. James, *Notable American Women*, 1:52; 2: 592, 3: 387. Mary Lyon preached that women should embark on careers as teachers in the spirit of missionaries and should eschew all materialistic gains. She encouraged her students to work for subsistence wages and, with her vast moral authority, effectively endorsed the practice of paying them less than men; Boas, *Woman's Education Begins*, pp. 36-37. Melder, "Mask of Oppression," p. 273, makes the same point.

23. McIntosh, *Origins of the Feminist Movement*, pp. 12-13. Rossi, *Feminist Papers*, pp. 258-65, emphasizes abolitionism in her discussion of the

social roots of the woman's rights movement. Keith Melder, "Ladies Bountiful: Organized Women's Benevolence in Early Nineteenth-Century America," *New York History* 48 (July 1967): 246-47. Mary P. Ryan, *Womanhood in America, from Colonial Times to the Present* (New York: New Viewpoints, 1975), pp. 180-85.

24. Gerda Lerner, *The Grimké Sisters from South Carolina* (New York: Schocken Books, 1971), p. 146.

25. Two excellent recent works on the Grimké sisters are Lerner's *Grimké Sisters* and Katharine Du Pre Lumpkin, *The Emancipation of Angelina Grimké* (Chapel Hill: University of North Carolina Press, 1974). Sarah Grimké, *Letters on the Equality of the Sexes and the Condition of Woman* (New York: Burt Franklin, 1970), is an essential document on the Grimkés and on the connection between abolitionism and feminism.

26. Lerner, *Grimké Sisters*, p. 162.

27. Ibid., p. 184. Beecher was answering Grimké's *Appeal to the Women of the Nominally Free States*.

28. Quoted in Rossi, *Feminist Papers*, p. 322.

29. Grimké, *Letters on the Equality of the Sexes*, p. 16.

30. Ibid., p. 10.

31. Quoted in Kraditor, *Up from the Pedestal*, p. 51.

32. Quoted in Flexner, *Century of Struggle*, pp. 50-51.

33. Kathryn Kish Sklar, *Catharine Beecher: A Study in American Domesticity* (New Haven: Yale University Press, 1973).

34. Daniel Scott Smith, "Family Limitation, Sexual Control, and Domestic Feminism in Victorian America," in *Clio's Consciousness Raised*, ed. Hartman and Banner, p. 123.

35. See above, pp. 59-60, and works cited in note 16.

36. McIntosh, *Origins of the Feminist Movement*, pp. 5-12.

37. James, *Notable American Women*, 1: 122-23.

38. Carroll Smith-Rosenberg, "Beauty, the Beast and the Militant Woman: A Case Study in Sex Roles and Social Stress in Jacksonian America," *American Quarterly* 23 (October 1971): 580-83.

39. Cott, *Bonds of Womanhood*, p. 201.

40. Ibid., p. 205.

41. Aileen Kraditor, *The Ideas of the Woman Suffrage Movement, 1890-1920* (Garden City, N.Y.: Doubleday, 1971), esp. chaps. 3-5.

42. Demos, "American Family in Past Time," p. 435.

43. Mary Roth Walsh, *"Doctors Wanted: No Woman Need Apply": Sexual Barriers in the Medical Profession, 1835-1975*. (New Haven: Yale University Press, 1977), pp. 88-89, 276. Two writers who deal more briefly with the subject agree with her on this point: John B. Blake, "Women and Medicine in

Ante-Bellum America," *Bulletin of the History of Medicine* 39 (March-April 1965): 104; and Richard Harrison Shryock, "Women in American Medicine," in *Medicine in America: Historical Essays* (Baltimore: Johns Hopkins University Press, 1966), p. 179. Shryock also feels, however, that the intensity of opposition to women doctors derived from the association of the women's medical movement and feminism: "One may conclude, therefore, with the paradoxical observation that the potency of the feminist crusade in this country explains both the pioneer character of the women's medical movement here and the intense opposition which it encountered" (p. 198). He is wrong on this point. Walsh's book shows conclusively that the medical profession's opposition to women doctors stemmed from economic and status considerations.

44. Quoted in James, *Notable American Women*, 3: 388.

45. Rossi thinks that Blackwell's real motive for adopting Kitty was to secure household help and that the reference to the need for relieving her loneliness was meant for the public only; Rossi, *Feminist Papers*, p. 336.

46. Walsh, *Doctors Wanted*, chaps. 2-3, for the material on Zakrzewska.

IV

Progress and Disappointment, 1860~1920

The outbreak of the Civil War in April 1861 ended the first phase of the woman's rights movement. As ardent abolitionists, the feminists decided to put their own cause aside to work for the victory of the North. Somewhat distrustful of Abraham Lincoln, they wanted to force the government to turn the war into a crusade against slavery. The last woman's rights convention met in February 1861, two months before the first shots were fired at Fort Sumter. Elizabeth Cady Stanton and Susan B. Anthony, two of the more radical feminist leaders, were uneasy about shelving the woman's issue. When the New York State legislature repealed two of the most controversial provisions in the Married Woman's Property Act of 1860, their fear that they had made a tactical error was confirmed. Therefore, when Charles Sumner introduced the Thirteenth Amendment into Congress in 1865, they seized the opportunity to form a new woman's organization, the National Women's Loyal League, which once again linked the cause of women and slaves. They attracted members from the feminist and abolitionist movements. At its first meeting, the league resolved, "There never can be a true peace in this Republic until the civil and political rights of all citizens of African descent and all women are practically established."[1] The league pledged to collect

1,000,000 signatures to support the Thirteenth Amendment, a number that represented one of every twenty persons in the northern states. Although they could not achieve this ambitious goal, two thousand persons circulated petitions and collected 400,000 names in fifteen months. [2]

The struggle for the Fourteenth and Fifteenth Amendments, which immediately followed the end of the war, demonstrated that Stanton and Anthony were correct in their reluctance to subordinate the woman's cause to any other. Freeing the slaves immediately raised the issue of giving them citizenship and the vote. Women, who had been active in the northern cause, expected to receive the franchise along with blacks of both sexes. They did not bargain with either the Republican politicians or their own male abolitionist allies. The Republicans refused to endanger the potential vote of two million black males by tying this issue to the vote for females. The abolitionists, for their part, spoke of "the Negroes' hour." To the feminists' horror, William Lloyd Garrison, Horace Greeley, Frederick Douglass, Wendell Phillips, and Garrett Smith, the men on whom they most counted for support, remained silent or actively opposed their efforts to link the two causes. Elizabeth Cady Stanton complained bitterly,

During the six years they [women] held their own claims in abeyance to those of the slaves of the South, and labored to inspire the people with enthusiasm for the great measures of the Republican party, they were highly honored as 'wise, loyal, and clear-sighted.' But when the slaves were emancipated, and these women asked that they should be recognized in the reconstruction as citizens of the Republic, equal before the law, all these transcendent virtues vanished like dew before the morning sun. And thus it ever is: so long as woman labors to second man's endeavors and exalt his sex above her own, her virtues pass unquestioned; but when she dares to demand rights and privileges for herself, her motives, manners, dress, personal appearance, and character are subjects for ridicule and detraction. [3]

Although the Civil War was disappointing to feminists from a political point of view, it was a major watershed in the history of American women. As the armies on both sides grew larger, the shortage of manpower made increased demands on females and forced them to undertake new activities and responsibilities. In rural areas, large numbers of women had to run farms and support families without the aid of male relatives. In more urbanized regions, they sought work outside the home in unprecedented numbers. For the first time females entered the civil service, office work, and the retail trades, while the proportion of women teachers increased dramatically.

Even more significant was the enormous effort that females made to ensure an adequate flow of money, supplies, medicine, and nurses to the battlefields and army hospitals. During the very month that the war began, Elizabeth Blackwell organized the Women's Central Association for Relief and began to train one hundred army nurses. June saw the organization of the United States Sanitary Commission, which united Blackwell's group and seven thousand other local societies to coordinate relief. During the war the commission spent over $50 million, most of it raised by females. They also collected supplies, sewed bandages, recruited nurses, and did volunteer work in hospitals. Louise Lee Schuyler and Mary Livermore engaged in fund-raising activities on an enormous scale and supervised complex organizations from their respective bases in New York and Chicago. Livermore raised two-thirds of the contributions sent to Grant's army. Her single greatest achievement was the Sanitary Fair of 1863, which raised over $70,000 and inspired similar fairs in other major cities. [4]

The most important effect of the Civil War on women's work was to turn nursing into a profession for women. Elizabeth Blackwell had foreseen a desperate need for nurses at the very beginning of the struggle. Her relief organization began to train women for service on the northern side almost immediately. In June 1861 the government appointed the well-known Dorothea Dix as superintendent of army nurses. Like many of her contemporaries, she worried about the moral temptations facing young women who served among so many men. She solved the problem by dictating that her nurses be over thirty, plain, and thick waisted.

Two of the most famous Civil War nurses, Mary Ann Bickerdyke and Clara Barton, worked outside Dorothea Dix's organization. Bickerdyke, a widow, had supported herself and two sons before the war by practicing what she called "botanic" medicine. In 1861 she began caring for the wounded and sick in hospitals and at the front. Her colorful personality, brusqueness, and courageous exploits won her more publicity than any of the other war nurses. In addition to nursing in the strict sense of the word, she did monumental amounts of laundry, prepared food, and distributed tons of supplies collected by the Chicago Sanitary Commission. In 1862 she became its official agent in the field.

Clara Barton, who also appeared on her own at the front, is much better known today than Mary Ann Bickerdyke. Barton was one of the first regularly appointed female civil servants. When the war broke out, she organized first aid facilities and collected supplies, which she then distributed in hospitals and on battlefields in Virginia and Maryland. She resisted all attempts to merge her activities with those of the Sanitary Commission or Dorothea Dix's division of female nurses. She short-circuited military routine and appeared time and time again with supplies at the front. Her activity reached its height in 1862. Two years later she became head nurse with Butler's Army of the James. The soldiers called her the Angel of the Battlefield.

Although women were much less active on the Confederate side, the southern government recognized female nurses in 1862. Sally Tomkins, to cite one example, established a hospital in Richmond and received a commission as captain in the Confederate army. Ella Newson supervised a military hospital in Kentucky. Before the war was over, 3,200 female nurses served on both sides.[5]

The four decades after the Civil War witnessed a dramatic expansion of higher education for women. Patricia Graham attributes it to ideological pressure from the feminist movement, centered in the East, and, even more, to the dire economic need of colleges and universities, which faced dropping enrollments due to the Civil War, economic depression, and dissatisfaction with the college curriculum.[6] In the East several private women's colleges were founded. In the West most institutions of higher learning were state supported, a pattern that the Morrill Education Act of 1862 encouraged. The state universities were coeducational from the start, because males did not enroll in sufficient numbers to support them and because taxpayers with daughters would not support institutions unless their children could attend along with the sons of their neighbors.

The first women's college in the East was Elmira, which opened six years before the outbreak of the Civil War. Nonetheless, the foundation of Vassar in 1861 marked a new epoch in women's higher education because of its high standards. Smith and Wellesley followed in

1875, Bryn Mawr in 1885, and Radcliffe in 1893. Mary Lyon's Mount
Holyoke became a college with degree-granting privileges in 1888.
The goal of all these schools was to give females the first-rate education that men received at Harvard and Yale. "It occurred to me,"
wrote Matthew Vassar, "that woman, having received from her creator the same intellectual constitution as man, has the same right as
man to intellectual culture and development." The goal of his institution was "to accomplish for young women what colleges of the first
class accomplish for young men: that is, to furnish them the means of
a thorough, well-proportioned, and liberal education, but one
adapted to their wants in life."[7] One of the major problems of the
early girls' schools was finding enough adequately qualified students.
Wellesley ran a preparatory school until 1880, Vassar until 1888.[8]

Most of the women who attended the girls' colleges were interested
in education for its own sake or in preparation for teaching careers.
Neither they nor their parents regarded their educations as preparation for homemaking, a distinct change from the outlook of the early
pioneers in female education, Catharine Beecher and Emma Willard.
The fathers of most of the girls had attended college and were businessmen or professionals. Scholarships went to daughters of professional families with modest incomes rather than to girls from working-class homes.[9]

As early as 1870, Wisconsin, Michigan, Missouri, Iowa, Kansas,
Indiana, Minnesota, and California had coeduational state universities. These institutions opened their doors to female students because political and financial reasons dictated it, not because their
faculty and administrators believed in principle in higher education
for women or had even given it much thought. They continued to educate women for marriage and appropriate female jobs, such as public
school teaching. The vast majority of their students were enrolled in
education and home economics programs and received much less rigorous intellectual training than male students. Their college experience discouraged them from challenging accepted ideas about
women, developing strong motives for pursuing independent careers,
or trying to break into "masculine" fields.[10]

A number of private coeducational institutions besides Oberlin and
Antioch were also founded in this period. Saint Lawrence University,

Boston University, and Swarthmore date from the 1860s and 1870s. Cornell opened its doors to women in 1875, although it had started as a men's college.

Opponents of these developments reacted with increasingly shrill and hysterical arguments against higher education for women. In keeping with the late nineteenth-century conviction that science could solve moral and social problems, they drew on Darwinism, physical anthropology, and physiology to prove their case. Darwin's ideas about women lent themselves easily to this use.[11] Various forms of the theory of evolution were among the most effective arguments against sending women to college. Physical anthropologists, particularly craniologists, contributed their share with the discovery that females had smaller brains than males. They explicitly, and incorrectly, linked brain size and intelligence. The physiologists applied the principle of the conservation of energy to the body. They concluded that women devoted so much energy to their reproductive organs and functions that they did not have enough left over to develop their intellectual abilities. The woman who violated her nature and went to college or devoted herself to mental activity would become sterile or give birth to feeble, unhealthy children because she had diverted energy from her uterus to her brain. In general, the physiologists believed that women's reproductive system dominated their entire physical and psychic existence.[12] The most influential, late nineteenth-century attack on higher education for women, Dr. Edward Clarke's *Sex in Education; or, A Fair Chance for the Girls*, was based on these kinds of physiological arguments.[13]

In the face of these attacks, the women's colleges felt very much on the defensive. To demonstrate the high quality of their schools, they self-consciously instituted the same admission requirements, curriculum, and examinations as the best men's schools. They started physical education programs, gave courses in physiology and hygiene, and hired doctors to live on campus in response to assertions that college education endangered female health. The Association of Collegiate Alumnae, forerunner to the American Association of University Women, submitted a report to the State Labor Commission of Massachusetts to prove that the health of college women was superior to that of noncollege women and college men.[14] Only M. Carey Thomas, president of Bryn Mawr from 1894 to 1922, objected to any concessions to social prejudice in the development of the curriculum for women.

Just because women have shown such an aptitude for a true college education and such delight in it, we must be careful to maintain it for them in its integrity. We must see to it that its disciplinary quality is not lowered by the insertion of so-called practical courses which are falsely supposed to prepare for life. . . . I am in consequence astounded to see the efforts which have been made within the past few years . . . to persuade, I might almost say to compel, those in charge of women's education to riddle the college curriculum of women with hygiene, and sanitary drainage, and domestic science, and child-study, and all the rest of the so-called practical studies.[15]

Opponents of female education noted that women with college degrees did not marry as frequently as those without a higher education. When they did, they had fewer children. This seemed to be the final proof that women should not go to college. In *A Century of Higher Education for American Women*, Mabel Newcomer says that the relevant statistics on marriage and childbearing are inconclusive.[16] She estimates that over 50 percent of all college women married.[17] In the female population as a whole, between 90 and 96 percent married throughout the nineteenth century.[18] Carl Degler believes that feminism often did take the form of a revolt against marriage and that this trend was most evident among educated women. He estimates that in 1900 25 percent of the females who received bachelor's degrees and 50 percent of the woman doctors remained single.[19] Seventy-five percent of the women who earned Ph.D.'s between 1877 and 1924 were spinsters.[20]

Among female college graduates, those from the eastern women's colleges were least likely to marry. Only 45 percent of those who graduated from Bryn Mawr between 1889 and 1908 did so. The comparable figure for Wellesley was 57 percent.[21] These were the women who more than any others created the stereotype of the educated spinster. Their impact on public attitudes was far greater than their numbers warranted because of their visibility as they fought their way into graduate schools and "masculine" professions[22] and assumed leadership roles in social reform movements.[23]

It is easy to understand why so many females with college educations chose to remain single. To a degree that is hard for us to appreciate, a woman had to make a choice: she either married and had children, or she remained single and had a career. Elizabeth Blackwell said explicitly that she decided to become a doctor because her choice put a "strong barrier" between her and matrimony.[24] Both Angelina Grimké and Antoinette Brown Blackwell disappeared from the ranks of feminist leaders after their marriages, although in both cases their husbands were in favor of women's rights. Alice Freeman Palmer resigned as president of Wellesley College when she married George Herbert Palmer, a philosophy professor at Harvard, in 1887. Propriety demanded that wives remain at home, and in many cases domestic chores and childbearing drained them of any energy that they might have devoted to intellectual activities or careers. Yet, after their exhilarating years at college, many women were far too committed to the pursuit of knowledge or the practical application of their educations to retreat willingly to the narrow confines of Victorian domesticity. And so, in surprising numbers, they chose the other alternative and rejected marriage.[25]

Another aspect of this situation is that in the ultimate sense Victorian notions about sexuality subverted the cult of domesticity. Women, who were raised to think of sexual relations as bestial, recoiled from marriage if presented with an alternative pattern of life.[26] In this regard, recent work on family limitation in the nineteenth century is very revealing. Daniel Smith attributes the dramatic fall in the birth rate to women. Smith notes that small families were more likely than large ones to end with girls or to consist solely of daughters. He assumes that women would be more satisfied than men with such families and that their existence indicates that wives—rather than husbands—controlled marital relations.[27] The major methods of controlling family size, *coitus interruptus* and abstinence, appealed to women, who were concerned about "marital excess," much more than to men. The revolt against frequent sexual relations seemed natural to females, who had been taught to regard sex as an activity alien to feminine nature and as one of the more unpleasant duties of the wife. If Smith is correct that Victorian views of sex influenced wives so strongly, it seems very likely that educated women with some choice about their lives would remain single and thus avoid sexual intercourse altogether. William O'Neill aptly asks "why beings as pure as themselves should be subjected to the lusts of men."[28]

Still another element in Victorian culture made marriage unattractive. The contrast between male and female nature and emphasis on female moral superiority created a strong sense of solidarity among nineteenth-century women.[29] Many of them felt that they had much more in common with each other than they ever could have with a man. Even nonsexual contact with males was bound to be degrading. The proliferation of women's clubs and reform groups after 1870 drew on these sororal feelings and on what contemporary feminists would call a recognition of sisterhood.[30] The small group of females who attended women's colleges lived for three or four years in relatively isolated communities that encouraged intense emotional ties among the students. One of the attractions of the settlement house movement at the end of the nineteenth century was undoubtedly that it enabled single women to continue to live together in relatively self-contained environments.[31]

One of the paradoxes of Victorian culture, therefore, is that it simultaneously exalted the cult of domesticity and made marriage unattractive. College-educated women were freer than any other group of females to reject matrimony because they could support themselves. The frequency with which they did so inspired opponents of higher education for women to fulminate about race suicide and the unnatural results of training beings designed for other functions. Nonetheless, the number of women going to college increased steadily between 1860 and 1920. By the latter year, 47.3 percent of the total enrollment was female, a figure that signified a major educational revolution.[32]

Although the college woman was no longer an isolated figure by 1900, social change had occurred so rapidly that many women active in the first decades of the twentieth century still saw themselves as the pioneers they had been in their youth. M. Carey Thomas delivered a speech at the twenty-fifth anniversary of the Association of Collegiate Alumnae in 1908 that illuminates the atmosphere in which the early women's colleges developed.

The passionate desire of the women of my generation for higher education was accompanied throughout its course by that awful doubt, felt by women themselves as well as by men, as to whether women as a sex were physically and mentally fit for it. . . . I cannot remember the time when I was not sure that studying and going to college were the things above all others which I wished to do. I was always wondering whether it could be really true, as everyone thought, that boys were cleverer than girls. Indeed, I cared so much that I never dared to ask any grown-up person the direct question, not even my father or mother, because I feared to hear the reply. I remember often praying about it, and begging God that if it were true that because I was a girl I could not successfully master Greek and go to college and understand things to kill me at once, as I could not bear to live in such an unjust world. When I was a little older I read the Bible entirely through with passionate eagerness, because I had heard it said that it proved that women were inferior to men. . . .

Before I myself went to college I had seen only one college woman. I had heard that such a woman was staying at the house of an acquaintance. I went to see her with fear. Even if she had appeared in hoofs and horns I was determined to go to college all the same. But it was a relief to find this Vassar graduate tall and handsome and dressed like other women. When, five years later, I went to Leipzig to study after I had graduated from Cornell. . . . I was thought . . . as much of a disgrace to my family as if I had eloped with the coachman. Now, women who have been to college are as plentiful as blackberries on summer hedges. [33]

Although the number of women entering the professions increased in the period 1860-1920, change in this area lagged behind the growth of higher education. A real disparity between the number of females receiving college degrees and the number of female professionals developed. The situation was all the more remarkable because more and more women sought work outside the home during these years. By 1900, 20.4 percent of all females were employed; by 1910, 25.2 percent. [34] The age and marital status of women workers also changed significantly. Most employed females in the 1890s were single, were under twenty-five, and left their jobs upon marriage. After 1900, however, the age of women workers began to rise, and an increasing number were married. In 1900, 5.6 percent of all American wives held jobs; in 1910, 10.7 percent. [35] An examination of this female labor force shows that its increasing size was due to economic necessity rather than to any dramatic change in attitudes about woman's proper sphere. Relatively few of the new female workers were native, middle-class, white women; the vast majority were immigrants or Blacks. As late as 1930, the latter groups constituted 57 percent of all employed women. [36] Of the women working in 1920, 11.9 percent were in the professions; 75 percent of this group were nurses or teachers, two careers often regarded as extensions of the proper female role. Women made few inroads into the so-called higher professions—medicine, law, and the ministry. [37]

In 1891 a book called *Woman's Work in America* appeared. Julia Ward Howe, a leading figure in the contemporary woman's movement, wrote the introduction, and well-known women contributed chapters on their fields of expertise. Written halfway through the period under consideration in this chapter, this book is a good starting point for estimating the position of professional women. Of its eighteen chapters, three were on higher education and seven on philanthropy. One entitled "Women in the State" dealt with the growing involvement of females in politics and in agitation for reform, while another, "Woman in Industry," discussed the working class. Five chapters concerned women in the professions. They surveyed literature, journalism, law, medicine, and the ministry. The book did not discuss either teaching or nursing, the two fields that employed the vast majority of professional women. The reason is that their position in these areas was so well established that it did not seem necessary. In the preface, editor Annie Nathan Meyer stated explicitly that "the fields of labor described here contain evidences of woman's progress; they are those in which women, if entrance were not absolutely denied them, were at least not welcomed, nor valued." [38]

Mary Putnam Jacobi, an outstanding doctor in the later nineteenth century, wrote the account "Woman in Medicine." [39] She considered the period before the Civil War as a kind of prehistory. Adequate medical schools rejected women. The handful of qualified female doctors received their training in Europe. The antebellum period saw the foundation of the first medical schools exclusively for women, Gregory's Medical School in Boston and the Women's Medical College in Philadelphia. Neither provided first-rate training since their students were excluded from hospitals and received no clinical experience. Elizabeth Blackwell founded the New York Infirmary in 1854 to remedy this situation.

Real progress began in the 1860s. Dr. Jacobi attributed it directly to the Civil War, which created an enormous interest in and need for hospitals and doctors: "It was amidst the exigencies of a great war that their opportunities opened, their sphere enlarged, and they 'emerged from obscurity' into the responsibilities of recognized public function.'' [40] These years saw "the transition for women physicians from the pre-medical period, when medical education was something attempted but not effected, to a truly medical epoch, when women could really have an opportunity to engage in actual medical work. Correlatively the theoretic education began to improve." [41] It was during this period that Marie Zakrzewska's New England Hospital grew into a model institution for treating women patients and training female physicians. By 1891, hospitals for women in New York, Philadelphia, Boston, Chicago, San Francisco, and Minneapolis employed female doctors. Women's medical colleges opened in New York, Chicago, and Baltimore.

These successes occurred in the midst of a continuing debate over whether women were capable of being competent doctors. The controversey began in Boston, where female physicians and their feminist supporters were relatively numerous and well organized and where the male medical establishment felt professionally and economically threatened. Horatio Storer and Edward Clarke, two doctors connected with Harvard Medical School and once considered friends of the women's medical community, raised the issue publicly in the first decade after the Civil War. Both argued against training women as physicians on physiological grounds. They virtually equated women with their reproductive systems, assumed that their menstrual cycles dominated their physical and mental lives, and saw their brains and uteri as competitors for a limited supply of vital energy. Clarke's book on the subject, *Sex in Education; or, A Fair Chance for the Girls*, was stated in terms that could be and were used to attack all higher education for women. Because he spoke with medical authority, women doctors and other advocates of female education recognized the importance of answering him. Beginning in 1874 a spate of scientific and statistical studies refuted his fundamental assertion that higher education ruined women's health and reproductive capacities. Jacobi wrote a monograph based on questionnaires sent to a thousand young women, while three doctors at New England hospital did a study of female physicians. Although this literature effectively destroyed the scientific case against women doctors, prejudice against them continued. As Mary Walsh has said, "In the final analysis, the opposition to the women physicians was more emotional than intellectual and thus impervious to statistical studies.... With this type of opposition, rational arguments about the capabilities of women, supported by mounting research data, might occasionally breach a barrier, but could not turn the battle."[42]

Mary Putnam Jacobi, Marie Zakrzewska, and Elizabeth Blackwell all thought that women would receive the highest quality training only in coeducational medical schools.[43] Dr. Blackwell opened a college in conjunction with her hospital only after she failed to secure the admission of females to existing medical schools in New York City. Determined that her students receive first-rate training, she instituted a uniquely demanding curriculum and system of education. At a time when the normal course was two years, she established a three-year graded curriculum with detailed laboratory work in the first two years and clinical experience in the third. She created an independent board of examiners composed of professors from other medical schools to test her students before they received their degrees. Zakrzewska hoped that the success of her hospital would convince Harvard Medical School to admit women.

In 1869 the University of Michigan opened the first coeducational medical school in the United States on the ground that a tax-supported institution had to be open equally to the children of its citizens. The school provided duplicate lectures in subjects liable to cause embarrassment to mixed audiences. Double courses existed in obstetrics, gynecology, and some branches of internal medicine and surgery. To ensure that both sexes received equal educations, its lectures, lecturers, and examinations were identical. Clinics were held in common. Boston, Syracuse, and Buffalo universities established coeducational medical schools before 1880. By 1893 the University of Oregon Medical School, Kansas Medical School, and three of the four medical schools in Boston (Boston University, Tufts, and the College of Physicians and Surgeons) admitted women. Their numbers in these institutions were impressive: 19 percent of the University of Michigan Medical School, 20 percent of the University of Oregon, and 31 percent of Kansas Medical School. By 1900, 42 percent of the graduates of Tufts Medical School were female.[44] In a footnote to her chapter, Dr. Jacobi noted with excitement that while *Woman's Work in America* was being printed, the trustees of Johns Hopkins University announced that their new medical school would be open to women in consideration of a gift of $100,000 given to the endowment fund on that condition. M. Carey Thomas of Bryn Mawr and a group of feminists had raised the money.

This is the first time in America that any provision for the medical education of women has been made at a university of the standing of the Johns Hopkins. It is expected that the medical education of the future school will be especially directed for the benefit of selected and post graduate students, for such as desire to make special researches and to pursue advanced studies in medical science. The admission of women to a share in these higher opportunities is a fact of immense significance, though only a few should profit by the advantage, the standing of all will be benefited by this authoritative recognition of a capacity in women for studies, on this higher plane, on equal terms and in company with men. [45]

The opening of Cornell Medical School to women in 1899 was another major landmark.

Professional recognition accompanied the spread of first-rate medical education for women. The American Medical Association admitted them as members and as delegates to the annual convention beginning in 1876. By the next decade, major hospitals were opening their lectures to females, who finally escaped from isolation in women's hospitals. Mount Sinai Hospital in New York City was the first in the country to give a female physician a regular staff appointment. Nonetheless, by 1891, Dr. Jacobi felt that Chicago was the city where hospital privileges were most equitably distributed between the sexes.

According to the census of 1880, 2,432 women were registered as doctors in the United States, but probably only a small percentage of them were genuinely professional in terms of their training and competence. Dr. Jacobi noted, for instance, that the 1880 census recorded 133 women physicians in New York, but that ten years later the medical register contained the names of only 48. [46] In 1890, 18 percent of the physicians in Boston were women. [47]

Despite the optimistic note on which Mary Putnam Jacobi ended her survey, the numbers of female physicians did not continue to grow in the next thirty years. According to the 1920 American Medical Association Directory, only 40 of 482 general hospitals accepted women interns. [48] The number of women in medical schools actually declined from 1,280 in 1902 to 992 in 1926. [49] The number of female physicians peaked at 6 percent of the national total in 1910 and declined steadily thereafter. [50]

The declining numbers of female medical students and doctors resulted from the convergence of two trends. [51] In the 1890s the opening of coeducational medical schools convinced many women that female medical colleges were obsolete. In a wave of optimism they closed the women's institutions or merged them with coeducational schools. By 1903 only three of the original seventeen were still open. The elimination of the women's medical colleges was carried out on the assumption that women would be admitted to coeducational institutions in equitable numbers. This hope proved to be totally false. During the first two decades of the twentieth century one after another of the medical schools adopted restrictive admissions policies designed to eliminate or reduce radically the numbers of female students. The effect on women was staggering. At Boston University, for example, 29.5 percent of the graduating classes between 1898 and 1918 were female; in the subsequent two decades the percentage fell to 9.9 percent. There was not a single woman in the class of 1939. [52] At Tufts the graduating class of 1910 was 7.6 percent female, compared to 42 percent only ten years earlier. The class of 1919 had only two women. [53] In 1902, without any prior warning to faculty or students, Northwestern University Medical School simply closed its women's division. [54] This pattern was repeated in one medical school after the other. [55] In 1925, American medical schools institutionalized their restrictive admissions policies by imposing a 5 percent quota on female students. [56]

What it was like to be a woman doctor in this period was suggested by Edmund Wilson in *Upstate*, writing about his cousin, Dorothy Reed Mendenhall, who became a physician early in the twentieth century.

In the eighties, medicine was still not considered an appropriate profession for a woman. The men doctors did not want them. The medical professors said that a woman's training was wasted because she would either not be up to finishing or would marry and fail to practice. But Dorothy had enough confidence in her own tenacity and her brains to accept the formidable challenge. ... I am a little shocked, though not really surprised, to learn from Dorothy's memoirs that when Dorothy was working in a hospital in New Jersey where my uncle Reuel, also a doctor, had placed her, his wife, my aunt Caroline, a model, as she thought, of conventional correctitude, wrote to Cousin Grace that she was very sorry that, in view of Dorothy Reed's then status, she would not be able to see her socially. . . . Her mother and her Talcottville family had been much upset by her studying medicine. "Aunt Lin, in all the years I was in Baltimore, always alluded to my 'being south for the winter.' Medicine was distinctly not a ladylike occupation."

. . . "I decided after much thought that as long as I was in medicine I would never object to anything that a fellow student or doctor did to me in my presence if he would act or speak the same way to a man . . . but if he discriminated against me because I was a woman . . . was offensive in a way he wouldn't be to a man, I would crack down on him myself, or take it up with the authorities if he proved too much for me alone. On the whole, this was the right way to take the position of women in medicine in the nineteenth century. . . . I was distinctly not such a nice person, but a stronger one, after Johns Hopkins. . . ."57

The years that saw the first significant entrance of women into the medical profession also witnessed the appearance of the first female attorneys. Women found it even more difficult to become lawyers than doctors, because the legal profession was institutionalized and had been granted licensing powers much earlier. Since English common law prohibited women from being called to the bar, the law had to be changed in each state by court decision or statute before they could practice as lawyers. Furthermore, practicing law was even more incompatible with nineteenth-century ideas about women than was practicing medicine. Female doctors could claim that their careers were natural extensions of women's nurturant, healing role in the home and that they protected female modesty by ministering to members of their own sex. By contrast, women lawyers were clearly intruding on the public domain explicitly reserved to men. Not unexpectedly, there were only 1,500 female lawyers in the United States compared to almost 9,000 women doctors in 1910.58

The first female to seek admission to the bar was Myra Bradwell of Chicago, whose husband was a distinguished attorney. Mrs. Bradwell studied law with him from the earliest days of their marriage. In 1868 she began to publish a weekly legal newspaper, the *Chicago Legal News*, which was a brilliant success. She was president of the journal without the usual disabilities of wifehood because the legislature passed a special law in her favor. She also printed legal forms, stationery, and briefs. After each session of the legislature, she published a revised edition of the Illinois Statutes. For twenty-five years she molded legal opinion in the Midwest. Mrs. Bradwell was also active in the Illinois Woman Suffrage Association. In 1869 the Bradwells, Elizabeth Cady Stanton, and Mary Livermore joined forces to secure passage of an act giving married women control over their earnings. Mr. Bradwell subsequently served in the state legislature and secured other reforms important to women.

In 1869, Mrs. Bradwell applied unsuccessfully for a license from the Illinois State Supreme Court to practice law. In its decision the court openly acknowledged Bradwell's competence to do so. It ruled, however, that it lacked power to grant her request because to do so would infringe on the powers of the legislature.

. . . when the legislature gave to this court the power of granting licenses to practice the law, it was not with the slightest expectation that this privilege would be extended equally to men and women. . . . Whatever, then, may be our individual opinions as to the admission of women to the bar, we do not deem ourselves at liberty to exercise our power in a mode never contemplated by the legislature, and inconsistent with the usages of the courts of the common law, from the origin of the system to the present day.59

On the substantive issue, the judges were clearly ambivalent.

There are some departments of the legal profession in which she can appropriately labor. Whether, on the other hand, to engage in the hot strifes of the bar, in the presence of the public, and with momentous verdicts the prizes of the struggle, would not tend to destroy the deference and delicacy with which it is the pride of our ruder sex to treat her, is a matter certainly worthy of her consideration.

But the important question is, what effect the presence of women as barristers in our courts would have upon the administration of justice, and the question can be satisfactorily answered only in the light of experience. If the legislature shall choose to remove the existing barriers, and authorize us to issue licenses equally to men and women, we shall cheerfully obey.60

Bradwell appealed to the United States Supreme Court on the ground that the denial violated her rights under the Fourteenth Amendment. The Supreme Court decided against her in 1873. The majority ruled on technical grounds, but a concurring minority opposed the entrance of women into the legal profession under any circumstances, in terms reflecting the values embodied in the cult of domesticity.

... the civil law, as well as nature herself, has always recognized a wide difference in the respective spheres and destinies of man and woman. Man is, or should be, woman's protector and defender. The natural and proper timidity and delicacy which belongs to the female sex evidently unfits it for many of the occupations of civil life. The constitution of the family organization, which is founded in the divine ordinance, as well as in the nature of things, indicates the domestic sphere as that which properly belongs to the domain and functions of womanhood. The harmony, not to say identity, of interests and views which belong, or should belong, to the family institution is repugnant to the idea of a woman adopting a distinct and independent career from that of her husband. . . .

The humane movements of modern society which have for their object the multiplication of avenues for woman's advancement, and of occupations adapted to her condition and sex, have my heartiest concurrence. But I am not prepared to say that it is one of her fundamental rights and privileges to be admitted into every office and position, including those which require highly special qualifications and demanding special responsibilities.[61]

The previous year the legislature had rectified the situation by statute.

In the next decade or so, women sought and won admission to the bar in most states through court decisions or legislative acts. In 1879, Belva Lockwood became the first women admitted to practice before the United States Supreme Court, a triumph that concluded a seven-year struggle to secure admission to all the courts in Washington, D.C.[62] Three years later fifty-six females practiced law in this country. Of that number, only thirty-one had gone to law school. The first woman to receive a law degree was Ada H. Kepley, who graduated from the Union College of Law in Chicago in 1870. Except for Harvard, Yale, Columbia, Georgetown, and the University of Virginia, most law schools admitted women by 1891.[63] Females also participated in bar associations. Despite this encouraging start, however, the number of women lawyers grew slowly in the thirty years before the passage of the Nineteenth Amendment. By 1920, although women constituted 47 percent of the total college enrollment, only 3 percent of the legal profession was female.[64]

Female ministers were even rarer than women lawyers. The largest churches—Roman Catholic, Episcopalian, Lutheran, Presbyterian, Methodist Episcopalian, and Baptist—excluded women from ordination and the pulpit.[65] By 1890 only smaller denominations, such as the Congregationalists, Universalists, Protestant Methodists, and German Methodists, had changed traditional practices.

Anna Howard Shaw, who studied for the ministry in the 1870s, faced the same prejudice and isolation that had confronted Antoinette Brown Blackwell and Olympia Brown in the 1850s. Shaw converted to Methodism and decided to enter the ministry while she was attending high school in Michigan. Her family was so appalled that they offered to pay for her entire education at the University of Michigan if she would give up the outrageous idea. When she refused, they broke all contact with her. Nonetheless, Shaw entered Albion College, a small coeducational Methodist institution, at the age of twenty-five. She supported herself by preaching and giving temperance lectures. After two years she left without taking a degree to go to Boston University to prepare for the ministry. She discovered that she could not live free in the dormitory provided for male theological students or eat at the club that provided them with cheap meals. She tried to support herself by preaching, but found it impossible because there were so many theological students in the city. Eventually she became so weak from inadequate diet that she could not walk the three flights of stairs to her classes without resting once or twice. At this crisis the Woman's Foreign Missionary Society rescued her by providing a weekly allowance of $3.50, plus $2.00 for rent. After she received her degree, the only woman in her class, two churches on Cape Cod employed her as their minister. Because the New England Conference of the Methodist Episcopal Church would not ordain her, Shaw could not baptize, administer the sacraments, or admit new members. When she appealed to the General Conference, it affirmed the action of the lower body and revoked her license to preach. She therefore applied successfully for ordination to the Protestant Methodist Church and became its first female minister in 1880. Her whole experience indicates that little had changed in America's most prestigious profession.[66]

The spread of higher education for women opened college teaching as a profession to females. Between 1890 and 1900 the first women began to appear on college faculties. The numbers involved were very small: in 1920 only 7.9 percent of the professors in American institutions of higher learning were women, although they earned 33.3 percent of the graduate degrees granted. [67] The disparity between these two percentages indicates how reluctant colleges and universities were to employ the females whom they themselves educated. The women's colleges were, of course, most receptive to hiring female professors. Maria Mitchell, one of the outstanding astronomers in nineteenth-century America, was one of the first members of the Vassar faculty. She discovered a comet that bears her name and was the first woman admitted to the Academy of Arts and Sciences. Katherine Lee Bates, author of "America the Beautiful," joined the faculty of Wellesley as an instructor in English in 1885. Six years later she became a full professor and the head of her department. Maria Louise Sanford taught English and history at Swarthmore, a new coeducational Quaker college. Because of a love affair with a married colleague, she resigned in 1879 and moved to the University of Minnesota. Margaret Floy Washburn, who graduated from Vassar in 1891, decided to continue her studies in psychology. Columbia University refused to admit her as a regular graduate student, so after a year there, holding a dubious status, she transferred to Cornell. She received her Ph.D. in 1894 in the new experimental psychology. In a long and distinguished career, she taught at Wells College, Cornell, the University of Cincinnati, and Vassar. She published her most important book, *The Animal Mind*, in 1908. From 1925 on, she was one of the four coeditors of the *American Journal of Psychology*.

Another Vassar graduate, Ellen Swallow Richards, chose an even more unreceptive field, chemistry. In 1870 she entered M.I.T. as a special student and became the first female ever accepted at a scientific institution. Three years later M.I.T. granted her a B.S. degree; Vassar, an M.A. Although she did graduate work at M.I.T., the institution refused to grant a Ph.D. to a woman, and she never received her doctorate. Swallow married a professor of metallurgy and mining and continued to work at M.I.T. in a somewhat irregular position. With the help of the Women's Educational Association of Boston, she established the Women's Lab at the university to train female scientists. In the seven years of its existence, she contributed about a thousand dollars a year of her own income to keep it running. Eventually,

M.I.T. appointed her a regular member of the faculty and integrated her pupils into the male student body.

The experience of female scientists in this period illustrates the crucial role that the eastern female colleges played in the careers of academic women. [68] The first three editions of James McKeen Cattell's *American Men of Science: A Biographical Directory* (1906, 1910, and 1921) listed 504 women. [69] Of a group of 483 of them, almost 40 percent attended just eight eastern women's schools, although they were relatively small institutions. Even more important, the women's colleges were major employers of female scientists. Between 1900 and 1920, for example, they employed 21 of the 23 female physicists listed by Cattell. In 1906, 57 percent of all the women whom he listed worked at these institutions. By 1921 the percentage fell to 36 percent, although the number of jobs doubled, because opportunities for female scientists were finally opening at the larger state and private universities. [70]

Throughout the period women scientists experienced discrimination that had the effect of segregating them from the mainstream of the profession. One of the first barriers that they faced was securing admission to graduate schools that would grant them a Ph.D. A number of women went through programs and then had the heart-breaking experience of being told that they would not be granted degrees. Johns Hopkins did this to Christine Ladd in 1882; Harvard, to Mary Witon Calkins in 1896. [71] By the latter decade, however, most graduate schools accepted women more willingly and granted them doctorates in large numbers. Of the scientists listed in Cattell's directory, 63 percent of the women and only 46 percent of the men had Ph.D.'s. [72]

Once they completed their education, women had many fewer employment opportunities than men. Men could choose between jobs in academic institutions and in industry, while women were confined to the former. Not a single female scientist held a job in industry before World War I. Within academia, women were concentrated in lower positions at less prestigious institutions. Most of the men worked in universities and medical schools; the women, in female colleges, nursing and normal schools, museums, and research institutions. Men's and coeducational colleges and universities rarely hired women. In

1921 they held .001 percent of the professorships at male colleges and 4 percent of the professorships at coeducational institutions, compared to 68 percent of the professorships at women's colleges. [73] The specific positions that they held revealed other kinds of discrimination and sex-role stereotyping. Many of the women with degrees in chemistry, for example, held positions in home economics departments. Not a single woman listed in Cattell was an engineer.

Given this situation, it is not surprising that female scientists had much higher unemployment rates than their male counterparts and that many more of them worked outside their fields. When Alice Hamilton returned to this country in 1896 after completing her medical training in Germany, where she had specialized in pathology and bacteriology, she could not find a job. She decided, therefore, to spend another year studying, this time at Johns Hopkins. The following summer she accepted an offer to teach pathology at the Women's Medical School of Northwestern University. In her autobiography she specifically expressed her gratitude "because it was employment in my own field." [74] Years later, when she was the leading expert in the United States on industrial diseases, Hamilton was appointed an assistant professor at Harvard Medical School. She had no illusions about their attitude toward women: "Industrial medicine had become a much more important branch during the war years, but it still had not attracted men, and I was really about the only candidate available." [75]

Finally, women received much less professional recognition than their male colleagues. They gradually won acceptance in scientific societies, but the prestigious National Academy of Science did not elect its first female member until 1925 (Florence Sabin) and its second until 1931 (Margaret Washburn). [76] Of the scientists listed in Cattell's directory, proportionately fewer women than men were considered outstanding by their colleagues. [77] Given the barriers that they faced at every stage of their careers, this was almost inevitable.

The professions under discussion were all considered "learned" in the sense that they required their practitioners to have a higher education. Women's entrance into medicine, law, the ministry, and college teaching was closely related to the revolution in female education that occurred in the last four decades of the nineteenth century. Between 1860 and 1920, women gained a foothold in the professions that they have never relinquished. These early pioneers proved that females were capable of the highest intellectual achievement, that they were physically able to meet the demands of professional life, and that they had the drive and tenacity to stick to their callings.

Undoubtedly, the feminist movement helped to create the environment that permitted these women to enter the careers of their choice. The general attack on deeply rooted prejudices and patterns of behavior encouraged and enabled determined females to break out of their traditional sphere. Political, economic, and social changes in the early nineteenth century had given birth to the woman's movement. By the end of the century it acted as an independent catalyst of further change.

Despite the significant progress that I have outlined, the achievements of this era were somewhat disappointing. Women remained a tiny, isolated minority in all of the learned professions. Less than 8 percent of the college professors, 3 percent of the lawyers, a small fraction of the doctors, and a mere handful of ministers were females. [78] What was most disturbing was the huge gap between women's educational and professional status. By 1920 almost half of the college students in the United States were women, and a third of the graduate degrees were awarded to them. [79] Nonetheless, strong pressures against female professionals survived. All too often choosing a career still meant forgoing marriage and confronting familial and social disapproval. Although some educated women revolted against matrimony in this period, they were always a small minority of all American females. The great majority preferred marriage and motherhood to any other vocation. Men did not welcome women into careers that they had monopolized and erected various obstacles to them. Although individual females successfully surmounted these barriers, the problem was not permanently solved as long as self-interest and prejudice combined to keep old attitudes alive. Whenever the opportunity presented itself, men reestablished the obstacles. The introduction of restrictive admission policies to medical schools and adoption of the 1925 quota on female entrance provide a cardinal example. The overriding concern of the early twentieth-century woman's movement with the vote and the demise of feminism in the 1920s were disastrous for professional women. Without the active ideological support of the movement, women succumbed to traditional ideas about the feminine role, which reappeared in the 1920s and 1930s in modern psychological and sociological form. The dwindling number of career women lacked the personal encouragement that females of an earlier generation had received from the woman's movement. [80]

The decades that witnessed the frustration of feminist hopes that women would win equal opportunities in the learned professions saw the continued expansion of the so-called female professions. These included new fields such as library science, home economics, and social work, as well as the now traditional careers in teaching and nursing. [81] Jobs in these areas were considered particularly appropriate for women because they drew on their natural talents for nurturance, sympathy, domestic management, and self-sacrifice. Advocates of the feminization of librarianship, for example, defended their position in much the same terms that Catharine Beecher had used to defend the female public school teacher in the 1830s and 1840s. [82]

College graduates, particularly from the eastern women's schools, played a leading role in the development of social work as a profession. [83] Although their alumnae were highly visible among the early generations of female college teachers, many more of them entered settlement houses than academia. Careers in social work harmonized perfectly with the ethos prevailing at the women's colleges.

Except at Bryn Mawr, where the indomitable M. Carey Thomas strove to prove that women could compare intellectually with men and where the emphasis was on independence, excellence, and competitiveness, the female schools extolled a peculiar blend of intellectual achievement, social service, and genteel femininity. Vassar, Smith, and Wellesley combined the cult of true womanhood with intellectual discipline and high academic standards. They also exposed their students to moderately advanced social thought and encouraged them to make practical use of their educations. While Bryn Mawr's ideal was androgynous, Vassar, Smith, and Wellesley sought to produce educated *women*, who combined intellectual achievement with feminine virtue. [84] Many of their alumnae consequently found social work the most appealing profession. It drew on their educations, satisfied their desire for social service, and conformed to their continued belief in the nurturant, self-sacrificing female temperament.

The women's professions were all underpaid and conferred little prestige on their members. As Susan B. Anthony had pointed out as early as 1853, no profession filled with women would be prestigious as long as the female sex was considered inferior.[85] Women accepted their low salaries because of the limited professional alternatives open to them, their internalization of the idea that it was unfeminine to be materialistic, and their acceptance of the social service ideal. Jill Conway has concluded that the "development of the women's professions should thus be interpreted as a conservative trend by which the potential for change inherent in changed educational experience was still-born and women's intellectual energies were channeled into perpetuating women's service role in society rather than into independent and self-justifying intellectual endeavor. It was also a trend by which the direction and support of most kinds of intellectual enquiry remained unquestionably male-controlled."[86]

Business was not a profession in the same sense as the careers that I have been discussing. Success—even a start—required not academic training, but rather a combination of ingenuity, capital, tenacity, and luck. Flourishing businessmen were essentially flourishing entrepreneurs. These conditions made business attractive to ambitious females. The lack of educational requirements and licensing bodies prevented men from erecting the kind of barriers to women that existed in fields like the law and medicine. The absence of any required training opened the field to women from the lower classes.

The sixty years from 1860 to 1920 saw the entrance into the field of business of a number of women who not only earned a living, but actually achieved extraordinary success. They were probably as numerous as women in the learned professions, although they are much less well known today. *Notable American Women* lists eleven in these decades who founded and ran enterprises that would have been a credit to any man.[87] These females differed from the women who had engaged in business or trade in the colonial period because they operated on a much larger scale and in an economic world entirely divorced from the home and because they were much less likely to be widows carrying on their husbands' businesses. Not one of these eleven women attended college, although some went to female seminaries and academies. They were an exceedingly diverse group. In terms of class, three came from very poor backgrounds, seven from middle-class circumstances, and one from a rich family. Two of them were southern Blacks. Eight married; three remained single. All the married women had children. Three of the wives worked with their husbands, although only one was involved in an enterprise that was *his* success before she participated. Their fields of endeavor included business promotion, investment, textiles, insurance, banking, and the food, beauty, and fashion industries.

Although it is tempting, I will not recount the biographies of all these successful businesswomen. However, I do want to talk about two whose activities seem closely related to contemporary females with business aspirations. The first is Miss Hetty Green, known as the "witch of Wall Street" because of personal eccentricity. Green inherited a large fortune from her mother, aunt, and father and used it to speculate in government bonds and railroads. She also invested heavily in real estate and owned some eight thousand parcels in major cities across the country. This property alone was worth $5-6 million when she died in 1910. Green was also a money lender. She had a remarkable sense of timing and liquidated her assets before panics started so that she had the cash to bail out less fortunate speculators. Her estate may have been as large as $100 million.[88]

The other woman, Mary Foot Seymour, was a schoolteacher in the 1870s when she saw the potential of the newly invented typewriter and shorthand for providing women with employment. In 1879 she established the Union School of Stenography at 38 Park Row, a property that now belongs to Pace University. She operated four schools, a business employing twenty-five stenographers, and an employment bureau. In 1889 she founded the *Business Woman's Journal*, a bimonthly that included accounts of successful females, articles of interest to businesswomen, and news of women's organizations. The paper had a regular distribution of about five thousand copies. In October 1892, Seymour launched the *American Woman's Journal*, which incorporated the original newspaper, in an effort to secure even wider circulation. She participated in women's groups and advocated female suffrage.[89]

I have recently discovered the autobiography of still another successful woman entrepreneur, Mrs. Alice Foote MacDougall, who was not included in *Notable American Women*.[90] MacDougall went into the wholesale coffee business in 1907 when her husband deserted her and their three children. She started out with $35 and a loan of $500. After some initial success, she expanded her operation to include tea and cocoa. Her most successful venture was opening a series of coffee-houses and restaurants. By 1928 her enterprises were worth about $2 million a year. In her autobiography, MacDougall discussed both the position of women in business and the feminist movement. She stated unequivocally, "No man ever unfairly discriminated against me. If one tried to, I, like everyone else, was equal to the emergency, and such experience really added a great deal to the zest of life."[91] She was hostile to the women's colleges and to the organized suffrage movement.

Explain the antagonism women showed me, as you will, members of the suffrage and feminist movements. I cannot. All I know is that while men sprang ever ready, ever chivalrous, to put business in my way . . . women almost invariably turned me down. There were exceptions, of course, as in the case of the superintendent of the hospital in Scranton, and in Martha Van Rensselaer, that amazing woman of the Department of Home Economics in Cornell. . . . But Smith College, Bryn Mawr, the Women's Exchanges, and hundreds of other similar institutions for women were impossible. . . . If their hesitancy could have been attributed to the quality of my coffee I would have been the first to acknowledge it. But by the time I approached places like these I was more or less of a specialist. I knew my market, both wholesale and retail. . . . my admiration of college intellect outside of scholastic matters had a severe blow, and my opinion concerning women in general and a certain type of college woman in particular was strengthened.[92]

By 1920, therefore, women had entered the male world of business and the learned professions. Despite discrimination, isolation, and ridicule, they proved that females could compete and succeed. Unfortunately, these brave spirits remained a tiny minority in their chosen fields. The great majority of American women hesitated to endure the personal sacrifices and practical difficulties involved in following their example. In the era after the passage of the Nineteenth Amendment, feminists faced the monumental task of turning these initial gains into more genuine economic equality between the sexes.

Notes

1. Elizabeth Cady Stanton, *Eighty Years and More, 1815-1897* (New York: Schocken Books, 1971), p. 238.

2. Eleanor Flexner, *Century of Struggle: The Woman's Rights Movement in the United States* (New York: Atheneum, 1971), pp. 110-11.

3. Stanton, *Eighty Years and More*, pp. 240-41. Many woman's rights leaders disagreed with Stanton and Anthony on this issue. Mott, Stone, Howe, and Antoinette Brown Blackwell supported the Fourteenth and Fifteenth Amendments. This was one of the issues behind the split in the movement in 1870.

4. Edward T. James, ed., *Notable American Women, 1607-1950*, 3 vols. (Cambridge, Mass.: Belknap Press, Harvard University Press, 1971), 2: 411-412.

5. Mary Elizabeth Massey, *Bonnet Brigades* (New York: Alfred A. Knopf, 1966), p. 52.

6. Patricia Albjerg Graham, "Women in Academe," in *The Professional Woman*, ed. Athena Theodore (Cambridge, Mass.: Schenkman Publishing Company, 1971), pp. 720-21.

7. Quoted in Mabel Newcomer, *A Century of Higher Education for American Women* (New York: Harper & Brothers, 1959), pp. 1, 55.

8. Ibid., pp. 21-22.

9. Ibid., pp. 57-58, 130-33.

10. Jill K. Conway, "Perspectives on the History of Women's Education in the United States," *History of Education Quarterly* 14 (Spring 1974): 5-7.

11. See pages 57-59.

12. Janice Trecker, "Sex, Science and Education," *American Quarterly* 26 (October 1974): 352-66. Elizabeth Fee, "Science and the Woman Problem: Historical Perspectives," in *Sex Differences: Social and Biological Perspectives*, ed. Michael S. Teitelbaum (Garden City, N.Y.: Doubleday, 1976), pp. 175-223. The ideas discussed in this paragraph were not effectively challenged until the 1890s and the opening decades of the twentieth century, accompanying the growth of a new, university-based science that emphasized experiments and statistical precision. Many of the scientists and social scientists involved in this assault on Victorian science were women. Despite their success from a scientific point of view, they made relatively little impact on public opinion before 1920. Fee, "Science and the Woman Problem," pp. 205-18. Rosalind Rosenberg, "In Search of Woman's Nature, 1850-1920," *Feminist Studies* 3 (Fall 1975): 146-52.

13. See Trecker, "Sex, Science, and Education," pp. 356-58; Rosalind Navin Rosenberg, "The Dissent from Darwin, 1890-1930: The New View of Woman among American Social Scientists" (Ph.D. diss., Stanford University, 1974), p. 30; and Mary Roth Walsh, *"Doctors Wanted: No Women Need Apply": Sexual Barriers in the Medical Profession, 1835-1975* (New Haven: Yale University Press, 1977), pp. 119-33, on Clarke and the public debate following the publication of his book.

14. Newcomer, *Century of Higher Education*, pp. 29-30.
15. Quoted in Aileen S. Kraditor, *Up from the Pedestal* (Chicago: Quadrangle Books, 1968), pp. 94-95.
16. Newcomer, *Century of Higher Education*, pp. 30-31.
17. Ibid., pp. 211-12.
18. Daniel Scott Smith, "Family Limitation, Sexual Control, and Domestic Feminism in Victorian America," in *Clio's Consciousness Raised*, ed. Mary Hartman and Lois Banner (New York: Harper Torchbooks, 1974), p. 120.
19. Carl N. Degler, "Revolution Without Ideology: The Changing Place of Women in America," in *The Woman in America*, ed. Robert Jay Lifton (Boston: Beacon Press, 1965), p. 206.
20. William Henry Chafe, *The American Woman, Her Changing Social, Economic, and Political Roles, 1920-1970* (New York: Oxford University Press, 1972), p. 100.
21. Roberta Wein, "Women's Colleges and Domesticity, 1875-1918," *History of Education Quarterly* 14 (Spring 1974): 37-38. Only 65 percent of the Bryn Mawr group and 76 percent of the Wellesley group who married had children. Jill Conway's estimate that 60 to 70 percent of the first generation of graduates from the women's colleges never married is certainly too high; "Perspectives on Women's Education," p. 8.
22. Among those who graduated from Bryn Mawr during the period 1889-1908, 62 percent went on to graduate school and 90 percent worked in paid positions. Among Wellesley graduates in the same period, 36 percent went on to graduate school and 65 percent held paid positions; Wein, "Women's Colleges and Domesticity," pp. 37-39, 45. Wein attributes the differences between the schools reflected in these statistics to the contrasting personalities and educational philosophies of the female presidents who dominated their formative years—M. Carey Thomas at Bryn Mawr and Alice Freeman Palmer at Wellesley.
23. J. Rousmaniere, "Cultural Hybrid in the Slums: The College Woman and the Settlement House, 1889-94," *American Quarterly* 22 (Spring 1970): 45-66.
24. Alice S. Rossi, ed., *The Feminist Papers: From Adams to de Beauvoir* (New York: Bantam Books, 1974), pp. 328-29.
25. Conway, "Perspectives on Women's Education," p. 8.
26. See pages 41-43 on nineteenth-century attitudes toward sexuality.
27. Smith, "Family Limitation in Victorian America," pp. 119-36.
28. William O'Neill, *The Woman Movement: Feminism in the United States and England* (Chicago: Quadrangle Books, 1971), p. 42.
29. Nancy F. Cott, *The Bonds of Womanhood: "Woman's Sphere" in New England, 1780-1835* (New Haven: Yale University Press, 1977), chap. 5, is a

perceptive and fascinating discussion of sisterhood among Victorian women.

30. Christopher Lasch and William R. Taylor, "Two 'Kindred Spirits': Sorority and Family in New England, 1839-1848," *New England Quarterly* 36 (March 1963): 23-41. John Demos, "The American Family in Past Time," *American Scholar* 43 (Summer 1974): 422-46. Carroll Smith-Rosenberg, "The Female World of Love and Ritual: Relations Between Women in Nineteenth-Century America," *Signs* 1 (Autumn 1975): 1-30.

31. Rousmaniere, "Cultural Hybrid in the Slums," pp. 45-66.

32. Chafe, *American Woman*, p. 58.

33. Quoted in O'Neill, *Woman Movement*, pp. 168-70.

34. Chafe, *American Woman*, p. 55.

35. Ibid., p. 56.

36. Ibid., p. 57.

37. U.S. Bureau of the Census, *Fourteenth Census of the United States Taken in the Year 1920, vol. 4, Occupations* (Washington, D.C.: Government Printing Office, 1923), pp. 34, 42. Of men in gainful occupations, 3.4 percent were professionals; of women, 11.9 percent. The large number of female professionals was due to their predominance in teaching and nursing, two low-prestige, low-paid fields. The only professions in which women outnumbered men were as teachers (122,525 males, 639,241 females), nurses (5,464 males, 143,664 males), and librarians (1,795 males, 13,502 females). Comparative figures for the learned professions are: architects, 18,048 males, 137 females; clergy, 125,483 males, 1,787 females; dentists, 54,323 males, 1,829 females; lawyers, judges, and justices, 120,781 males, 1,738 females; physicians and surgeons, 137, 758 males, 7,219 females; technical engineers, 136,080 males, 41 females; veterinary surgeons, 13,493 males, 1 female.

38. Annie Nathan Meyer, ed., *Woman's Work in America* (New York: Henry Holt and Co., 1891), iv.

39. Mary Putnam Jacobi, "Woman in Medicine," in *Woman's Work in America*, ed. Meyer, pp. 139-205.

40. Ibid., p. 167.

41. Ibid., p. 169.

42. Walsh, *Doctors Wanted*, chap. 4 (pp. 132-33 quoted).

43. Jacobi, "Woman in Medicine," in *Woman's Work in America*, ed. Meyer, pp. 170-71. Walsh, *Doctors Wanted*, pp. 104-05.

44. Walsh, *Doctors Wanted*, p. 182.

45. Jacobi, "Woman in Medicine," in *Woman's Work in America*, ed. Meyer, p. 204n.

46. Ibid., p. 197.

47. Walsh, *Doctors Wanted*, pp. 181-82.

48. Chafe, *American Woman*, p. 60.

49. Ibid., p. 90.

50. Walsh, *Doctors Wanted*, p. 185.

51. Ibid., chap. 6.

52. Ibid., pp. 198-99.

53. Ibid., p. 202.

54. Ibid., p. 204-5.

55. Ibid., p. 193, for a table showing the decline at eighteen coeducational medical schools.

56. Ibid., p. 224. Also Chafe, *American Woman*, p. 60.

57. Edmund Wilson, *Upstate* (New York: Farrar, Straus and Giroux, 1971), pp. 60-62.

58. W. Elliot Brownlee and Mary M. Brownlee, *Women in the American Economy: A Documentary History, 1675-1929* (New Haven: Yale University Press, 1976), p. 264.

59. Quoted in ibid., pp. 293-94.

60. Quoted in ibid., pp. 295-96.

61. 83 U.S. (16 Wall) 130 (1872).

62. Brownlee and Brownlee, *Women in the American Economy*, pp. 296-307.

63. Ada M. Bittenbender, "Woman in Law," in *Woman's Work in America*, ed. Meyer, p. 234.

64. Chafe, *American Woman*, p. 58.

65. Rev. Ada C. Bowles, "Woman in the Ministry," in *Woman's Work in America*, ed. Meyer, pp. 208-13.

66. Anna Howard Shaw, *The Story of a Pioneer* (New York: Harper & Brothers, 1915), chaps. 3-4.

67. Chafe, *American Woman*, p. 60.

68. This discussion of female scientists is based on Margaret W. Rossiter, "Women Scientists in America Before 1920," *American Scientist* 62 (May-June 1974): 312-23.

69. Ibid., p. 312.

70. Ibid., pp. 317-18.

71. Ibid., p. 319.

72. Ibid., p. 314.

73. Ibid., p. 316.

74. Brownlee and Brownlee, *Women in the American Economy*, p. 284.

75. Quoted in Walsh, *Doctors Wanted*, pp. 211-12.

76. Rossiter, "Women Scientists in America," p. 321.

77. Ibid., p. 320.

78. Chafe, *American Woman*, pp. 58-60.

79. Ibid.

80. Walsh, *Doctors Wanted*, pp. 214-15, makes this point in connection with women doctors.

81. On the development of home economics, see page 135.

82. On this whole subject see Dee Garrison's excellent essay, "The Tender Technicians: The Feminization of Public Librarianship, 1876-1905," in *Clio's Consciousness Raised*, ed. Hartman and Banner, pp. 158-78.

83. Rousmaniere, "Cultural Hybrid in the Slums," pp. 45-66.

84. Ibid. Also Wein, "Women's Colleges and Domesticity," pp. 31-47.

85. Gerda Lerner, *The Female Experience: An American Documentary* (Indianapolis: Bobbs-Merrill, 1977), pp. 235-36.

86. Conway, "Perspective on Women's Education," p. 9.

87. They are Elizabeth Eaton Boit, Ellen Louise Curtis Demorest, Kate Gleason, Hetty Howland Robinson Green, Margaret Gaffney Haughery, Rose Marrward Knox, Margaret Getchell La Forge, Nettie Fowler McCormick, Mary Foot Seymour, Maggie Lena Walker, and Sarah Bredlove Walker; James, *Notable American Women*, vols. 1-3.

88. Ibid., 2: 81-83. For a biography of Green, see Boyden Sparkes and Samuel Taylor Moore, *The Witch of Wall Street: Hetty Green* (Garden City, N.Y.: Garden City Publishing Co., 1930).

89. James, *Notable American Women*, 3: 271-72.

90. Alice Foote MacDougall, *The Autobiography of a Business Woman* (Boston: Little, Brown, 1930).

91. Quoted in ibid., p. 85.

92. Ibid., pp. 84-85.

V

The Vote, but Not the Answer, 1920~1945

On August 26, 1920, the Tennessee legislature ratified the Nineteenth Amendment and enfranchised 26 million American women. For thirty years a united woman's organization, the National American Woman's Suffrage Association, had worked for that day, promising that the addition of the superior sex to the electorate would purify politics, aid the cause of Progressive reform, and add a powerful force for peace to political life.

Slightly over a decade later, in an article called "Discouraged Feminists," Emily Newell Blair wrote,

Feminism, in this country at least, expressed the desire of women once more to have a part in making the world. . . . Queerly enough, in an age where politics counted less than before, they concentrated first on the effort to get political equality. . . .

What these feminists wanted was not merely a chance to work for some man but a chance to rise to positions of authority so they could again be effective in determining the conditions under which they lived. What these women hoped for was a world in which men and women would work in competition with each other and the best individual win. The sex line was to be dropped and the world become the composite work of individuals of both sexes.

But it did not work out that way. The best man continued to win, and women, even the best, worked for and under him. Women were welcome to come in as workers but not as co-makers of the world. For all their numbers they seldom rose to positions of responsibility or power. The few who did fitted into the system as they found it. All standards, all methods, all values continued to be set by men, even those as regards food and clothes, once distinctly women's business. . . .

Is this, then, the end of the feminists' effort to find a place in this man's world?[1]

Blair was not alone in her disappointment. By the mid-1920s, groups ranging from the moderate League of Women Voters to the radical National Woman's party were bewailing their lack of influence on the national scene. Sylvia Kopald and Ethel Puffer Howe noted with despair that women had not yet approached economic equality with men, that questions were still raised about their intellectual abilities, and that the generation of females coming into adulthood was bored with or even hostile to the whole woman's movement.[2] In short, the achievement of the vote had little, if any, impact on the status of females. One remembers with admiration the astuteness of Elizabeth Cady Stanton's remark half a century earlier that the vote alone was "not even half a loaf . . . only a crust, a crumb."[3]

Part of the reason the Nineteenth Amendment proved to be a disappointment was the character of the suffrage movement in the thirty years before its victory in 1920. The first generation of feminists, the women who adopted the Seneca Falls Resolutions, had defined the woman's problem in the broadest possible sense. They had seen that to achieve equality it was necessary to reform practically every area of human life. As early as 1853, Stanton remarked, "I do not know whether the world is quite willing or ready to discuss the question of marriage. . . . I feel, as never before, that this whole question of woman's rights turns on the pivot of the marriage relation, and, mark my word, sooner or later it will be the topic of discussion." Seven years later she reiterated, "How this marriage questions grows on me. It lies at the foundation of progress."[4] She understood that the real cause of inequality between the sexes was rooted in ideas about female nature and a multitude of social and economic institutions and relationships that assumed and depended upon the subordination of women. Therefore, drawing on the egalitarian philosophy of the Enlightenment, she launched a sweeping attack on the cult of domesticity and all its assumptions. For her, deprivation of the vote was not the core of the problem.

Unfortunately, the feminist movement lost this radical perspective in the last quarter of the nineteenth century. It focused increasingly on the issue of the vote and paid less and less attention to such matters as marriage, divorce, child rearing, and economic opportunity. From a tactical point of view, this was good strategy, since suffrage was one issue on which a broad spectrum of women could agree. It could be supported without challenging widespread assumptions about woman's nature and about separate male and female spheres. Increasingly, suffragists argued for the vote on the ground not that feminine and masculine nature were the same, but that women were different—even superior to—men. Stanton's egalitarian ideology was discarded for arguments based on acceptance of the Victorian notion that women were biologically different from men and, therefore, had different capacities, talents, and contributions to make to society.[5]

One of the first prominent feminist intellectuals to move in this direction was Antoinette Brown Blackwell. After her marriage and retirement from active participation in the movement, she turned to the problem of reconciling Darwinism with the demand for equality for women. She accepted the fundamental Darwinist idea that biology determined mental capacity and character. Physical differences between males and females meant that they were also different in their emotional and intellectual qualities. Blackwell did not, however, equate differentiation with inferiority. For Stanton's conviction that men and women were the same, except for their reproductive functions, she substituted the idea of equivalency. Without matching each other in any specific characteristics, the sexes balanced each other in the sum of their attributes. Blackwell's actual description of woman's separate, equivalent nature conformed closely to the Victorian ideal of the emotional, mothering, dependent female.[6]

In order to avoid surrendering to the conventional judgment that this distinct, feminine nature was intellectually inferior and properly destined women for their traditional roles, Blackwell's ideological followers turned Darwinism on its head and asserted the female's superiority. Since the nineteenth century already believed women to be superior morally, this adjustment simply gave scientific sanction to pervasive notions about women. Increasingly, therefore, women demanded legal reform because of their special needs and their ability to purify the world outside the home. In 1893, for example, Carrie Chapman Catt, the leading suffragist of her day, declared, "It is because of the differences between men and women that the nineteenth century more than any other demands the enfranchisement of women." [7] The deep involvement of females in social reform movements in this period reinforced the notion that, if given the vote, they would carry their concerns as mothers and ethical models into the outside world. [8]

Even Charlotte Perkins Gilman, the most radical feminist thinker of these decades, believed in biologically based differences between the male and female minds. Nature made women more nurturant, tender, passive, and patient than men to fit them for their roles as mothers. Gilman regarded this distinction between the sexes as beneficial. Unfortunately, she felt, the process of evolution had created other, less desirable differences between male and female personalities because women were economically dependent on men. Since women's survival depended on their ability to seduce and hold husbands, they developed characteristics attractive to men during the long process of evolution. These included an exaggerated eroticism, frailty, and ignorance and created a type of "oversexed" femininity. If women became economically independent, these undesirable characteristics would gradually disappear. However, women would still retain the special virtues connected to their maternal functions. In short, the feminist Gilman followed the cult of domesticity in defining women as mothers. Her radicalism consisted of separating the role of mother from economic dependence and confinement to the home. [9]

These changes in the character of the feminist movement and its ideology meant that in their period of greatest influence, feminists fought exclusively for the franchise, rather than for a broad spectrum of reforms to ensure equality between the sexes. Their triumph in 1920 did not signify a commitment to the ideal of equality or the wide range of goals enunciated at Seneca Falls. In fact, given the growing influence of a feminist ideology that incorporated biologically based notions of separate male and female spheres, probably only a small portion of the women who worked for the Nineteenth Amendment actually held views as radical as Elizabeth Cady Stanton's.

The females who won the vote expected to use it to extend their beneficent maternal influence and thus reform the world outside the home. With almost millenarian overtones, they promised to end war, corruption, immorality, exploitation, and urban squalor. The very vagueness and loftiness of their hopes masked the fact that the women who supported the suffrage movement came from very diverse class and regional backgrounds and would never agree on the concrete changes necessary to achieve their exalted aims. The coalition had little chance of surviving its victory. Even more crucial, the suffragists failed to recognize that by arguing for the vote on the ground that it would produce good results, rather than on the basis that it was just, they made it conditional. Once the Nineteenth Amendment failed to usher in the promised new world, there was no basis for continuing to support organized feminism.[10] Finally, because the suffrage movement had concentrated so single-mindedly on the vote, it had failed to work for the other reforms that were essential to make the enfranchisement of women meaningful. As the leaders of the major political parties could have told them, and as the city bosses whom they attacked demonstrated day after day, politics was a full-time business. To participate on an equal basis with men, to run for office as well as to vote, women had to give up their notions of special female functions and talents. They had to make the same full-time commitment to politics that they had made to their great crusade for the franchise. This meant rethinking the whole way in which society raised and educated its young, handled domestic chores, and conceived of the proper relations between husband and wife. Yet this is the very kind of radical thought that the latter-day suffragists so studiously avoided.

Given these facts, it is not surprising that the Nineteenth Amendment made little difference to American politics. Women did not vote or run for office as women. Except on issues of personal morality, their political views were similar to those of men in their class. Most females voted like their husbands. The majority showed an indifference to politics that stood in sharp contrast to their efforts to win the suffrage. Fewer women voted than men, only a tiny percentage ran for office, and even a smaller percentage were elected.

The final cause of political disaster was the National Woman's party demand for an Equal Rights Amendment in 1923. The majority of suffragists, allied with the social reform movement, regarded the amendment as a threat to the protective legislation for which they had fought so hard since the turn of the century.[11] The reformers believed that women differed fundamentally from men and should be treated as a separate class. The extreme feminists who supported the Woman's party, however, disapproved of laws singling out women for special treatment on the ground that, unlike men, they could not take care of themselves. They also felt that under the guise of concern for females, many laws actually discriminated against them. The purpose of the Equal Rights Amendment was to obliterate sex as a functional, legal classification. The Wisconsin Equal Rights Law showed that compromise between the two positions was possible. It provided for complete equality except for "the special protection and privileges which they [women] now enjoy for the general welfare."[12] However, the personal and ideological conflict between the feminists and reformers was so great that neither side would make any concessions, and they moved toward an irrevocable split. At the core of the dispute was the fact that the hard-core feminists called upon women to put their own interests first, in defiance of the whole tradition of altruism associated with organized womanhood.[13] By the end of the decade, the woman's movement had ceased to function as a major force in American politics.[14]

The decade that saw the demise of organized feminism also saw the triumph of ideas preaching the sexual liberation of women. The propagandists for sexual freedom encouraged females who considered themselves progressive to accept the idea of a unique feminine character that suited them for special functions. These ideas were associated with people like Havelock Ellis, Edward Carpenter, and Ellen Key. A British physician, Ellis believed in feminine distinctiveness and superiority. In his best-selling book, *Man and Woman*, he defended women against charges of inferiority. Nevertheless, he described females within the parameters of Darwinist theory. He believed, for example, that due to their physiological constitutions, women were both less variable and more emotional than men. He especially stressed the importance of the menstrual cycle, which influenced feminine strength, intelligence, and dexterity so that women's abilities fluctuated with their monthly cycle. Menstruation particularly affected their powers of self-control. In Ellis's view, this cycle raised serious questions about the fitness of females for business positions.[15]

As a Darwinist, Ellis integrated both men and women into the animal kingdom. In this context, he asserted that women were as sexually passionate as men. He even argued that some of their ostensible intellectual inferiority was due to the extraordinary inhibitions resulting from the sexual repression on which society insisted. Despite comparable levels of passion, male and female sexuality were, according to Ellis, very different in character. Sexual differences extended to every aspect of behavior. Therefore, although he called for an unprecedented liberation of female sexuality, Ellis emphasized the differences between males and females and analyzed women in terms of their biological character.[16] Charlotte Perkins Gilman felt that Ellis used Darwinism simply to confirm as normal the overdevelopment of female sexuality, which she regarded as an unfortunate product of women's economic dependence.[17]

Ellen Key, an outspoken advocate of free sexual expression for women, thought that love and motherhood were the two spheres most suited to female nature. According to Key, a mature female is completely devoted to maternity. On these grounds, she opposed the suffrage movement, the campaign for legal equality, and the feminist insistence on woman's right to work.[18] Her contemporary, Margaret Sanger, also urged females to seek power in their own spheres and concentrate on the distinctive "feminine element." One of the reasons that she advocated contraception was that it would liberate female sexuality.[19] As William O'Neill stated succinctly,

It became possible in the 1920's to simultaneously take a radical stand on sex and a conservative one on women's social role. . . . Thanks to the Ellen Keys, Margaret Sangers, Grant Allens, and Havelock Ellises, it was easy to be thoroughly liberated sexually while maintaining a social pattern and a domestic life much like one's unemancipated neighbors. It was possible, then, to fall away from the old feminist standards, to abandon paid employment and public service, and to lapse into familism while at the same time feeling thoroughly up to date.[20]

In conjunction with the collapse of the organized woman's movement and widespread acceptance of separate male and female spheres by those who considered themselves feminists, this new emphasis on women's sexuality gave rise to what Andrew Sinclair calls "the New Victorianism."[21] It prescribed a sexually determined role for all nor-

mal women and assumed that they would function best as wives and
mothers, although these functions were now updated somewhat by
giving them "a higher erotic charge and a greater cultural burden." [22]
Fewer and fewer of the girls entering adulthood in the 1920s had the
crusading spirit and desire for professional success that had characterized so many of their predecessors in the previous generation. This
change was particularly marked among college graduates, an increasing number of whom expressed a preference for marriage over any
other life-style. This change began in the early twentieth century, but
first became a matter of concern to feminists in the 1920s. Roberta
Wein suggests that a significant contrast existed between those who
graduated from the women's colleges before and after 1910. [23] At the
end of the nineteenth century, half of the graduates of the best wom-
en's schools remained single and formed the core of the increasing
number of female professionals. In sharp contrast, a survey of alumnae from Hollins, Bryn Mawr, Barnard, Vassar, and Smith showed
that 80 percent of those graduated by one school between 1919 and
1923 married, while at another the figure was 90 percent. A newspaper poll of Vassar students in 1923 indicated that 90 percent
wanted to marry, while only 11 of 152 preferred a business or professional position to a husband. Seven years later, 70 percent of the girls
at the New Jersey College for Women expressed such views. [24]

Frank Stricker questions whether the fact that more and more female college graduates were marrying meant that they were rejecting
careers. He quotes figures to show that increasing numbers of professional women combined marriage with their careers. The proportion
of professional women who married rose from 12.2 percent in 1910 to
19.3 percent in 1920 and 24.7 percent in 1930. [25] These figures hardly
prove Stricker's point, however, because the vast majority of the wom-
en classified as professionals were nurses and teachers who did not go
to college at all in this period. [26] To estimate the impact of marriage
on college-educated women, it is necessary to treat them as a separate
group. At Bryn Mawr, the only school for which I have figures, there
seems to have been a correlation between remaining single and commitment to a career, though the increase in numbers of married alumnae occurred before 1920. Of those who graduated between 1889 and
1908, only 45 percent married, while 62 percent went on to graduate
school and 90 percent held paid positions at some point in their lives.

Among those who graduated between 1909 and 1918, the comparable figures are 67 percent, 49 percent, and 77 percent, respectively. [27]

The New Victorianism encouraged women to think of childbearing and homemaking as complicated, lofty enterprises demanding a skilled mixture of exact science and inspiration. Interest in home economics burgeoned. The pioneer in this field was Ellen Swallow Richards, discussed earlier as one of the first academic women in chemistry. [28] From about 1890 on, she was more and more concerned with the home economics movement, which applied modern science to cooking, nutrition, sanitation, and hygiene. She took the lead in developing syllabi for women's clubs and courses for public schools, agricultural and extension schools, and colleges. She prescribed standards for training teachers in these subjects and compiled bibliographies. In 1908 she was instrumental in organizing the American Home Economics Association and served as its president until 1910. [29] As interest grew in the 1920s, Marion Talbot pioneered a graduate program in home economics at the University of Chicago. Cornell, under the leadership of Martha Van Rensselaer, acquired preeminence in the field. The land grant colleges had had home economics departments from the beginning, and the public schools employed increasing numbers of their graduates to teach hygiene and cooking.

Most disturbing was the impact of these trends on the leading women's colleges. These institutions had opened to provide their students with educations comparable to those which men received at Harvard and Yale. In the 1920s they were under attack for not preparing their graduates for their chief vocations—wifehood, maternity, and homemaking. Ethel Puffer Howe, a graduate of Radcliffe, urged them to develop courses in domestic science, eugenics, hygiene, and aesthetics of the home. [30] In 1924 the Vassar Board of Trustees created an interdisciplinary School of Euthenics to focus on the development and care of the family. The college offered a series of courses on Husband and Wife, Motherhood, and The Family As an Economic Unit. [31]

Women's magazines like the *Ladies' Home Journal* and *McCall's* joined in the rising tide of opinion that proclaimed the domestic sphere to be the most satisfying for women. They exalted the skills necessary to run a home efficiently, raise children, and ensure the happiness of every member of the family. At the same time they attacked feminism and, especially, career women. One of the ironies of the situation was that women who were themselves successful professionals, like Dorothy Thompson and Claire Callahan, advised their sisters not to follow them out of the home.

The collapse of the woman's movement and the triumph of the New Victorianism made the 1920s a discouraging period for the dwindling number of feminists. Nonetheless, a few staunch souls continued to protest against these developments. In *Woman's Dilemma* (1925), Alice Beal Parsons exposed the retrogressive implications of the argument for feminine uniqueness. Modern theories glorifying woman's biological capacities kept her in the home just as surely as older theories that preached female inferiority. Parsons questioned Havelock Ellis's insistence that women's happiness depended solely on a satisfactory sex life. Like men, they needed economic and social independence as well as healthy sexual relations and were just as capable of productive work. There was nothing about the unique feminine biological makeup that made women unfit for serious employment. If they were behind males in achievement, it was because historically their energies had been consumed by child bearing and rearing. [32]

Ethel Puffer Howe was expressing similar views when she queried, "The man demands of life that he have love, home, fatherhood, and the special work which his particular brain combination fits. Shall the woman demand less?" She maintained that "women as a class have been too humble, too timid, to claim as an ultimate principle of life for themselves, what every man has without asking. . . . The ultimate principle of integration would demand full provision, in all educational plans, professional codes, and social arrangements for the ideally complete woman which would eliminate forever the necessity of an 'intolerable choice.'"[33] From 1925 to 1931, Howe headed the Institute to Coordinate Women's Interests at Smith College. The goal of the institute was to explore ways of enabling college-educated wives to enter professional occupations by experimenting with cooperative nurseries, communal laundries, shopping groups, and central kitchens. Howe hoped to initiate a revolution in the organization of the home along lines described by Charlotte Perkins Gilman in *Woman and Economics*. [34]

To Suzanne La Follette, whom William O'Neill considers the

"most original feminist writer of the 1920s," Howe's institute was itself a capitulation to male prejudice. [35] Since its expressed purpose was to reconcile marriage with women's educational and professional concerns, it rested on "the tacit assumption that marriage is the special concern of woman, and one whose claims must take precedence over her other interests . . . that marriage and motherhood constitute her normal life, and her other interests something extra-normal." [36] This seemed particularly true since the institute suggested that most of its proposals worked best for part-time workers. At best, therefore, women would be trapped in dead-end jobs. According to La Follette, the real solution to the female employment problem was public day nurseries, free marriage, and the equal sharing of domestic and child-rearing tasks by husband and wife.

La Follette felt that the basic source of the female problem was the economic system, which treated her as property, a situation institutionalized in marriage. Real freedom depended on a complete reform of the economic system. Until such time, however, she recommended the abolition of marriage in its traditional form and a recognition that women are entitled to equality because it is just, not because it is necessary for better mothering or the application of maternal virtues to social problems. Suffragists who argued for equality on the basis of women's special functions fell into the serious error of assuming that marriage and motherhood were their unique province and that they existed for the good of the species. Achievement of the vote and political equality was a desirable first step, but that was all. By relying ultimately on an economic revolution, Suzanne La Follette revealed just how hopeless the feminist cause was in the 1920s, since massive change seemed highly unlikely in the decade of the "return to normalcy." [37]

It is in the context of this unfavorable ideological and political environment that the position of professional women in the 1920s and 1930s has to be evaluated. On the surface, advances that had begun sixty years earlier continued. The percentage of women going to college increased, while one out of every seven Ph.D.'s was awarded to a woman. In 1920, 11.8 percent of all female workers were professionals; in 1930 the figure has risen to 14.2 percent. [38] The October 1927 issue of *Current History* was devoted to "The New Woman" and extolled her professional achievements. In an article entitled "Woman's Achievements Since the Franchise," Charlotte Perkins Gilman spoke in exuberant terms of their progress. [39]

Despite Gilman's optimistic survey, the situation was not really one that could satisfy feminist aspirations. Although the number of female professionals was growing, most of them were concentrated in teaching and nursing. The percentage of female lawyers and architects remained stable at 3 percent. [40] In the whole country there were only 60 female C.P.A.'s and 151 dentists. [41] In New York women professionals included 63,637 teachers and 21,195 nurses, but only 11 engineers and 7 inventors. [42] The percentage of women doctors declined from 6 percent in 1910 to 5 percent in 1920 and to 4.4 percent in 1930. The absolute numbers fell from 9,015 in 1910 to 6,825 in 1930. [43] There was a 5-percent quota on female admissions to medical schools from 1925 to 1945. [44] In addition to restrictive admission policies, women who wanted to become doctors had to face even greater difficulties in securing internships once they graduated from medical school. The number of medical students who went on to hospital training grew throughout the early twentieth century. By 1932 seventeen state boards included successful completion of an internship among their licensing requirements. Yet most hospitals would not accept female interns, a fact that was often cited as a reason not to admit them to medical school in the first place. In 1921, for example, only 40 of 482 general hospitals accepted female interns. Twelve states had no internships open to women. As late as the 1930s, 250 female medical graduates competed for 185 internships, while 4,844 males chose from among 6,154. [45]

The position of academic women was equally deplorable. By 1927, Bryn Mawr had graduated 1,088 Ph.D.'s, most of whom went into teaching. However, by the end of the 1920s only 21 of them held full professorships in women's colleges, 4 in men's colleges. [46] While they earned 33 percent of the graduate degrees granted, females occupied only 4 percent of the full professorships. [47] The percentage of women on college and university faculties peaked in 1930 and declined thereafter. [48] A survey of 844 academic women in 1929 concluded dismally:

It would appear that the field of college teaching holds comparatively little promise for women. . . . Training represented in degrees and years of teaching experience contributes little to the advancement of women in the college teaching field. . . . The rank and file of the respondents seem to have developed a defensive attitude bordering on martyrdom, and complained, waxed bitter, and voiced resentment toward the conditions of which they were the victims. [49]

Emily Blair discussed the situation at length in an article entitled "Discouraged Feminists." She quoted a remark that Dr. Anna Howard Shaw, a leading feminist, made a few months before her death.

You younger women will have a harder task than ours. You will want equality in business and it will be even harder to get than the vote, for you will have to fight for it as individuals and that will not get you far. Women will not unite, since they will be competitors with each other. As soon as a woman has it for herself she will have entered the man's world and cease to fight as a woman for other women. [50]

Blair observed in despair that men who belonged to the chamber of commerce were bankers, presidents of factories, owners and managers of stores, lawyers, doctors, and local executives of large companies, while the women who joined the business and professional women's clubs were predominantly stenographers, clerks, and teachers, with an occasional doctor or lawyer. They earned from $750 to $5,000 a year; the members of the chambers of commerce, from $5,000 to $50,000. [51]

On the basis of the statistics cited here and the remarks of feminists like Emily Blair, most historians see the 1920s as a period when the movement of women into the professions slowed down and in some areas, such as medicine, reversed itself. They attribute this development to the resurgence of attitudes emphasizing women's maternal and marital roles, the declining interest of young female college graduates in the careers that had appealed so strongly to their mothers and grandmothers, the persistence of discrimination, and the collapse of the feminist movement, which had supplied encouragement and a sense of mission to the women growing up in the half-century before 1920.

In a recent article Frank Stricker challenges this interpretation of the 1920s. [52] He uses statistical data to show that women's experience varied from one field to another and concludes that it is impossible to make a valid statement about professional women in general. He shows that the actual numbers of professional and business women increased, even though their percentages relative to men decreased because the number of male professionals rose significantly after 1920.[53] According to him, these increasing numbers demonstrate that women had not turned their backs on careers, as so many historians have claimed.

In fact, Stricker's statistics prove a good deal less than he claims. While they establish that professional women existed in the 1920s and that in some areas their numbers increased, they do not alter the basic picture. The movement of women into the professions *had* lost momentum compared to the period 1860-1920. As a group they displayed much less determination to crash professional barriers than the previous two generations.

Despite this, Stricker's article makes a valuable contribution to the history of women in the professions by questioning interpretations that overemphasize the importance of women's attitudes in shaping their experience in the 1920s.[54] He stresses external factors such as discrimination, the practical difficulties of combining a profession with marriage and children, and the absence of support from an organized feminist movement with a coherent ideology. Mary Walsh's recent book on women doctors certainly supports Stricker's point of view. She proves conclusively that discrimination and the disintegration of the woman's rights movement were the primary factors behind the declining numbers of female physicians.[55] In support of the latter argument, she notes that 96 percent of the doctors listed in *Notable American Women* were either affiliated with female institutions at some point in their careers or were active feminists.[56] One of the most successful of them, Alice Hamilton, claimed explicitly that it was easier for female physicians to succeed when they "could count on the loyalty of a group of devoted feminists who would choose a woman doctor because she was a woman."[57]

The whole significance of the 1920s is epitomized by the fact that the symbol of the decade was not the emancipated career woman, but the flapper. Although she was sexually liberated and had greater social freedom than her predecessors, the flapper fit easily into a society that saw women in predominantly sexual terms. When her dancing and drinking days were over, she settled down as wife and mother.[58]

The story of Zelda and F. Scott Fitzgerald, who symbolized the irresponsible, madly happy youth of affluent high society in the 1920s, is as adequate as any feminist commentary could be on the flapper ideal. Zelda was a southern belle, trained to be beautiful, decorative, and amusing. She was the model for her husband's most famous heroines, Daisy Buchanan and Nicole Diver. In the early days of their marriage, the Fitzgeralds ran through the enormous profits of his novels and short stories in endless parties, big houses, extended trips to the Riviera, and rivers of champagne. Zelda's tragedy was that her husband expected her to amuse herself quietly while he wrote and to be playfully available when he chose to relax. The emptiness and boredom of this life led her into an affair and then produced an increasingly insistent desire on her part to express herself creatively. At first Zelda turned to the ballet, an impossible choice given the age at which she began. Then, amidst increasing signs of mental breakdown, she tried to write. Fitzgerald totally opposed her efforts to become an author because he was the professional in the family, supported her with his earnings, and felt entitled to the sole use of their common experience as material for his books.

I am a professional writer, with a huge following. I am the highest paid short story writer in the world. . . . Everything we have done is my . . . [sic] I am the professional novelist, and I am supporting you. That is all my material. None of it is your material. . . . I would like you to think of my interests. That is your primary concern, because I am the one to steer the course, the pilot. . . . I want you to stop writing fiction.[59]

Their lives together ended tragically: Zelda died in an insane asylum, Scott became an alcoholic.

If the 1920s saw a slowing down of the entrance of women into the professions, the 1930s spelled disaster. Under the impact of the depression, hostility to female employment reached new levels of intensity. There was virtually unanimous opinion that women should not compete for scarce jobs with men who had families to support. Implicit in this view was the assumption that females did not have families to support and therefore had less right to employment than men. For feminists who agreed with Charlotte Perkins Gilman that economic independence was absolutely essential for women, the views dominant in the 1930s were tantamount to the defeat of their cause.

There was particular antagonism to working wives. A Gallup poll in 1936 reported that 82 percent of those questioned answered no when asked if women with employed husbands should be allowed to work. Of the women questioned, 75 percent answered in this way. From 1932 to 1937 the federal government prohibited more than one member of a family from working in the civil service, a law that essentially discriminated against wives. Many states passed legislation restricting the employment of married women, while whole cities went on crusades to fire them. The National Educational Association reported in 1930-31 that of 1,500 school systems surveyed, 77 percent refused to hire wives and 63 percent dismissed female teachers when they married. Private businesses also followed these policies in many instances. The executive committee of the American Federation of Labor resolved that "married women whose husbands have permanent positions ... should be discriminated against in the hiring of employees."[60]

Opportunities for professional women declined along with other jobs during the depression. Teaching jobs almost disappeared, a matter of grave importance since it was one of the few professions that they dominated. The percentage of women teachers fell from 85 percent in 1920 to 78 percent in 1940.[61] The situation among college professors was not very different. During the 1930s the proportion of women receiving doctorates relative to men declined, and those who earned them were less likely than ever to put them to use in paid employment.[62] The percentage of female college teachers fell from 32.5 percent to 26.5 percent and continued to decline until the late 1950s.[63] This trend was evident even in the women's schools.

The experience of Ruth Benedict at Columbia University is almost the archetypal story of the female academic in this period. She was graduated from Vassar, Phi Beta Kappa, in 1909 and was married in 1914. After a few happy years, Benedict became increasingly dissatisfied and enrolled in the New School of Social Research, where she discovered anthropology. In 1923 she received her doctorate from Columbia under Franz Boas, the leading anthropologist in this country.

She began to publish in 1922, even before she received her degree. Although she was soon virtually running the anthropology program at Columbia, she held only peripheral jobs because Boas thought that married women could get along on low pay. From 1923 to 1931 she was a lecturer on annual contract, although she had sufficient standing in the field to become editor of the *Journal of American Folklore*. When she separated from her husband in 1930, Boas recognized that she needed a more lucrative position and secured her an assistant professorship. In 1934 she published *Patterns of Culture*, the best-known introduction to anthropology for the next quarter of a century. During the late 1930s and World War II, she and Boas became involved in publishing literature to combat Hitler's theory of race. She worked for the Office of War Information from 1943 to 1945, analyzing Rumania, Thailand, and Japan for the government. Her analysis of Japanese culture, *The Chrysanthemum and the Sword*, was another major landmark in American anthropology. In 1947 the United States government awarded her a huge grant to establish and direct a program of research into contemporary cultures. By the time Franz Boas died in 1942, Benedict was one of the leading anthropologists in the United States. She was president of the American Anthropological Association for two years; and in 1948, Columbia finally promoted her to a full professorship. [64]

For most female college graduates, there simply were no jobs during the depression. Only one-third of those who graduated from Barnard in 1932 took paying jobs. [65] Whether they accepted the current belief that they should not compete with men in times of high unemployment or felt that it was hopeless even to make the effort is unclear. The few who managed to gain a foothold in careers suitable for college graduates found the experience enormously frustrating. Advancement was slow and in many cases could not go beyond established ceilings. According to the American Association of University Women, 80 percent of the female college graduates surveyed reported that they received less pay than men for comparable work. [66] The overall result was that 12.3 percent of all women workers were in the professions by 1940, a figure comparable to that of 1920, but down from that of 1930. [67] During the depression, therefore, women professionals lost any gains that they had made since the passage of the Nineteenth Amendment.

American entrance into World War II almost instantaneously changed the economy from one characterized by massive unemployment to one in which labor was in short supply. To fill the needs of the enormous defense industry and government bureaucracy while also supporting a huge army, society turned to women. Where a few years earlier they were chastised for seeking employment and depriving men with families of support, they were now encouraged, even praised, for springing to their country's aid in time of need. Almost overnight the attitude toward working women—even working wives— changed. As a result, World War II was a landmark in the growth of female employment. Almost 7 million women entered the labor force for the first time; the proportion of working women rose from one-quarter to one third. [68] More females were employed outside the home than at any previous time in American history. Equally important, most of the new members of the labor force were married and significantly older than the prewar group. In the 1930s the average age of working women was thirty-two or under; in 1945 it was over thirty-five. [69] Middle-aged women were clearly one of the large untapped labor pools.

Most of the new jobs were in defense industries and the government bureaucracy, which sought relatively uneducated, inexpensive employees. For college-educated, middle-class women, interested in professional and executive positions, the war was somewhat less significant. However, even here, certain employers found that if they were to function at all, they would have to hire females. Rensselaer Polytechnic Institute enrolled its first woman student. The Curtiss-Wright Company sent eight hundred female engineering trainees to college, while giant corporations like Montsanto, Du Pont, and Standard Oil hired women chemists for the first time. The government employed women attorneys, and Wall Street brokerage houses recruited female analysts and statisticians. [70]

The shortage of doctors created new opportunities for women physicians, who were treated as "valuable national assets" for the first time. [71] Their successful campaign to secure commissions in the army and navy medical corps symbolized their new status. By the middle of the war, medical schools were accepting more women in order to meet the growing demand for doctors and to fill their classes with qualified students. The percentage of female medical students rose from 5 percent in 1941 to 8 percent in 1945. [72] For similar reasons more and more hospitals opened their internships to women. In the fall of 1945, after a century of obdurate resistance, Harvard Medical School bowed to the necessity of the times and enrolled twelve women in the freshman class. [73]

Even in this favorable wartime situation, however, women were not treated equally. They rarely received the same salaries as men who had held the positions before them. Businesswomen often complained that they were expected to remain as trainees instead of moving into the ranks of management. Whatever the progress, the real question was whether the change would be permanent. Would the experience of seeing females succeed in positions that they had never filled before break down traditional attitudes about their abilities and the jobs best suited for them? Would the massive employment of wives, even those with young children, destroy prejudice against working mothers? There was no way of knowing until the return to a peacetime economy. Since the post-World War II period opened a new era in the history of women, I will turn to these questions in my next chapter.

The experience of women with professional aspirations in the quarter of a century after the passage of the Nineteenth Amendment is very instructive for contemporary feminists. It was a period in which the entrance of females into the professions slowed down and then actually declined in relative terms. A major reason was that women no longer had the support of an organized feminist movement and a coherent feminist ideology. Without a militant woman's movement pressuring the government and employers and influencing public opinion, females will never achieve economic equality with men. On an individual basis, they are relatively ineffectual in changing the status quo, as Anna Howard Shaw foresaw. The history of this era demonstrates that as long as they acquiesce, women function as a marginal economic group consigned to relatively low-paid, low-prestige positions. They are discouraged or prevented from working in periods of unemployment and encouraged only when a crisis, such as a major war, creates a labor shortage that men cannot fill. It is no accident that the only professions that they dominate numerically are public school teaching, nursing, and library science.

From 1920 to 1945 the ideological defense of this economic reality rested on an elaborate exaltation of woman's biological role, which supported a sharp distinction between male and female functions that was not very different from the Victorian cult of domesticity, with the exception that it recognized female sexuality. The only answer to this is for women to adhere consistently to a philosophy, for which there is certainly a great deal of evidence, that the sexes are equal in capacity in everything except their biological role in reproduction. Every ideology that has focused on the difference between the sexes, no matter how it is phrased, has been used historically to consign women to the home. [74] Women must, in short, uphold the Seneca Falls Declaration of Sentiments: "Resolved, That woman is man's equal—was intended to be so by the Creator, and the highest good of the race demands that she should be recognized as such." [75]

Notes

1. Quoted in Aileen S. Kraditor, *Up from the Pedestal* (Chicago: Quadrangle Books, 1968), pp. 342-43.

2. Ibid., pp 331-39. William O'Neill, *The Woman Movement: Feminism in the United States and England* (Chicago: Quadrangle Books, 1969), pp. 196-204.

3. Quoted in William Henry Chafe, *The American Woman, 1920-1970*, (New York: Oxford University Press, 1972), p. 25.

4. Quoted in Miriam Schneir, ed., *Feminism: The Essential Historical Writings* (New York: Vintage Books, 1972), p. xvii.

5. The interpretation of the suffrage movement in this and the following paragraphs is stated most extensively in Aileen S. Kraditor, *The Ideas of the Woman Suffrage Movement, 1890-1920* (Garden City, N.Y.: Doubleday, 1971). While I agree with her thesis that the movement became more conservative and relied increasingly on arguments of expediency, I think the contrast between the first and second generation of feminists is often overstated. Even in her own day, Elizabeth Cady Stanton was more radical intellectually than most of the other pioneers in the movement. Furthermore, despite her reliance on Enlightenment philosophy in the Seneca Falls Declaration and other pronouncements, she also asserted woman's special maternal nature in her autobiography and other writings. See, for example, "The Matriarchate," in *Up from the Pedestal*, ed. Kraditor, pp. 140-47. On occasion, she used this conviction to argue for giving females the vote. Another early feminist, Antoinette Brown Blackwell, was one of the first intellectuals in the movement to integrate Darwinism into her ideology. See pages 129-30 above on Blackwell

in this connection. Even racist arguments for woman's suffrage appeared among the first generation, particularly during the struggle for the Fourteenth and Fifteenth Amendments. See Henry Blackwell, "What the South Can Do," in *Up from the Pedestal*, ed. Kraditor, pp. 253-57; and Elizabeth Cady Stanton, Susan B. Anthony, and Matilda J. Gage, "The Kansas Campaign of 1867," in *The Feminist Papers: From Adams to de Beauvoir*, ed., Alice S. Rossi (New York: Bantam Books, 1974), pp. 430-70.

The suffrage movement was more conservative in the last decades of its existence than the woman's rights movement was in the mid-nineteenth century because the former became large and respectable. It attracted women who would never have joined or supported the woman's movement in the early years when feminists were a tiny, ridiculed minority. As success became a real possibility, the leadership itself became more concerned to defend its program in ideological terms that would command the widest possible support. In the context of late nineteenth-century America, this meant arguing for the vote on the basis of the cult of domesticity or as an expedient measure to defend and improve the American way of life.

Many of the first generation of leaders were still alive and in positions of power when this shift began in the 1870s and 1880s. Their changing emphasis can be attributed to advancing age, disillusionment with the abolitionists and Blacks after the fight over the Fourteenth and Fifteenth Amendments, or a decision (conscious or unconscious) to narrow their aims and ideology in order to achieve some success. The longevity of many of the early feminists masked this gradual ideological transition. The only early leader who never accepted the reduction of the woman's movement to pursuit of the vote and who remained an intellectual maverick was Elizabeth Cady Stanton. The suffrage organization formally disavowed her when she published the *Woman's Bible* in 1896. The rise of new leaders in the 1890s and the first decades of the twentieth century made the change in the woman's movement much more apparent, but there was never a sharp break that can easily be connected to a generational change in the leadership.

William O'Neill's view of the evolution of the suffrage movement is similar to Kraditor's; "Feminism as a Radical Ideology," in *Dissent: Explorations in the History of American Radicalism*, ed. Alfred F. Young (DeKalb: Northern Illinois University Press, 1968), pp. 275-300.

6. Antoinette Brown Blackwell, "Sex and Evolution," in *Feminist Papers*, ed. Rossi, pp. 356-77.

7. Quoted in Rosalind Navin Rosenberg, "The Dissent from Darwin, 1890-1930: The New View of Woman among American Social Scientists (Ph.D. diss., Stanford University, 1974), p. 46.

8. Jill Conway, "Women Reformers and American Culture, 1870-1930,"

in *Our American Sisters: Women in American Life and Thought*, 2d ed., ed. Jean E. Friedman and William G. Shade (Boston: Allyn and Bacon, 1976), pp. 301-12, discusses leading social reformers who continued to hold conservative ideas about women at the same time that they created radically new patterns of behavior.

9. R. Rosenberg, "The Dissent from Darwin," pp. 52-53, 57-60. Chafe, *American Woman*, pp. 7-10.

10. O'Neill, "Feminism as a Radical Ideology," pp. 282-90.

11. During the Progressive era, social reformers associated with such groups as the National Consumers League, the National Women's Trade Union League, the Settlement House Movement, and the General Federation of Women's Clubs had fought for state and federal legislation to protect women and children, as particularly vulnerable groups, from the worst forms of economic exploitation. They sought laws prohibiting child labor, regulating the hours that females could work, setting minimum wages for women, and regulating labor conditions. By the 1920s, they had won major victories on the state and federal levels. Many females first joined the suffrage movement when their activities as reformers convinced them that women needed the vote to achieve their legislative goals. The Supreme Court declared minimum wages for women unconstitutional in 1923; O'Neill, "Feminism as a Radical Ideology," pp. 288-89.

12. Chafe, *American Woman*, pp. 117-18.

13. O'Neill, "Feminism as a Radical Ideology," p. 296.

14. J. Stanley Lemons, *The Woman Citizen: Social Feminism in the 1920's* (Urbana: University of Illinois Press, 1975), argues that women's social reform movements survived the passage of the Nineteenth Amendment and provided one of the important links between Progressivism and the New Deal. This view is consistent with a recognition that the movement for female emancipation and woman's rights disintegrated. Lemon's thesis is stated clearly in the preface to his book. Clark A. Chambers, "The Campaign for Women's Rights in the 1920's," in *Our American Sisters*, ed. Friedman and Shade, pp. 323-44, argues along similar lines.

15. Paul Robinson, *The Modernization of Sex: Havelock Ellis, Alfred Kinsey, William Masters and Virginia Johnson* (New York: Harper & Row, 1976), pp. 34-37.

16. R. Rosenberg, "The Dissent from Darwinism," pp. 47-51.

17. Ibid., p. 57. See page 130 on Gilman.

18. William L. O'Neill, *Everyone Was Brave* (Chicago: Quadrangle Books, 1971), pp. 312-13.

19. Ibid., p. 313. David M. Kennedy, *Birth Control in America: The Career of Margaret Sanger* (New Haven: Yale University Press, 1970), chap. 5.

20. O'Neill, *Everyone Was Brave*, p. 313.

21. Andrew Sinclair, *The Emancipation of the American Woman* (New York: Harper Colophon Books, 1965), chap. 31. Conway, "Women Reformers," p. 301.

22. O'Neill, *Everyone Was Brave*, p. 309.

23. Roberta Wein, "Women's Colleges and Domesticity, 1875-1918," *History of Education Quarterly* 14 (Spring 1974): 43-45.

24. Chafe, *American Woman*, p. 102.

25. Frank Stricker, "Cookbooks and Law Books: The Hidden History of Career Women in Twentieth Century America," *Journal of Social History* 10 (Fall 1976): 8.

26. See note 37 to chapter 4 above. Robert W. Smuts, *Women and Work in America* (New York: Schocken Books, 1971), pp. 20, 49-50, 73-4, 80-81, 83, shows that in the early twentieth century teachers and nurses were not college educated and came from very different class backgrounds than the women who entered the "learned" professions.

27. Wein, "Women's Colleges and Domesticity," pp. 37, 43-45.

28. Emma Seifrit Weigley, "It Might Have Been Euthenics: The Lake Placid Conferences and the Home Economics Movement," *American Quarterly* 26 (March 1974-December 1974): 79-96, on the early development of home economics.

29. Edward T. James, ed., *Notable American Women, 1607-1950*, 3 vols. (Cambridge, Mass.: Belknap Press, Harvard University Press, 1971), 3: 143-46. For a recent biography, see Robert Clarke, *Ellen Swallow: The Woman Who Founded Ecology* (Chicago: Follett Publishing Company, 1973).

30. Chafe, *American Woman*, p. 103.

31. Ibid.

32. Discussed in O'Neill, *Everyone Was Brave*, pp. 323-25.

33. Quoted in O'Neill, *Woman Movement*, p. 203.

34. Chafe, *American Woman*, pp. 100-1.

35. O'Neill, *Everyone Was Brave*, pp. 325, 331.

36. Ibid., pp. 325-28, 331-32 (p. 331 quoted).

37. Suzanne Lafollette, "Concerning Women," in *Feminist Papers*, ed. Rossi, pp. 541-65.

38. U.S. Department of Commerce, Bureau of the Census, *Sixteenth Census of the United States: 1940, Population, Comparative Occupation Statistics from the United States, 1870-1940* (Washington, D.C.: Government Printing Office, 1943), p. 101. Of all men in gainful employment 3.4 percent in 1920 and 4.5 percent in 1930 were professionals. See note 37 to chapter 4 above for an explanation of the higher percentages of female professionals.

39. *Current History* 27 (October 1927). Gilman's article is on pp. 7-14.

40. Chafe, *American Woman*, p. 58.

41. Ibid., p. 90.

42. Ibid.

43. Mary Roth Walsh, *"Doctors Wanted: No Women Need Apply: Sexual Barriers in the Medical Profession, 1835-1975* (New Haven: Yale University Press, 1977), pp. 185-86.

44. Chafe, *American Woman*, p. 60.

45. Walsh, *Doctors Wanted*, pp. 219-24.

46. Chafe, *American Woman*, p. 91.

47. Ibid.

48. Stricker, "Cookbooks and Law Books," pp. 2, 6.

49. Quoted in O'Neill, *Everyone Was Brave*, p. 306.

50. Quoted in Kraditor, *Up from the Pedestal*, p. 339.

51. Ibid., p. 340.

52. Stricker, "Cookbooks and Law Books," pp. 1-19.

53. Ibid., p. 7.

54. O'Neill, "Feminism as a Radical Ideology," pp. 287-93, and Carl Degler, "Revolution Without Ideology: The Changing Place of Women in American Society," in *The Woman in America*, ed. Robert Jay Lifton (Boston: Beacon Press, 1965), pp. 193-210, apply to the history of feminism as a whole the kind of interpretation that Stricker is attacking. Sinclair, *The Emancipation of the American Woman*, chap. 13, esp. p. 149, employs it in a discussion of professional women.

55. On the significance of the decline of the woman's rights movement, see Walsh, *Doctors Wanted*, pp. 260-67. The whole book is an argument in support of the thesis that discrimination was the key factor restricting the numbers of women doctors.

56. Ibid., p. 261.

57. Quoted in ibid., p. 260.

58. Although the sexual revolution is associated with the emergence of the flapper as a cultural symbol in the 1920s, a number of recent historians have shown that the shift in sexual mores and attitudes toward divorce actually occurred before World War I. James R. McGovern, "The American Woman's Pre-World War I Freedom in Manners and Morals," in *Our American Sisters*, ed. Friedman and Shade, pp. 345-65. William L. O'Neill, "Divorce in the Progressive Era," in *American Family in Social-Historical Perspective*, ed. Michael Gordon (New York: St. Martin's Press, 1973), pp. 251-66. John C. Burnham, "The Progressive Era Revolution in American Attitudes Toward Sex," *Journal of American History* 59 (June 1972-March 1973): 885-908.

59. Nancy Milford, *Zelda* (New York: Avon, 1971), p. 328.

60. Quoted in Chafe, *American Woman*, pp. 108, 111.

61. Ibid., p. 59.

62. Ibid., p. 91.

63. Ibid., p. 94.

64. James, *Notable American Women*, 1: 128-31.

65. Chafe, *American Woman*, p. 59.

66. Ibid., p. 61.

67. Ibid., p. 92.

68. Ibid., pp. 148, 246.

69. Ibid., pp. 144-46.

70. Ibid., p. 141.

71. Walsh, *Doctors Wanted*, pp. 225-26.

72. Ibid., p. 230.

73. Ibid., p. 233.

74. Ideologies, such as the cult of domesticity, that were based on differences between the sexes were of course used in specific instances to argue for expanding women's roles. Catharine Beecher, Emma Willard, and Mary Lyon all did this. See pages 59-60 above. Jane Adams argued that women's role should be extended into the area of social reform and politics because females had a special beneficent contribution to make on account of their unique innate character. Nonetheless, arguments of this sort can never be used to argue for genuine equality since they concede from the beginning that females have special talents and weaknesses. One of the reasons for the movement's developing in the way that it did during the period 1890-1920 was its conservative ideological base. The suffragists did not fight for the reforms that would make the vote meaningful because they accepted the nineteenth-century view of women and, therefore, could not imagine a genuinely radical transformation in the female role in the family and society. See pages 129-33 above for an elaboration of this argument.

75. Quoted in Kraditor, *Up from the Pedestal*, p. 187.

VI

Change and Reaction, 1945~1960

World War II drew unprecedented numbers of American women into the labor force. Three million females took jobs outside the home for the first time. Unlike their prewar sisters, many of them were married, had children, and were over thirty-five. Women who already worked outside the home took advantage of the labor shortage to move from low-paying work in restaurants, laundries, and small shops to high-paid factory jobs. Both government and private industry recognized that female labor was essential to the war effort; Rosie the Riveter became a national heroine. Although the war had less of an impact on professional women, even they were able to break down certain barriers because of the extreme shortage of available men.[1]

If, as Charlotte Perkins Gilman believed, the key to equality between the sexes was that women become self-supporting, it appeared that the war was a major landmark in the history of women. However, as everyone clearly recognized, the war was an emergency. The real question was whether the new acceptability of working wives would carry over into peacetime and whether the experience of seeing females in new roles would have a permanent impact on traditional attitudes.

Even during the war there were signs that it was premature to be overly sanguine about the long-term effect of the wartime situation.

Despite a formal commitment to equal pay for equal work, for example, females in manufacturing in 1945 still earned only 65 percent of male's pay, the same proportion that prevailed in 1940.[2] The National War Labor Board consistently weakened its initial insistence on equal pay and provided employers with a series of loopholes. It maintained, for example, that the requirement did not apply to jobs that were "historically" women's and that employers could assume compensation was fair in jobs to which women alone were assigned. Separate job categories along sex lines continued, and different plants of the same company were permitted to have different pay scales. Finally, when fear of runaway inflation led President Roosevelt to order that employers hold the line on wages, the National War Labor Board postponed thirty cases involving wage parity between the sexes. Other sorts of discrimination continued. Businesswomen complained, for example, that they could not enter top management positions commensurate with their ability. Despite the extreme shortage of physicians, the army did not commission female doctors until 1943.[3]

One of the clearest indications that traditional attitudes had changed little was the government's lack of response to the need for child care and other community services as more and more wives with families entered the working force. The war effort was directly involved, because the absentee and turnover rates of women workers were twice those of men. Forty percent of those who left employment cited domestic, marital, and related difficulties.[4] Females with young children stayed home when their offspring were ill, when school vacations were held, and when haphazard child-care arrangements broke down. It was abundantly clear that they could not maximize their contribution to winning the war without special government services. By extension, such services were also necessary in peacetime if women were to achieve genuine economic equality.

The need for community programs to support the wife and mother, particularly child-care arrangements, clashed with traditional values about woman's proper place, the crucial role that she played in child rearing, and the general feeling that the domestic sphere was peculiarly hers. Therefore, in spite of the extreme need, very little was done in this country to provide support for the female war worker. Despite a great deal of rhetoric, the federal government allowed rivalry between competing agencies to retard the development of an effective child-care program. Federal centers aided less than 10 percent of the mothers who needed assistance.[5] The contrast with the situation in Great Britain was striking. With a population less than one-third of the United States', the British government cared for three times as many children. Other adjustments were also made to ease the difficulties of British women who ran homes and held jobs simultaneously. "Priority certificates" permitted them to order food in the morning and pick it up at night on the way home so that they could avoid long lines. Many stores remained open in the evening for their convenience and industry often gave them one afternoon a week off to shop. Welfare officers were assigned to each war plant to handle problems. The Food Ministry set up more than two thousand "central kitchens," which prepared over 3 million meals a week for females to carry home at cost. In this country, where the emergency was less severe, traditional attitudes prevailed and precluded this kind of constructive action.[6]

Despite the assumption among leaders in government and industry that most women were anxious to return to their homes as soon as possible, a high percentage indicated that they wanted to retain their jobs when the war was over. A survey by the United Auto Workers showed that 85 percent of those interviewed wanted to continue working, while the Women's Bureau of the Department of Labor received an affirmative response from 80 percent of those whom it questioned.[7] The greatest enthusiasm was among women over forty-five.[8] They were least likely to have young children and therefore probably experienced the least role conflict when they took jobs. The primary motive of all these females was financial; only 8 percent of those who wanted to continue working gave feminist reasons.[9] According to the New York State Division of Industrial Relations in 1946, "Women, like men, work because their earnings are needed to support themselves and their families and to meet home expenses. . . . Single women support themselves and aged parents. . . . Married women support themselves and dependents."[10]

Whatever they preferred, fears about a postwar recession, desire to give employment priority to returning veterans, and traditional notions about woman's place led to massive layoffs of female workers in 1945 and 1946. Within a year after the end of the war, women doctors were being removed from hospital and staff positions to make room for returning veterans.[11] Sixty percent of all those dismissed were women; their rate of dismissal was 75 percent higher than that of men.[12] In New York State the percentage of the work force which was female declined from 33 percent to 25 percent. In some industries the numbers laid off were staggering: Aluminum Company of Ames dismissed 50 percent of its women employees; Ford Motor Company at Willow Run, 81 percent; the Hoover Company, 84 percent; American Brake and Block, 90 percent; American Leather Products, Asbestos Manufacturing Company, and Baker Rouland Company, all 100 percent.[13] Industry revised age restrictions to throw women over forty-five out of work and reimposed prohibitions about hiring wives.[14] Once again protective legislation that kept females out of certain jobs was enforced, although these laws had been suspended without ruining the health of American women during the wartime emergency.[15] There was hardly a better illustration of how correct the advocates of the Equal Rights Amendment were when they argued that the effect of these laws was prejudicial to females.

Despite massive layoffs, the number of working women did not decline permanently. Within a relatively short period, female war workers were employed once more. Between September 1945 and November 1946, 2.25 million women voluntarily left jobs and 1 million were laid off; in the same period, 2.75 million were hired. By 1947, female employment had reached wartime levels and was setting new records in the economic boom of the late 1940s and early 1950s. What had happened, however, was that women were driven back to their lower-paying, less secure jobs in traditional fields. In Baltimore, for example, females' average wages fell from $50 a week in 1944 to $37 in 1946. Most of the new female workers were wives; indeed, for the first time the majority of employed women were married. The number of couples in which both husband and wife worked increased from 3 million, or 11 percent, in 1940 to almost 7 million, or 20 percent, in 1948. One-quarter of the female labor force had children under eighteen years old. The median age of employed women was thirty-six-and-a-half, compared to thirty-two before the war. Increasingly, the working wife was a common feature of middle-class America.[16]

As during the war, high levels of female employment coexisted with economic inequality. Wage discrimination continued. Wherever women constituted more than 50 percent of the labor force in an in-

dustry, its wages fell below the national average. The dollar gap between full-time male and female employees continued. In 1963, the
year that Congress passed the Equal Pay Act, working women earned
only 59 percent of the average male income.[17] Although the absolute
numbers of females going to college increased, they constituted a
smaller proportion of total enrollment than before the war. The percentage of women in the professions continued to decline, slipping
from 15 percent in 1930 to 11 percent in 1960.[18] The number of female lawyers and school superintendents decreased. The quota on female admissions to medical school continued, and 70 percent of all
hospitals rejected female interns. The New York Obstetrical Society
would not admit women physicians. Although 25 percent of all government workers were female, only 3 percent held high-level positions. A survey of banks in Chattanooga, Tennessee, showed that
males and females served as tellers in equal numbers, but men were
senior tellers; women, junior. Business executives had little confidence in feminine ability to handle management positions. Fifty-three
percent of those interviewed in 1946 by *Fortune* magazine said women
handled people less well than men did, while 66 percent said they were
less able to make decisions.[19]

What seems to have happened was that a revolution occurred in female employment in the 1940s and 1950s without a corresponding
shift in attitudes toward women. While more and more wives and
mothers held jobs, most Americans still subscribed to the idea that
their proper place was in the home. The lag between cultural norms
and everyday behavior was possible because the new feminine role was
conceived in economic terms rather than as a commitment to new
social values. The crucial justifications for the working wife and
mother were inflation and rising expectations. Often it was the
woman's salary that enabled a family to rise into the middle class or to
pay for a home and a college education for their children. In a sense,
the wife simply fulfilled the ideal of being a helpmate in a new way.
Before the war, employment was expected only of wives whose husbands' income placed them below the poverty line; after the war, it
was expected to fulfill the family's dreams of a better life. What was
significant was the impression that wives went to work out of necessity
rather than out of a desire to find individual fulfillment. Often there
was even verbal expression of the notion that the wife's job was tempo-

rary, long after it was clear that this statement did not correspond to reality. In short, women sought jobs, not careers.

Given the gap between social attitudes and reality, it is not surprising that the revolution in female employment did not generate a revival of feminism. A hard core still advocated passage of the Equal Rights Amendment, and there was even some talk in congressional circles that it ought to be passed to reward women for their magnificent contribution to the war effort. However, even female leaders like Eleanor Roosevelt and Mary Anderson maintained that protective legislation was more important than the abstract principle of legal equality. [20] There was no protest when all federal support for child-care centers ended on March 1, 1946. Despite the growing numbers of employed wives and mothers during the late 1940s and the 1950s, there was little demand for child-care centers or other forms of community support for working women. For most of them, employment outside the home simply meant holding two jobs instead of one.

The enormous expansion of private nursery schools since World War II was undoubtedly one way in which middle-class women solved the problem created by their dual roles. [21] Since it was increasingly accepted that nursery school was good for the youngsters, mothers could free themselves for employment without challenging the assumption that child rearing was their primary responsibility. Just as they went to work for the good of the family, they sent their three-year-olds to school for unselfish reasons. In growing circles, a distinct suspicion existed that women who could afford nursery school but did not send their children were too possessive. A real revolution in middle-class child-rearing patterns had occurred, but, once again, in a form that failed to undermine traditional ideas about women's roles.

The persistence of traditional views about feminine nature and woman's proper sphere was reinforced by the enormous influence of Freudian psychoanalytic theory in the postwar period. It was only after 1945 that Freudianism became a pervasive influence in American culture. On the broadest level, Freudianism was hostile to any feminist ideology because it sought the source of female dissatisfaction in the individual rather than in the social situation. [22] More specifically, Freud and his followers prescribed traditional roles for women and defended customary attitudes toward them in up-to-date scientific terminology. To Freud the first crucial experience in the formation of the female personality was penis envy, an emotion little girls felt as soon as they noticed that little boys had something that they lacked. Girls wanted a penis because it was superior for masturbation, although Freud did not make clear how they knew this. Because of their deficiency, girls had contempt for their own bodies and an inferiority complex. Out of anger at their mothers, whom they blamed for their lack, they turned to their fathers in the hope that they would supply them with the missing organ and entered what Freud called the Oedipal stage. When daughters realized their fathers could not fulfill this wish, they developed a substitute desire to bear the fathers' baby. In psychoanalytic terms, the baby was a substitute for the penis. In adulthood, normal women transferred this desire from their fathers to another man. It was natural for females to desire maternity; if they did not, it was because they were suffering from unresolved penis envy and a masculinity complex. Intellectual and professional ambitions in women stemmed from penis envy.

Freud also traced temperamental differences between men and women to biology. He defined femininity as essentially passive, masochistic, and narcissistic. Divergence from this norm, a restatement of Victorian prescription in scientific terminology, was unhealthy. Modesty and jealousy, both peculiarly feminine traits, originated in penis envy.

The difference between the childhood Oedipal complex in boys and girls, again rooted in biology, accounted for the differing development of the male and female superego, or conscience. The boy, who had a penis, feared castration by his father in retaliation for his desire to possess his mother. He developed a superego to conceal and transcend his anxiety. Since the girl lacked a penis to begin with, she had no stimulus for developing a superego, which explained her lack of moral sense and idea of justice, as well as her subjection to emotional bias rather than judgment.

The female's weak superego[23] and an inferior capacity for sublimating her libido (sex drive) explained why women have contributed little to civilization and culture in the past and have little hope of doing so in the future. The female was less able to sublimate than the male because she possessed weaker libido to start with.[24] Her involvement in pregnancy and childbirth also undermined her capacity for sublimation.[25] In *Civilization and Its Discontents*, Freud postulated an inherent opposition between women and culture.[26] Finally, he maintained that repressive sexual patterns carried over into every area of the woman's life and explained her unquestionable intellectual inferiority. These repressive patterns began in childhood, when the girl gave up masturbation in the period of penis envy, and were reinforced by the whole character of her upbringing.[27]

Because of the female's weak libido, men had to take the initiative in sexual relations to ensure continuation of the race, although this hardly seems consistent with Freud's conviction that normal women desired maternity. Sexual aggressiveness was natural to and appropriate to men; sexual passivity, to women. Freud also maintained that intercourse was painful to women and that any pleasure they felt was masochistic.[28] Although his language was different, there is really little distinction between Freud's woman and the Victorian stereotype.

What is most curious about Freudianism is that it evolved in a circle distinguished by creative and active women, including Lou Andreas Salome, Anna Freud, Karen Horney, Clara Thompson, Helene Deutsch, and Marie Bonaparte. Although they themselves scarcely fit the Freudian stereotype of the uncreative, passive woman, many of these early Freudians, particularly Helene Deutsch and Marie Bonaparte, expanded the original psychoanalytic equation of femininity and passivity, masochism, and narcissism. Perhaps the definitive statement of the Freudian view appeared in Helene Deutsch's *The Psychology of Women*.[29]

One of the earliest dissents from within psychoanalytic circles came from Karen Horney, a German psychoanalyst who emigrated to the United States in 1932. Departing from the basic Freudian assumption, she questioned whether the feminine type is the result of instinctual factors or cultural influences, particularly the patriarchal ideal. She was also skeptical about assuming that what was true of middle-class Viennese society was true in all human societies across time and place. Turning to the substantive detail of Freudian theory, Horney questioned the whole masculine orientation of psychoanalysis. She maintained that the concept of penis envy ignored the joy that women felt in pregnancy and motherhood. She even suggested that it was envy of women's biological capacity that men sublimated into culture building. She also disputed the notion that frigidity was the normal sexual attitude of women, regarding it as illness, not health, and the result of cultural factors. [30]

Most Freudian psychoanalysts were much more conservative on the woman's problem than Horney or another dissenter, Clara Thompson. The influx of psychoanalysts from Europe in the 1930s was probably important in giving American theory its traditionalist cast. These immigrants not only made the United States, particularly New York, one of the world centers of psychoanalysis, but also defended ideas about women that had been developed in the conservative environment of central Europe. [31]

All psychoanalysts today are not, of course, Freudians in the strict sense. The movement has splintered and resplintered since its earliest days, leaving Freudians, Adlerians, and Jungians in well-defined, hostile camps. Even those who have not discarded Freud's major theories have often modified them considerably. A good deal of the most creative recent work in psychoanalytic theory has focused on the evolution of the ego and the development of identity, neither of which issues were central to Freud's work. Nonetheless, it seems to me, the basic thrust of Freudian psychoanalytic theory, however cautious, sophisticated, and revisionist, is to retain the assumption that men and women are innately different in character and behavior as well as in their specialized reproductive roles. A good example of this is the famous essay by Erik Erikson, "Inner and Outer Space: Reflections on Womanhood," which appeared in *Daedalus* in 1964. [32] Erikson opened by asserting that women were innately different from men in instinct, interests, and function in human society because of their childbearing and child-rearing functions. He believed that as mothers they might save the world from nuclear holocaust, the end product of male technology. With a little imagination one hears speaking in him the suffragists who believed that giving women the vote would usher in an era of peace and prosperity.

The basic thesis of Erikson's essay was that the woman's kinesthetic and psychic sense of inner space was more important than classic Freudian penis envy in the development of her psychology. As proof he cited the play constructions of 150 boys and 150 girls aged ten, eleven, and twelve. Erikson asked them to create a scene for him from blocks and such toys as furniture, automobiles, and human figures. In two-thirds of the cases, girls constructed low, interior, peaceful, essentially domestic scenes. Most of the animals and human figures were placed inside enclosed space. The boys, however, built high walls and towers, placed most of their figures outside buildings and enclosures, included many more moving animals and automobiles, and were the exclusive architects of accidents and ruins. Ignoring the significance of deviation in one-third of the children and rejecting the purely social interpretation of his observations, Erikson concluded,

The spatial phenomenon observed here would then express two principles of arranging space which correspond to the male and female principles in body construction. These may receive special emphasis in pre-puberty, and maybe in some other stages of life as well, but they are relevant throughout life to the elaboration of sex-roles in cultural space-time.33

The inner space of the girl's play constructions corresponds to the physical inner space of their wombs and the inner-direction of their essential reproductive function. The domestic and tranquil character of their scenes reflects their qualities as future mothers.

The human foetus must be carried inside the womb for a given number of months; and . . . the infant must be suckled or, at any rate, raised within a maternal world best staffed at first by the mother (and this for the sake of her own awakened motherliness as well as for the newborn's needs), with a gradual addition of other women. . . . It . . . makes sense that she is able earlier than boys to concentrate on details immediate in time and space, and has throughout a finer discrimination for things seen, touched, and heard. To these she reacts more vividly, more personally, and with greater compassion. More easily touched and touchable, however, she is said also to recover faster, ready to react again and elsewhere. That all of this is essential to the "biological" task of reacting to the differential needs of others, especially infants, will not appear to be a farfetched interpretation. . . . The little girl also learns to be more easily content within a limited circle of activities and shows less resistance to control and less impulsivity of the kind that later leads boys and men to "delinquency." All of these and more certified "differences" could be shown to have corollaries in our play constructions. . . .

Thus only a total configurational approach—somatic, historical, individual—can help us to see the differences of functioning and experiencing in context rather than in isolated and senseless comparison. . . .

Am I saying, then, that "anatomy is destiny"? Yes, it is destiny, insofar as it determines the potentials of physiological functioning, and its limitations.

But anatomy also, to an extent, codetermines personality configurations. The modalities of woman's commitment and involvement, for better *and* for worse, also reflect the groundplan of her body.[34]

Erikson's argument strikes me both as patently absurd and illogical, despite its wide influence. On a theoretical level there is a fatal flaw in the argument: no one can argue anything meaningful about biologically based differences between the sexes from play constructions of children ten to twelve years old. By that time, they are far too socialized; on the most obvious level, they have been to school and have seen too many television shows and advertisements that depict boys and girls and men and women in the most traditional ways. Although it is enormously clever to draw parallels between play constructions, anatomy of the male and female bodies, and differences between the functions and characters of the two sexes, it strikes me as too clever by half. As a woman, as someone who was once a little girl, I doubt very much that females, particularly before puberty, have a sense—kinesthetic, somatic, psychic, or otherwise—of any kind of inner space. While a woman certainly feels (and, of course, knows as an objective fact) that she has something inside of her while she is pregnant, the opposite—that she has a sense of an empty inner space when she is not—does not necessarily follow.

There is also built into Erikson's theory an automatic and necessary connection between childbearing and child rearing. This connection is, and always has been, one of the basic issues between feminists and anti-feminists. It is one of the basic assumptions of every variety of psychoanalytic theory, but one that has not, in my view, been proven. Indeed, one of the few modern experiments in rearing children in a totally different way, on the kibbutzim in Israel, has suggested that it is perfectly possible to break the connection between the biological and social function without doing untold damage to the children concerned. Bruno Bettelheim's study, *Children of the Dream*, demonstrated that children raised on the kibbutzim were quite different from children raised in traditional nuclear families, but were certainly not more psychologically incapacitated.[35]

Finally, as a historian, it seems to me that Freudianism has gone or is going through the kind of evolution in its theories about women that characterized Darwinist theory in the nineteenth century. All Darwinists believed that there was a connection between biological evolution, character, and intellectual capacity. Initially, they affirmed that biology proved the inferiority of women and used their findings to define distinct feminine spheres suited to their reproductive functions and lesser abilities. Later many Darwinists continued to assert the biologically based differences between the sexes in character and talent, but maintained that although they were different, women were equivalent and in some areas even superior. The belief in separate spheres survived, but without the stain of inferiority. Likewise, original Freudian theories depicted females as inferior in many crucial areas because of physiologically based differences between the sexes, particularly in their genitals and level of libido. Erikson continued to affirm that there were emotional and behavioral differences derived from women's distinctive physical construction and reproductive role, but that these differences made them superior in certain areas. Indeed, he ventured that only the maternal instinct can save humanity from nuclear destruction. Feminist acceptance of the notion of separate female and male spheres at the end of the nineteenth century was one of the factors narrowing the scope of the woman's movement, limiting the impact of the passage of the Nineteenth Amendment, and destroying feminism in the 1920s. Subscription to psychoanalytically based sexual differences has had a comparable effect in the period since World War II.

Freudianism has had as pervasive an influence on popular culture in the last three decades as Darwinism had in the late nineteenth and early twentieth centuries. One of the best-selling books in the immediate postwar period was *Modern Woman: The Lost Sex* by sociologist Ferdinand Lundberg and psychiatrist Marynia F. Farnham. Their book discussed women as "one of modern civilization's major unsolved problems." [36] Their thesis was that one of the keys to the ills of the twentieth century was woman's failure to accept that the ultimate goal of her life is motherhood and that her appropriate relationship to man is one of biological and psychological dependence. They considered the sex act itself, in which women are passive and receptive, a paradigm of the ideal female personality. Using simplified Freudian concepts, they argued that feminism was a neurotic reaction to male dominance, which encouraged females to reject their natural sex-based instincts and become imitation men. The pernicious influence of feminism was responsible for a good deal of contemporary cultural pathology. Lundberg and Farnham based their general picture of feminists as neurotic on an extended analysis of Mary Wollstonecraft, who wrote the first systematic argument for equality between the sexes, *Vindication of the Rights of Woman*, in 1792.

Two years later, Lynn White, Jr., president of Mills College, one of the best female schools west of the Mississippi, published *Educating Our Daughters*. [37] He addressed himself to the fact that American colleges did not consider the special interests, aptitudes, and accomplishments of women in their curricula. He stated as fact, and accepted as desirable, that females had very different life patterns from males. Particularly, they faced two "big" choices that men did not—whether to marry or have careers and what to do when their children grew up. White clearly did not favor women having both careers and marriage, although he saw no incompatibility when men did so. White also referred to "rapidly mounting evidence that cultural creativity is very nearly sex-linked." [38] He asserted as fact that males had higher numerical ability and females higher verbal skill and that women were factual and concrete, while men tended to generalization and abstraction. On the basis of his convictions about women's intellectual capacities, White felt that female colleges should once and for all discard the false purpose for which they were founded—that is, to provide women with the same education as men. Specifically, the curriculum must prepare women to handle the life crises that they faced in their twenties and forties and must respect their special interests and abilities as females. A liberal arts program designed for them would emphasize psychology, sociology, and anthropology at the expense of literature, history, philosophy, and political economy. It would concentrate on the minor arts instead of the fine arts, which were a particularly masculine domain. White's ideas on women's intellectual capacities were virtually the same as those of nineteenth-century Darwinists. Both White and the Darwinists, in turn, espoused a modern version of the ancient Western tradition that asserted the intellectual inferiority of females.

Vocational training for women, according to White, ought not to be too specific, since most females would be spending the decades after college in the home. By implication, of course, professional schools were not appropriate places for them. Female education should emphasize the importance of the family, and family values ought to permeate history, literature, and philosophy when they were taught to girls. Women's colleges ought, also, to develop courses that deal with the technical problems of running a home and handling a family. Specifically, White mentioned food and nutrition, textiles and clothing, health and nursing, house planning and interior decoration, garden design and applied botany, and child development. His ideas echoed those of the early home economics movement, although they sounded increasingly anachronistic in a highly industrialized, market economy.

Marriage and family patterns from 1945 to 1960 reflected the ideological environment just described. The average age of marriage for American women dropped to the lowest level anywhere in the Western world. The birth rate soared, especially among the college educated. For the first time they had as many children as the poor. Even among the best-educated females, marriage took precedence over professions. There was an increasing feeling that families and careers could not be combined, and most women opted for the former. The early feminist ideal of the single, professional woman almost completely disappeared. In the 1870s, two out of five Vassar graduates married before the age of twenty-seven; in 1920, three out of five; in 1960, four out of five. [39] Fewer and fewer females earned the highest professional degrees. In the 1950s women received 10 percent of the Ph.D.'s granted, while they had earned 14 percent in the 1920s and early 1930s. [40] Of outstanding female graduate students at Columbia University from 1946 to 1951, only 50 percent had what they described as satisfactory careers. [41] The 1950s also saw a mass exodus to suburbia, where the wife's primary role was to make her home an oasis of comfort and serenity for the harried male who returned in the evening from the race for economic success in the city. It all seemed like a strangely modern version of the Victorian ethos.

Nonetheless, despite the apparent triumph of what Betty Friedan later called "the feminine mystique," all was not well in suburbia, nor was the reality of women's lives quite so static and traditional as it appeared on the surface. The female labor force continued to grow, particularly among well-educated wives with children. Among women whose husbands earned from $7,000 to $10,000, the percentage who worked outside the home grew from 7 percent in 1950 to 25 percent in

1960. Two years later, 53 percent of all female college graduates were employed, while 36 percent of those with high school diplomas held jobs. Seventy percent of all females who had five or more years of higher education worked. [42] There was, in short, a continuing revolution in female employment, especially among the comfortable, suburban women who were allegedly finding contentment in domesticity. What was even more significant was that many of these women reported receiving more gratification from their jobs than they did from their roles as wives and mothers. In one survey two-thirds of those who responded said that it was their jobs that made them feel important and useful. [43] Women who tried to conform to the image of the affluent, suburban wife with three or four children increasingly suffered from what Friedan called the "problem without a name" and turned to extramarital affairs, alcohol, tranquilizers, and psychiatry. In short, the gap between social reality and ideals, which began in the post-World War II revolution in female employment, continued and posed serious problems for more and more women. They suffered because they failed to find contentment and fulfillment in prescribed roles, but felt guilty if they tried to break out of them.

It was certainly the fact that she spoke to a real, if unexpressed—even unconscious—need that accounted for the extraordinary success of Simone de Beauvoir's *Second Sex* when it appeared in English in 1952. [44] Beauvoir is a French writer who completely revolted against the conservative, bourgeois, Catholic background in which she was raised. Her family educated her for a career because they could not afford to marry her in circles that they considered socially acceptable. Her father, therefore, always considered her profession and success a mark of his own failure. At the age of twenty-one, she met Jean-Paul Sartre and entered the relationship that has dominated the rest of her life. As lovers and intellectual partners, Sartre and Beauvoir took their mutual affection and responsibilities seriously, However, neither of them believed in marriage, since they both denied that human beings were meant to be monogamous and felt that each of them should be free to enter serious relationships with others. They maintained separate residences, although they met almost every day. Today their relationship is over thirty years old and still vital; Beauvoir has declared it the single greatest success of her life.

In *The Second Sex*, Beauvoir brought biology, history, psychology, sociology, anthropology, literature, and philosophy to bear on the question "What is a woman?" She used the philosophical concept of "the other" to explain the peculiar relationship of attraction and repulsion that has characterized men and women since the beginning of history. Strongly influenced by Engels, she attributed the subjection of females to their relative physical weakness and the development of private property. What is perhaps most shocking in her book is her analysis of the different stages in a woman's life. In her conclusion she suggested that socialism is the only way to solve the female problem at its root. For the individual woman in a capitalist society, however, economic independence was essential. In recent years, Beauvoir has specifically repudiated her earlier belief that socialism would solve the woman problem and has supported organized feminism.[45] Although the sales indicated that people were reading *The Second Sex*, it did not spark a resurgence of feminism in this country, partly because the purpose of the book was not political and it avoided any kind of immediate call to action. Much more important, of course, was the whole ideological environment that I have been discussing.

Eleven years later, however, there appeared a book that smashed the complacency of the 1950s and initiated the first serious resurgence of feminism in this country since the 1920s. The book, Betty Friedan's *Feminine Mystique*, was a blistering attack on affluent surburban America and the functions that it assigned to women.[46] Unlike Beauvoir's book, it was an explicit, even strident, call to action and succeeded in arousing middle-class American women in a way that they had not been stirred for over a generation. McCarthyism, fear of nuclear confrontation, and suspicion of nonconformity had prevented Americans from asking any meaningful questions about the status quo in the early 1950s. A decade later, however, the civil rights movement was in full swing. Just as the birth of feminism had been connected with the abolitionist movement in the mid-nineteenth century, its resurrection in the twentieth century was closely related to the struggle for racial equality. At the time Friedan's book appeared, the civil rights movement was at the height of its influence among the suburban women to whom she appealed most directly. They were in a less conservative frame of mind than they had been for years. Furthermore, female college students, often their daughters, who traveled to the South in connection with the movement were horrified to discover that while their male colleagues wrote statements, made policy, and organized demonstrations, the women were expected to make endless pots of coffee and do the typing. The sexual exploitation of women in the movement was expressed for all time by Stokley Carmichael's infamous remark, "The only place for women in the movement is prone." Thus, by 1963, there were two distinct audiences for Betty Friedan's message: radicalized, but disillusioned, college students and discontented, middle-class, suburban housewives.

By the "feminine mystique" Friedan meant a definition and glorification of the female role that focused exclusively on the woman's sexual and reproductive functions. It implied the same kind of separation between male and female spheres that characterized Victorian America and stimulated the first feminist meeting at Seneca Falls in 1848.

It is my thesis that the core of the problem for women today is not sexual but a problem of identity—a stunting or evasion of growth that is perpetuated by the feminine mystique. It is my thesis that as the Victorian culture did not permit women to accept or gratify their basic sexual needs, our culture does not permit women to accept or gratify their basic need to grow and fulfill their potentialities as human beings, a need which is not solely defined by their sexual role.[47]

Friedan blamed the pervasiveness of the feminine mystique on Freudian psychoanalytic theory, functionalist social scientists, educators, and self-interested advertisers. Labeling Freudianism the "ideological bulwark of the sexual counter-revolution in America," she introduced a theme repeated later by a much more radical feminist, Kate Millett.[48] In Friedan's view, much of what Freud attributed to biology and instinct was due in fact to cultural causes and social conditioning, a point of view that she derived from behavioral psychology and social science. She flatly rejected the notion of penis envy: "You cannot explain away woman's envy of man, or her contempt for herself, as mere refusal to accept her sexual deformity, unless you think that a woman, by nature, is a being inferior to man. Then, of course, her wish to be equal is neurotic."[49] She also pointed out, most pertinently, that all psychoanalytic theory was developed to help the individual adjust to society, not to change it, and is, therefore, inadequate once one perceives the need for reform.

Betty Friedan felt that the pervasiveness of these ideas in American culture resulted from the conjunction of a number of influences. In the immediate postwar period, a rush for matrimony and motherhood resulted naturally from postponements forced by the conflict. Even more fundamentally after the trauma of the war years, many Americans, particularly men, were anxious to retreat into the overidealized image of domesticity that had sustained them during the war. The feminine mystique was therefore particularly appealing in the social context of the late 1940s and early 1950s. Its Freudian theoretical base became part of American mass culture through the joint efforts of popularizers like Lundberg and Farnham, functionalist social scientists, educators who accepted the ideas uncritically, the women's magazines, and self-interested advertisers. The immigration of many conservative psychoanalysts from Europe in the 1930s ensured that Freudianism would bolster the status quo in respect to female roles. Friedan was harshest when she attacked the women's magazines and advertisers. She noted, relevantly, that by the 1950s most of the editors of the women's magazines were men, a situation that had not prevailed earlier. Here one can see the direct result of the retreat from feminism and the ideal of the career women that occurred from 1920 to 1945. In conjunction with advertisers, on whom women's magazines were financially dependent and who perceived correctly that the affluent suburban housewife was an inexhaustible market for new blue Ajax and the latest model refrigerator, the *Ladies Home Journal*, *McCalls*, and others endlessly preached the gospel that full-time wives and mothers had happy husbands and well-adjusted children.

The motivational researchers must be given credit for their insights into the reality of the housewife's life and needs—a reality that often escaped their colleagues in academic sociology and therapeutic psychology, who saw women through the Freudian-functional veil. To their own profit, and that of their clients, the manipulators discovered that millions of supposedly happy American housewives have complex needs which home-and-family, love-and-children, cannot fill. But by a morality that goes beyond the dollar, the manipulators are guilty of using their insights to sell women things which, no matter how ingenious, will never satisfy those increasingly desperate needs. They are guilty of persuading housewives to stay at home, mesmerized in front of a television set, their nonsexual human needs unnamed, unsatisfied, drained by the sexual sell into the buying of things.

The manipulators and their clients in American business can hardly be accused of creating the feminine mystique. But they are the most powerful of its perpetuators.... If they are not solely responsible for sending women home, they are surely responsible for keeping them there.50

Betty Friedan rejected and attacked the feminine mystique partly because it made women unhappy, something she documented over and over again in her critique. However, the reader feels clearly that happiness was not for her the cricial issue. The crux of her complaint was that the feminine mystique discouraged women from making mature choices about their lives and developing their talents. Because they were conditioned from early childhood to follow a road that led to full-time domesticity and motherhood, they avoided the identity crisis and conscious choices that all males encounter. The price of avoiding these issues was perpetual immaturity and the sacrifice of their potential. Deeply embedded in Friedan's book was the notion that true growth and fulfillment as an individual involve a commitment to what Protestant theologians once termed a "calling."

Notes

1. See pages 144-46 above on World War II's positive effect on the situation of women doctors.

2. William Chafe, *The American Woman, 1920-1970* (New York: Oxford University Press, 1972), p. 158.

3. Ibid., pp. 152-57.

4. Ibid., p. 160.

5. Ibid., p. 170.

6. Ibid., pp. 161, 170. I attribute the very different British response to a strong labor movement, a greater need to organize the whole society efficiently for the war effort, and a reaction to the social problems revealed during the bombings and evacuations from slums in London and other cities.

7. Sheila Tobias and Lisa Anderson, "Whatever Happened to Rosie the Riveter," *Ms*, June 1963, p. 93.

8. Chafe, *American Woman*, p. 179.

9. Ibid., p. 191.

10. Quoted in Tobias and Anderson, "Rosie the Riveter," p. 93.

11. Mary Roth Walsh, *"Doctors Wanted: No Women Need Apply"*: *Sexual Barriers in the Medical Profession, 1835-1975* (New Haven: Yale University Press, 1977), pp. 234-35.

12. Chafe, *American Woman*, p. 180.

13. Tobias and Anderson, "Rosie the Riveter," p. 93.

14. Chafe, *American Woman*, p. 180.

15. Tobias and Anderson, "Rosie the Riveter," p. 94.

16. Chafe, *American Woman*, pp. 180-83.

17. Ibid., p. 185. U.S. Department of Labor, Women's Bureau, *Fact Sheet on the Earnings Gap*, Publication no. 71-86 (Washington, D.C.: Government Printing Office, 1971), p. 1. In 1973 the income of women in full-time employment was 57 percent that of men. The Equal Pay Act does not seem to have made much of an impact.

18. William O'Neill, *Everyone Was Brave* (Chicago: Quadrangle Books, 1971), p. 338.

19. Quoted in Chafe, *American Woman*, pp. 184-85.

20. Ibid., p. 188.

21. Jesse Bernard, *The Future of Motherhood* (New York: Dial Press, 1974), p. 281n.

22. This interpretation of Freud's ideas about women is based primarily on three of his late essays on the subject: "Some Psychical Consequences of the Anatomical Distinction Between the Sexes" (1925), in *The Standard Edition of the Complete Psychological Works of Sigmund Freud*, 23 vols., ed. James Strachey (London: Hogarth Press, 1961), 19: 248-58; "Female Sexuality" (1931), in ibid., 21:225-43; "Psychology of Women" (1933), in *New Introductory Lectures on Psychoanalysis* (New York: W. W. Norton, 1933), pp. 153-85. I provide citation for specific views attributed to Freud only in cases in which I think my interpretation is particularly controversial.

23. "Psychology of Women," pp. 176-77; "The Passing of the Oedipus-Complex" (1924), in *Collected Papers*, ed. Joan Riviere (New York: Basic Books, 1959), 2: 274-75.

24. "Psychology of Women," pp. 179-80; "'Civilized' Sexual Morality and Modern Nervous Illness" (1908), in *The Standard Edition*, 9: 192. In the latter essay Freud explicitly states that woman "possesses a weaker sexual instinct."

25. "Psychology of Women," pp. 183-84; "'Civilized' Sexual Morality," p. 195. "Civilization and Its Discontents" (1930), in *The Standard Edition*, 21: 103, refers to "instinctual sublimations of which women are little capable," but does not give any reasons for this incapacity.

26. "Civilization and Its Discontents," pp. 103-4. Also see "Psychology of Women," pp. 183-84.

27. "'Civilized' Sexual Morality," pp. 198-99; "Psychology of Women,"

pp. 172-73; and "Female Sexuality," pp. 229-30, 232, for repression of sexuality as one female response to the discovery of her organic inferiority. Also "Some Consequences of the Distinction Between the Sexes," pp. 255-58.

28. "Psychology of Women," pp. 156-57, 180.

29. Helene Deutsch, *The Psychology of Women*, 2 vols. (New York: Bantam Books, 1973).

30. Karen Horney, *Feminine Psychology* (New York: W. W. Norton, 1967). See especially "The Flight From Womanhood" and "The Problem of Feminine Masochism."

31. I am indebted to Rosalind Navin Rosenberg of Columbia University for pointing out the importance of this factor to me.

32. Erik Erikson, "Inner and Outer Space: Reflections on Womanhood," in *The Woman in America*, ed. Robert Jay Lifton (Boston: Beacon Press, 1965), pp. 1-26.

33. Ibid., p. 11.

34. Ibid., pp. 17-21.

35. Bruno Bettelheim, *Children of the Dream* (New York: Macmillan, 1969), chap. 5, for a summary of his views.

36. Ferdinand Lundberg and Marynia F. Farnham, M.D., *Modern Woman: The Lost Sex* (New York: Harper & Row, 1947), p. 1.

37. Lynn White, Jr., *Educating Our Daughters: A Challenge to the Colleges* (New York: Harper & Row, 1950).

38. Ibid., p. 46; see chapter 3 for White's argument on innate intellectual differences between the sexes.

39. Andrew Sinclair, *The Emancipation of the American Woman* (New York: Harper Colophon Books, 1965), p. 359.

40. Patricia Albjerg Graham, "Women in Academe," in *The Professional Woman*, ed. Athena Theodore (Cambridge, Mass.: Schenkman Publishing Company, 1971), p. 721; O'Neill, *Everyone Was Brave*, p. 305.

41. O'Neill, *Everyone Was Brave*, p. 345, citing a survey by Eli Ginzberg.

42. Chafe, *American Woman*, pp. 218-19.

43. Ibid., pp. 219-20.

44. Simone de Beauvoir, *The Second Sex* (New York: Bantam Books, 1961).

45. Simone de Beauvoir, *All Said and Done* (New York: Warner Books, 1975), pp. 469-71. Alice Rossi, review of *All Said and Done* by Simone de Beauvoir, *Psychology Today* 9 (October 1975): 16-17. Caroline Moorehead, "A Talk With Simone de Beauvoir," *New York Times Magazine*, June 2, 1974, p. 18.

46. Betty Friedan, *The Feminine Mystique* (New York: Dell, 1963).

47. Ibid., p. 69.

48. Kate Millett, *Sexual Politics* (New York: Avon Books, 1970), pp. 176-220.

49. Friedan, *Feminine Mystique*, p. 109.

50. Ibid., pp. 218-19.

VII

The New Feminism, 1960~1975

Nineteen sixty-three was a landmark year in the history of American women. After a hiatus of over four decades the woman's movement burst into life again and revived the demand for equality between the sexes that had first been sounded at Seneca Falls over a century earlier. Betty Friedan's *Feminine Mystique* was the ideological keynote and call for action of the new feminism.

The same year saw the publication of the report of the President's Commission on the Status of Women, established two years earlier by John F. Kennedy to investigate and suggest remedies for "prejudices and outmoded customs [that] act as barriers to the full realization of women's basic rights."[1] The report was based on the analyses and recommendations of seven committees—civil and political rights, education, federal employment, private employment, home and community, social security and taxes, and protective labor legislation. Although in many cases the committee reports were much stronger in tone and recommendations than the final document, the report proved beyond a shadow of a doubt that in almost every area of life women were indeed second-class citizens. The commission was somewhat ambivalent about woman's proper sphere, which certainly accounts for the moderate tone of its report. On one hand, it assumed that the nuclear family is vital to the stability of American society, that women have a unique and unchangeable role in the family, and that wives and mothers who work must play a dual role to a much greater extent than men. On the other, it maintained that every obstacle to women's full participation in society should be removed. Its acceptance of much of the feminine mystique was evident in the extended discussion of education, counseling, and the female's contribution to the home and community life. Most feminists argue that full equality is a chimera until basic patterns of marriage and child rearing are modified and society provides support services to the employed wife and mother. Whatever its deficiencies in their eyes, however, there can be little doubt that by its very existence the Presidential Commission on the Status of Women "generated for the first time in nearly a half-century a general interest in women's issues."[2]

Shortly after publication of the commission's report, Congress passed the Equal Pay Act, which outlawed wage discrimination on the basis of sex. It was the first major piece of legislation against inequality between the sexes since the Nineteenth Amendment. The Wage and Hour Division of the Department of Labor, which enforces the law, carries out routine compliance checks of employers and investigates any complaints that it receives. Between 1972 and 1975 its activities resulted in the payment of almost $17 million in back pay to 47,553 employees, most of them female. In addition, the equal pay provisions of two major consent decrees each won back pay of $7 million to employees.[3] Furthermore, the very existence of the law has had a salutary effect on establishments that have never been subject of a complaint or a review. Most feminists knowledgeable in the area consider the Equal Pay Act the most effective of all the legislation passed to eliminate sex discrimination in employment.

In 1964, Congress passed Title VII of the Civil Rights Act, which prohibited discrimination in employment on the basis of race, religion, color, national origin, and sex by private employers, unions, employment agencies, and colleges and universities. It specifically excluded federal, state, and local governments. The main purpose of the bill was to deal with racial inequality. The work *sex* was added to Title VII as a joke by Representative Howard Smith of Virginia, who apparently wanted to defeat the whole law by enveloping it in controversy and ridicule.[4] Nonetheless, his amendment was retained and the law passed. The Equal Employment Opportunity Commission

(EEOC) was formed to enforce Title VII. Much to the surprise of the first chairman of the EEOC, Franklin D. Roosevelt, Jr., he was deluged with complaints from women, rather than racial minorities. Since he perceived correctly that the real purpose of the 1964 Civil Rights Act was to deal with racial discrimination, he was less than energetic in investigating and handling cases involving females. The EEOC's executive director, Herman Edelsberg, publicly labeled the sex provision of Title VII a "fluke . . . conceived out of wedlock."[5] More effective enforcement of Title VII has been a major concern of feminists ever since.

The combined effect of all these developments was not only to bring the issue of equality between the sexes into public consciousness again, but also to stimulate a resurgence of organized feminism. One branch of the revived movement is primarily concerned with women's rights. It works through political and legal channels to achieve legislative, economic, and educational reforms to eradicate sex discrimination.[6] Women's rights groups include the National Organization for Women (NOW), Women's Equity Action League (WEAL), Federally Employed Women (FEW), National Federation of Business and Professional Women's Clubs, National Women's party, and National Women's Political Caucus.

The most controversial and important of these organizations is the National Organization for Women, NOW, founded in 1966 by Betty Friedan and a group gathered in Washington for the National Conference of State Commissions on the Status of Women. NOW describes itself as a civil rights organization to bring women into "truly equal partnership with men" in all areas of American society.[7] It lobbies for women's rights and disseminates feminist ideology. It was the first militant woman's group in the twentieth century to combat sex discrimination in all spheres of life: social, political, economic, and psychological. Its 1968 bill of rights demanded passage of the Equal Rights Amendment, enforcement of laws banning sex discrimination in employment, maternity leave rights in employment and social security benefits, tax deduction for home and child-care expenses for working parents, child-care centers, equal and unsegregated education, equal job-training opportunities and allowances for poor women, and the right of women to control their reproductive lives.[8]

Although most Americans considered the way NOW linked the

issues of legal and economic equality to the necessity of providing government support for the wife and mother to be quite radical, many younger women did not think it had gone far enough in its analysis of the female problem or in its program. Most of them came to the movement from the radical student and civil rights groups of the early 1960s. Their dissatisfaction with NOW stemmed from a number of sources. Many felt its concentration on legal remedies would lead the movement into the same kind of dead end and ideological compromise that faced the suffragists in 1920. Others believed that there could be no cure for the woman problem within the framework of a capitalist society; this was Simone de Beauvoir's initial assumption. Still others were simply impatient with what they considered the middle-class and reformist character of organized feminism.

Women's liberation groups sprang from these far more radical circles.[9] Whether or not they explained sexual inequality in Marxist terms as a by-product of capitalism or as a primary and independent problem, these women were far less interested in fighting for specific legal reforms than in analyzing the origins, nature, and extent of women's subservient role in society, with particular attention to the psychology of oppression. They assert that social, not individual, factors determine the context and problems of female lives and that therefore the solution lies in a new feminist consciousness and pattern of behavior. The original unit and primary technique of women's liberation is "consciousness raising." The formative idea of the consciousness-raising group is that a small number of women should meet regularly to discuss their attitudes and experiences as females. The assumption is that these discussions will demonstrate in the most concrete way how much of their experience is determined by social attitudes and conditions. It will also break down the barriers of hostility and distrust that many women feel for each other because they perceive other females as sexual rivals and because they have internalized the contempt for women expressed in countless ways in our sexist society.

Whether they are primarily concerned with woman's rights or with female liberation in the more radical sense, the leaders of the contemporary movement are acutely aware that they are trying to revive a cause that collapsed ignominiously at the movement of its greatest victory. They have studied the rise and fall of the earlier movement in order to avoid its unhappy fate. Most historians of the subject have concluded that the suffragists failed to win equality between the sexes because of their ideological compromise with the doctrine of separate female and male spheres, their failure to propose changes in the institutions of marriage and the family, and their general overcommitment to political and legal issues. The way in which current activists have tried to avoid these pitfalls has had a major impact on the character and direction of the movement today. For one thing, there is a great emphasis on ideology and a rejection of all biological and psychological theories that serve as a basis for doctrines of separate male and female spheres. [10] The marked anti-Freudianism of the movement is most notable, although the recent publication of Juliet Mitchell's defense of Freud, *Psychoanalysis and Feminism*, may indicate that a revision of this attitude is underway in some feminist circles. [11]

Another difference between the movement today and its predecessor is that current feminists have raised the issue of marriage and the family as central to the problem of women. They have returned to the radical perception of Elizabeth Cady Stanton, who saw way back in the 1850s that sexual equality was unattainable if these institutions remained unchanged, but was very much alone in her willingness to raise the subject in public. Today, few females who have given it any thought would deny that if women are to achieve on a par with men in the world outside the home, the housekeeping and child-rearing functions within it must be radically restructured. Although men often treat it as a trivial subject, few questions are more crucial to the future of women than what Pat Mainardi called the "politics of housework." [12]

Still a third distinguishing characteristic of the contemporary woman's movement is its concern with what psychologists and social scientists call sexual stereotypes. Sexual stereotypes are assumptions about the nature of men and women that are held by members of both sexes and influence their behavior in every area of life. By and large, they incorporate the most traditional notions about female nature and woman's proper sphere. The importance that feminists attach to sexual stereotypes and their pernicious and pervasive influence fits in well with the emphasis on psychology and the behavioral social sciences in contemporary culture.

One area in which there has been more continuity than contrast be-

tween the nineteenth-century and the present-day woman's movements has been in the attitude toward work outside the home. From
the Seneca Falls Declaration of Sentiments and Resolutions in 1848—
which demanded equal access to the "various trades, professions, and
commerce"—to Charlotte Perkins Gilman's *Woman and Economics*
in 1898—which attributed the female's subjection to her financial dependence and asserted that she can never be equal without first becoming self-supporting—nineteenth-century feminists constantly
reiterated the pernicious effect of confining women to the home and
depriving them of economic independence. Virtually all contemporary feminists also take this position. To a woman, they agree with
Gilman that fundamentally the housewife exchanges sexual and domestic services for support and that as long as employment is not a
viable alternative, due either to her lack of training or to her own and
her husband's attitudes, she cannot deal with him as a genuine equal.
As expressed by Simone de Beauvoir in *The Second Sex*,

A woman supported by a man—wife or courtesan—is not emancipated from
the male because she has a ballot in her hand; if custom imposes less con-
straint upon her than formerly, the negative freedom implied has not profoundly modified her situation; she remains bound in her condition of vassal-
age. It is through gainful employment that woman has traversed most of the
distance that separated her from the male; and nothing else can guarantee
her liberty in practice. Once she ceases to be a parasite, the system based on
her dependence crumbles; between her and the universe there is no longer any
need for a masculine mediator.[13]

The development of the American family since World War II provides factual evidence to confirm this theoretical position. The level of
employment among wives has been growing steadily since 1947, despite the fact that the feminist movement was dormant until very recently. Sociologists and psychologists who have studied the relations
between husbands and wives in families in which both are employed
have noted significant differences between their relationships and
those of couples in which the wife remains at home. Men married to
employed females share in domestic and child-rearing tasks to a
much greater degree than men married to full-time housewives.[14]
Chafe discusses a number of studies that speak explicitly about the
blurring of sex roles and the obliteration of firm boundaries between

the husband's and wife's spheres. Even more important, working women play a much greater part in making major family decisions than housewives, so there is a major shift in the distribution of power between husband and wife. Most men recognize the justice of allowing women to participate in decisions about spending money that they have helped to earn. Furthermore, employed wives develop the confidence from success in their jobs that enables them to challenge their mates' authority and unilateral decisions. Finally, many of them draw support for their new assertiveness from coworkers who share their views about the proper distribution of power within the family. Thus, without reference to any feminist ideology, "holding a job significantly affected the distribution of roles within society and the family."[15]

In addition to seeing an intimate connection between economic independence and equality between the sexes, feminists in the tradition of Betty Friedan see careers as a means to self-fulfillment and satisfaction in one's life. Friedan stated explicitly in *The Feminine Mystique* that vocations were the cure for the emptiness, unhappiness, and purposelessness characteristic of the lives of many of the suburban women whom she had observed and about whom she was writing.[16] As Simone de Beauvoir recognized in *The Second Sex*, long before Friedan wrote, this kind of argument in favor of female employment has definite class limitations in its relevance and applicability.[17] There are, as a matter of fact, only a limited number of professional, high-status, challenging jobs in society; a good deal of the work that has to be done is routine, takes little skill, and yields little sense of satisfaction. Much of it even has negative status implications, whatever the pay. Access to the relatively few desirable jobs is normally limited by educational requirements. Since education is still closely correlated to socioeconomic status, this means in effect that it is predominantly members of the upper and middle classes who have access to jobs that can really develop into the kind of careers and vocations about which Friedan was talking. This is true, of course, for both men and women. Because of sexual stereotypes, different patterns of child rearing, education, socialization, and overt discrimination, a smaller percentage of females than males have entered the professions and other creative careers in the past. The impact of feminism may be to raise the percentage just as it spurred the initial breakthrough at the end of the nineteenth and beginning of the twentieth centuries. The great majority of women workers, however, will hold the same kind of relatively routine, low-satisfaction jobs as the majority of men.

In making this point, I certainly do not wish to discourage females from working outside the home, but am simply trying to present a more realistic picture of what employment means for the great majority. Even if they do not have vocations in the sense that Friedan was talking about, women certainly gain many benefits from jobs, the most important being the income that they earn and the redistribution of power and roles in the family. Furthermore, many wives gain as much, if not more, satisfaction from their work—even from relatively unchallenging positions—than they do from their functions as wives and mothers, in spite of traditionalist assumptions to the contrary. I suspect that this is because many of them have experienced the disadvantages of being full-time housewives: the sense of powerlessness connected with financial dependence, the boredom of housework, the overreliance on close family relationships for emotional satisfaction, and the diffuse sense of isolation within the home. As a result, many of them have a much clearer appreciation of the positive functions of work than do men, who often regard jobs as an unavoidable burden connected with their responsibilities as fathers and husbands.

Whatever the validity of feminist arguments for work outside the home, and whether or not the current movement continues at its present active level, more and more American women will hold jobs for longer and longer periods for economic and demographic reasons. The major stimulus for the entrance of wives into the labor market since World War II has been financial.[18] The only way in which many American families can achieve the standard of living to which they aspire is for the wife to work. The steady process of inflation since 1945, which has now reached almost catastrophic proportions, has kept up the monetary pressures. Indeed, one of the results of the rapid price rises of the last few years has been to push more women than ever into employment. Even if the unacceptable inflation that we are now experiencing is brought under control, there is little reason to assume that the more gradual, but steady, price rise of the last thirty years will be eliminated.

Equally important are the two most striking demographic patterns affecting females in the last decades—the fall in the birth rate, so that we are now approaching zero population growth in the United States, and the gradual lengthening of the woman's life span. What this means in simple terms is that a smaller and smaller proportion of the female's life is going to be taken up by childbearing and child rearing. A woman who marries at the age of twenty-two, has her first child at twenty-five and her second at twenty-eight, a not unlikely pattern, will be only thirty-four years old when the younger starts going to school for a full day. If we assume a retirement age of sixty-five, she still has over thirty years left for gainful employment. Even if she stays home until her younger child graduates from high school, she will be only forty-six years old when her full-time occupation as a mother ends, and she can work for almost twenty years before retiring. Although some women will certainly occupy themselves with domestic, social, and philanthropic activities along traditional lines, this real life situation guarantees that ever greater numbers will seek jobs for significant portions of their adult years. In *Women's Two Roles*, Alva Myrdal and Viola Klein estimate that in the last three decades of the twentieth century, being a housewife and mother will be a full-time job for only one-quarter to one-third of the average woman's life. [19] The most recent statistics reflect the trends that they anticipated. In March 1976, 47 percent of all women and 50 percent of all mothers with children under eighteen were in the labor force. [20]

One of the major concerns of the contemporary feminist movement is to ensure that the growing numbers of employed women receive the same wages and other benefits as men holding comparable positions and that females have equal access to the professions and other high-paying, high-status positions. A virtual legislative revolution has given them the legal weapons with which to combat sex discrimination in these areas, and they have entered the fray with enthusiasm. The woman's rights wing of the movement spends much of its time, energy, and money pressuring government agencies to enforce the relevant laws and resorting to the courts when they fail. Whatever their frustrations and failures, congressional and presidential action in the last decade has redrawn the rules governing the labor market so that, for the first time, females have some hope of achieving the economic equality and independence about which Charlotte Perkins Gilman wrote so rhapsodically.

The passage of the Equal Pay Act of 1963 and Title VII of the 1964

Civil Rights Act opened this legal revolution. Then, in 1965, Executive Order 11246, as amended by Order 11375 two years later, outlawed discrimination by federal contractors and subcontractors on grounds of race, color, religion, national origin, and sex. The order is administered by the Office of Federal Contract Compliance (OFCC). Revised Order 4, issued by the secretary of labor in December 1971, outlines the kinds of programs necessary to alleviate discriminatory practices by federal contractors. The Department of Health, Education, and Welfare (HEW) administers the program in educational institutions. Any business or college or university that receives more than $50,000 a year in federal contracts must file an affirmative action program with HEW or OFCC. The executive orders also extend the prohibition against discrimination embodied in Title VII to the federal government. Enforcing this part of the orders is the responsibility of the Civil Service Commission, which designed the Federal Woman's Program to carry it out.

Nineteen seventy-two saw major advances all along the legislative front. The Equal Pay Act was expanded to cover professional and administrative employees for the first time. Title IX of the Educational Amendments Act forbade discrimination on the basis of sex in all federally assisted educational programs. In the area of admissions, the bill specifically applies to all public undergraduate institutions, all professional schools, all graduate schools, and all vocational schools, including vocational high schools. Private undergraduate institutions, religious institutions, and military schools are exempt. Whether or not they are exempt for admissions, the other provisions of the bill apply to all institutions when they admit students of both sexes. The act covers virtually all areas of student life and activities, including financial aid, athletics, housing, services provided to students, and parietal rules. The same year Title VII of the 1964 Civil Rights Act was extended to state and local government employers. The State and Local Fiscal Assistance Act, which instituted revenue sharing, prohibits recipients from discriminating in the use of those funds. Ironically, considering his stated views on women's issues, Richard Nixon's first administration is a landmark in the battle for sexual equality in employment.

The crucial issue, of course, is whether this impressive array of laws is enforced strictly. Here, women have been less than satisfied—and with good reason. Many responsible officials at the highest levels have stated openly that they are more concerned with the problems of racial minorities than of females. Criticism has been directed at the EEOC, at the OFCC, and at the way in which HEW has handled the major universities. On the positive side, both organized women's groups and individual females have been energetic and persistent in filing complaints with the designated enforcement agencies and the courts in order to maintain pressure on the government. In 1970, for instance, the Wage and Hour Division received complaints against 700 employers for wage discrimination. By late in the following year, it had awarded $36.5 million to 88,000 employees, mostly women. By 1971, formal charges of discrimination were brought against more than 300 colleges and universities, over 10 percent of the national total. [21] Seventy percent of the complaints received by the EEOC are about sex, not racial, discrimination. [22]

Despite all this legislation and activity, women have not achieved genuine equality in employment. The most obvious indication of this is the persistence of a wide earnings gap between men and women who work full-time. In 1973, the median income of white men was $11,633; of minority men, $8,363; of white women, $6,544; and of minority women, $5,772. [23] The median income of male high school graduates was $2,246 more than that of the female with four or more years of college. [24] On a national level, women's average earnings were 57 percent of men's, a lower ratio than prevailed in 1940. [25] The median income of women with four-year college degrees was 59 percent of that of men in the same category. [26] In 1973, of all jobs paying $15,000 or more per annum, 94 percent were held by white males, the remaining 6 percent being divided between minority men and all females. [27] Or, to put it another way, just over 1 percent of the women, compared to 17 percent of the men, earned more than $15,000 per annum. [28]

The salary gap exists in the professions as well as in the work force as a whole. In 1973 the median income of women in professional and technical jobs was 63.6 percent of men's in that category. The median income for men was $14,306; for women, $9,093. [29] Female scientists earned from $1,600 to $6,200 a year less than male scientists in 1973, the gap varying with age and from field to field. [30]

In academia in 1974-1975, the median salary for women was 77.8 percent of that earned by male faculty at universities and 85.7 percent at colleges, compared to 84.9 percent of male faculty salaries in all four-year institutions in 1959-60.[31] The Women's Bureau of the Department of Labor reported that business companies consistently offered women college graduates lower salaries than men, although the gap decreased from 1970 to 1971. In accounting, for example, the average monthly salary offered to males was $845 a month; to females, $793.[32] Men with M.B.A. degrees earned $1,000 to $3,500 a year more than women M.B.A.'s in 1968, 1969, and 1970.[33] In 1970, 38.3 percent of all male nonfarm managers and administrators earned $15,000 or more, while only 6.5 percent of the women in this category earned at that level. The median income of the female managers was $7,539; of the male, $13,629.[34] On Wall Street, women financial analysts earned an average of $17,500; men, $27,000.[35]

A survey of the professions and of managerial levels in business indicates that women still hold only a small percentage of all positions in these areas and tend to be concentrated in the lower levels of their fields.[36] They frequently suffer from wage discrimination. However, after declining throughout the 1930s, 1940s, and 1950s, the percentages of female professionals began to rise in the last decade. In 1971, females constituted 9 percent of the physical scientists, 7 percent of the physicians, 3 percent of the lawyers, 2 percent of the dentists, and 1 percent of the engineers and federal judges.[37] On the other hand, they were 27 percent of the mathematicians, 18 percent of the biological scientists, and 19 percent of the social scientists.[38] Between 1960 and 1970 the number of female engineers and accountants more than doubled.[39] Between 1974-5 and 1975-6 the percentage of women in college and university faculties decreased slightly, while the gap between the salaries of female and male professors widened.[40] In 1973 only 5 percent of employed women were classified as managers and administrators, and they earned only 52.8 percent of men's wages in that category.[41] The American Society for Personnel Administration and the Bureau of National Affairs surveyed 150 companies in 1970 and found that 39 percent had no women managers, 88 percent had less than 5 percent, and 93 percent had less than 10 percent.[42] While more than half of all small companies and 85 percent of larger ones recruit on college campuses, only 30 percent go to women's colleges. Even when they do, they rarely bring females into the key entry-level positions, which are the important first step in the managerial hierarchy. [43] Few companies include women in their training programs. The President's Commission on the Status of Women reported slightly over a decade ago that females received only 10 percent of the money available for on-the-job training although they constituted over 30 percent of the labor force. [44]

In a fascinating article that appeared in *Ms.* in June 1973, Lisa Wohl stated that the securities industry was a bastion of white male America and that the few women in top positions were tokens. By and large, the number of females in any job was in inverse ratio to the amount of client contact and financial reward. Ninety percent were in clerical or back-office positions, 5 percent in sales, and not quite 7 percent in management. [45] In Wohl's opinion even the small latter figure was inflated, because many of the jobs listed as management did not actually involve any genuine executive functions. For example, Bruce Cobden, the personnel director of the New York Stock Exchange (NYSE), reported that 60 of 600 managerial or official posts were held by women. On further questioning, however, he admitted that none of them supervised professional-level men. [46] Of the 55,000 registered brokers working for firms that belong to the NYSE, 5,000 were female. Many of these were secretaries who registered so that they could take orders when their bosses were out of the office. [47] Such female brokers as there were dealt with individual clients rather than the large institutions that yielded big commissions. The real tycoons of Wall Street were investment bankers or underwriters. Not one of the largest investment banking or underwriting firms had a female senior vice-president or full partner. In the last decade a handful of women have broken through what appeared to be insuperable barriers. Julia Walsh and Phyllis Peterson became the first female members of the American Stock Exchange in 1965; Muriel Sieber, of the NYSE in 1967. Merrill Lynch, the largest brokerage firm in the industry, picked its first woman vice-president in 1968. [48] Whether this indicates a permanent breach in the masculine world of Wall Street or is simply a form of tokenism that bespeaks little real change is something that only the future will tell.

In a survey of the banking industry in 1972, Nancy Giges wrote optimistically, "Fortunately for those women just beginning their careers, the atmosphere is apparently changing." The statistics that she supplied about the industry indicated that whatever the prognostication for the future, banking in 1972 was as male a world as Wall Street. In 1972 the National Association of Banking Women reported that 70 percent of the employees in banking were females, but only 10 percent were officers—and these at the most junior levels. Of the organization's 9,000 members, 12 were chairmen of the board; 2, vice-chairmen; 41, bank presidents; 1,700, vice-presidents; and 53, bank directors. [49] A more recent study of twenty-four large banks shows that women have made gains since 1971, although they are still concentrated in clerical and office jobs. Sixty-three percent of the workers in the banks surveyed were female; they filled 83 percent of the banks' office and clerical jobs. Only 2 percent of the senior officials were women at the eight institutions that supplied data on that particular point. On the other hand, in all twenty-four banks, 13 percent of all bank officers and 26 percent of all bank officials were female, compared to 6 percent and 16 percent, respectively, in 1971. [50]

What is most significant for the future is the increasing number of women in professional school. In 1960, 10.7 percent of the Ph.D.'s granted in this country went to women, a decline from 1920, when they earned 15.7 percent. The figure rose slowly throughout the 1960s, but did not reach the level of 1930 until 1972, when 16 percent of all doctorates were awarded to females. The figure is still rising, having reached 21.9 percent in 1975. [51] The influx of women into law schools has been the most dramatic change. By 1974 they constituted 16 percent of total enrollment. [52] The Comprehensive Health Manpower Act of 1971, prohibiting discrimination in all federally funded programs in the health fields, covers medical schools and schools of dentistry, pharmacy, veterinary medicine, optometry, and nursing. The greatest change has been in medical schools, where quotas were customary. Between 1964 and 1973 the number of female medical students increased 138.6 percent. Only 6.8 percent of the graduating class in 1965, they constituted 10.7 percent in 1974. In 1974 just under 20 percent of the total enrollment was female. [53] During the same year, they constituted 27.3 percent of the students in pharmacy school. [54] Although the numbers and percentages are still minute, there has been an increase in the number of female engineering students in the last few years, too. From 1968-69 to 1974-75 the number of women receiving bachelor's degrees in engineering rose from .82 percent to 2.3 percent. The comparable figures for master's degrees were .71 percent and 2.41 percent and for doctorates .68 percent and 1.74 percent. [55] In 1975 they comprised 6.9 percent of the full-time enrollment in undergraduate programs and 4.3 percent in graduate programs. [56] In 1968 over 600 women received M.B.A.'s, compared to only 167 in 1960. [57] In 1975-76, 20 to 35 percent of the enrollment in M.B.A. programs, depending on the school, was female. [58] These figures indicate that the next decade will see substantial increases in the number of women seeking positions in the professions and the higher reaches of business.

The persistence of inequality in the professions and managerial levels of business and the resistance to enforcement of legislation against discrimination are testimony to the strength of the social attitudes and patterns of behavior that caused the situation to develop in the first place. Despite the rebirth of feminism in the 1960s, an androgynous ideal has not displaced the long-standing belief that men's and women's biological differences create different talents and personalities in the two sexes and suit them for different economic and social roles. The doctrine of separate spheres is still with us. Consequently, many men in positions of authority still do not believe that women have an equal right to jobs or that they ought to be out of the home in the first place.

They also believe that women will cause extra problems as employees and therefore feel that they are acting rationally when they prefer to hire men. The two most common accusations are that women's absentee and job-turnover rates are much higher than men's. In *Women's Two Roles*, Myrdal and Klein stated that women were absent from work two or three times more than men and changed jobs more often. However, they noted that the rate of absenteeism declined as job responsibility increased, so one factor in this negative situation might be the concentration of females at the lower end of the employment ladder. According to Myrdal and Klein, many married women wanted part-time jobs; unable to find them, they converted full-time positions by taking time off. High job-turnover rates were due primarily to younger women who left employment when they married or had babies or when their husbands were transferred. Discrimination also discouraged females from taking their jobs seriously: they had little opportunity for advancement, received less pay than men in the same positions, and were the first fired in hard times. Finally, for deep-rooted historical and social reasons, women did not think in terms of careers and were therefore relatively indifferent to the seniority and chance of promotion that they might gain by staying in one job for a long time.[59]

A study of job turnover by the U.S. Civil Service Commission in the early 1960s showed that although the overall rates of turnover for women were significantly higher, there was little difference if females and males within the same grade were compared. The higher turnover rates for women were due to their concentration in the lower ranks of the civil service. The study concluded that the length of time in a job was much more closely correlated to rank, salary, and age than to sex. Indeed, the commission noted that the few women at the highest levels tended to remain in a position longer than equivalent men because they had less opportunity to move into better positions elsewhere.[60]

The major justification for paying women less than men is that they do not need the money since they are not supporting families; indeed, many come from dual-income homes. The argument has just enough truth to protect those who advance it from seeing themselves as the sexists that they really are. For one thing, if it were not totally disingenuous, employers would pay single men the same reduced rates as females, something which has never happened, to my knowledge. Much more important, the argument is totally false. In 1973, women headed 12 percent of the families in the United States, but accounted for 45 percent of those below the poverty line.[61] In 1974, 29 percent of the families with employed wives had incomes under $10,000.[62] In 1974, 14.4 percent of the women holding jobs were widowed or divorced, and 23.3 percent were single. Another 4.6 percent were married with absent husbands.[63] Finally, I question whether the use of need is relevant at all; my instinct is that it is raised only as an excuse to discriminate. When an employer hires a male, he offers him the going wage; he does not ask him if he needs it or can make do with less. It should be no different for women.

Such rationalizations for discrimination affect all working women. Committed professional women face an additional set of prejudices, most of which are rooted in social attitudes, as well as certain disadvantages that stem from their actual position in the labor force.[64] In general, career women have less bargaining power than comparable men and therefore can extract less favorable salaries and promotion opportunities from their employers. They have less mobility because they are likely to be tied to the place where their husbands work; they have less opportunity to move laterally into comparable jobs; and they are generally less secure in the positions that they hold. By and large, men take women's career aspirations less seriously than men's and equate female ambition and drive with unpleasant aggressiveness. Here again, traditional sexual stereotypes that derive ultimately from the cult of domesticity still condition male responses to females. Finally, professional women are victimized by the social attitudes and patterns of behavior that they themselves have internalized. They often lack confidence in their own abilities and therefore fail to push for advancement that a comparable male would consider his just due. Or, in some cases, they avoid success because they adhere to traditional definitions of femininity and interpret success as a threat to their gender identity.[65] Furthermore, the very patterns of behavior and response encouraged in women may be counterproductive in the professional and business world. That, in fact, is the thesis of Margaret Hennig and Anne Jardim's recent book, *The Managerial Woman*.[66] They argue that women entering the corporation are traveling into a foreign country created by men, one in which success depends on their ability to understand and adapt to male values, responses, and patterns of behavior. Their point can obviously be extended to practicing law or accountancy in a large firm or teaching in a large university— indeed, to any profession carried on in a bureaucratic setting. Finally, professional women often feel guilty and fragmented by their domestic and maternal responsibilities, even when they have adequate housekeeping and child-care arrangements. If they are unfortunate in the latter respects, they have the added burden, which few men ever face, of trying to excel at two or three jobs at once.[67] All in all, as Caroline Bird made abundantly clear in *Born Female*, only the rare professional woman advances as rapidly as a comparable man; all too many fall by the wayside or settle for positions far below their talents and training.

Many women are profoundly shocked when they encounter prejudice and resistance to antidiscrimination laws for the first time. Coming to grips with this reality is often a disillusioning experience for those who have always assumed that they would be judged on their merits. Instead of being crushed, however, professional women should realize that in pursuing careers they are not only seeking and achieving personal success, as important as that is. They are also participating in a magnificent struggle for sexual equality that began over 125 years ago at Seneca Falls. Females who face discrimination should take heart from the experiences of the heroic women who opened higher education, law, medicine, the ministry, and countless other opportunities to members of their sex. When they fight to use their talents and energies in their chosen fields, they are continuing along paths first marked out by these noble predecessors. Contemporary women owe a large debt to the "strong-minded" females of the nineteenth and early twentieth centuries. The debt should be repaid by continuing the crusade to build a society founded on sexual equality. This task is the professional woman's particular inheritance from history.

Notes

1. Quoted in Judith Hole and Ellen Levine, *The Rebirth of Feminism* (New York: Quadrangle Books, 1971), p. 18.
2. Ibid., p. 24.
3. U.S. Department of Labor, *1975 Handbook on Women Workers*, Bulletin 257 (Washington, D.C.: Government Printing Office, 1975), p. 289.
4. Caroline Bird, *Born Female*, rev. ed. (New York: Pocket Books, 1971), chap. 1.
5. Quoted in ibid., p. 13.
6. Hole and Levine, *Rebirth of Feminism*, p. ix.
7. Quoted in ibid., p. 85.
8. Ibid., p. 88.
9. Ibid., pp. ix-x.
10. Today, sociobiology, a new form of biological determinism, is functioning as the ideological counteroffensive to the androgynous social ideal advocated by feminism. In a recent article in *Daedalus*, Alice Rossi, a well-known feminist sociologist, accepts the basic tenets of sociobiology and tries to show that it is not incompatible with feminism, though it casts doubt on certain feminist assumptions, goals, and tactics. Her effort reminds me of Antoinette Blackwell's equally futile attempt to harmonize Darwinism with feminism in the late nineteenth century. See Rossi, "A Biosocial Perspective on Parenting," *Daedalus* 106 (Spring 1977): 1-32. On Blackwell, see pages 129-30 above.
11. Juliet Mitchell, *Psychoanalysis and Feminism* (New York: Pantheon,

1974). Mitchell does not advocate a return to Lundberg and Farnham or any use of Freudianism to defeat feminism. Her goal is to demonstrate that Freudian psychoanalytic theory is not inherently opposed to equality between the sexes. Ultimately, I think she fails.

12. Pat Mainardi, "The Politics of Housework," in *Sisterhood Is Powerful*, ed. Robin Morgan (New York: Vintage Books, 1970), pp. 447-54.

13. Simone de Beauvoir, *The Second Sex* (New York: Bantam Books, 1961), p. 639.

14. William Chafe, *The American Woman, Her Changing Social, Economic, and Political Roles; 1920-1970* (New York: Oxford University Press, 1972), pp. 221-24. It should be noted that *none* of these studies claims that working wives and husbands shared domestic and child-rearing tasks equally. They do show that there was more sharing than in homes in which the wife did not work.

15. Ibid., p. 223.

16. Betty Friedan, *The Feminine Mystique* (New York: Dell, 1963), chap. 14.

17. Beauvoir, *Second Sex*, pp. 639-41.

18. Valerie K. Oppenheimer, "A Sociologist's Skepticism," in *Corporate Lib: Women's Challenge to Management*, ed. Eli Ginzberg and Alice M. Yohalem (Baltimore: Johns Hopkins University Press, 1973), pp. 34-35. Jean Curtis, *A Guide for Working Mothers* (New York: Simon & Schuster, 1976).

19. Alva Myrdal and Viola Klein, *Women's Two Roles: Home and Work* (London: Routledge and Kegan Paul, 1956), p. 12.

20. *Spokewoman* 8 (October 15, 1977): 6.

21. Hole and Levine, *Rebirth of Feminism*, pp. 29, 47.

22. *Women as Economic Equals*, Proceedings of conference held at the Shoreham Hotel, Washington, D.C., March 21, 1973 (San Francisco, 1973), p. 62.

23. Department of Labor, *1975 Handbook on Women Workers*, p. 136.

24. Ibid., p. 134.

25. Ibid., p. 127.

26. Ibid., p. 134.

27. Gloria Steinem, "If We're So Smart, Why Aren't We Rich?" *Ms.*, June 1973, p. 126.

28. Department of Labor, *1975 Handbook on Women Workers*, p. 128.

29. Ibid., pp. 130, 135.

30. Betty M. Vetter, "Women in the Natural Sciences," *Signs* 1 (Spring 1976): 714.

31. Marion Kilson, "The Status of Women in Higher Education," *Signs* 1 (Summer 1976): 937, and note 14.

32. U.S. Department of Labor, Women's Bureau, *Fact Sheet on the Earnings Gap*, Publication no. 71-86 (Washington, D.C.: Government Printing Office, 1971), p. 6.

33. "Discrimination in the Professional Job Market," *MBA*, March 1971, p. 28.

34. Hilda Kahne, *Women in Management: Strategy for Increase* (Washington, D.C.: Business and Professional Women's Foundation, 1974), pp. 3-4.

35. Lisa Cronin Wohl, "What's So Rare as a Woman on Wall Street," *Ms.*, June 1973, p. 128.

36. Department of Labor, *1975 Handbook on Women Workers*, pp. 83-101.

37. "Discrimination in the Professional Job Market," p. 28. Rosalind Loring and Theodora Wells, *Breakthrough: Women into Management* (New York: Van Nostrand Reinhold, 1972), p. 29.

38. *Graduate and Professional Education of Women*, Proceedings of AAUW Conference, May 9-10, 1974 (Washington, D.C.: 1974), p. 87.

39. Department of Labor, *1975 Handbook on Women Workers*, p. 93.

40. *Spokeswoman* 7 (December 15, 1976): 5.

41. Phyllis A. Wallace, "Sex Discrimination: Some Societal Constraints on Upward Mobility for Women Executives," in *Corporate Lib*, ed. Ginzberg and Yohalem, p. 70.

42. Loring and Wells, *Breakthrough*, pp. 7-8.

43. "Discrimination in the Professional Job Market," p. 28.

44. *American Women: Report of the President's Commission on the status of Women* (Washington, D.C.: Government Printing Office, 1963), p. 30.

45. Wohl, "What's So Rare as a Woman on Wall Street," p. 83.

46. Ibid., p. 83.

47. Ibid., p. 84.

48. Ibid., p. 83.

49. Nancy Giges, "Bankwomen: The Atmosphere is Changing," *MBA*, 6 (March 1972), p. 5.

50. "Women Making Job Gains in Banking Industry," *Spokeswoman* 7 (January 15, 1977): 6-7.

51. Betty M. Vetter and Eleanor L. Babco, *Professional Women and Minorities* (Washington, D.C.: Scientific Manpower Commission, 1975), p. 52.

52. *Graduate and Professional Education of Women*, p. 38.

53. Ibid., p. 32.

54. Ibid., p. 86.

55. Vetter and Babco, *Professional Women nd Minorities*, p. 317.

56. Ibid., p. 318.

57. "Discrimination in the Professional Job Market," p. 29.

58. Helen Du Pont, "The MBA: Ticket to Where the Jobs Are?" *Women's Work* 2 (May-June 1976): 10.

59. Myrdal and Klein, *Women's Two Roles*, chap. 6.

60. *American Women: Report on the Status of Women*, p. 33.

61. Department of Labor, *1975 Handbook on Women Workers*, p. 141.

62. Ibid., p. 124.

63. Ibid., 17.

64. The best general studies of discrimination in business and the professions are Bird, *Born Female*, and Cynthia Fuchs Epstein, *Woman's Place: Options and Limits in Professional Careers* (Berkeley and Los Angeles: University of California Press, 1971).

65. Matina Horner, "Fail: Bright Women," *Psychology Today* 3 (November 1969): 36-38, 62. Juanita Kreps discounts this factor as important among the kind of women who seek to become executives; "The Source of Inequality," in *Corporate Lib*, ed. Ginzberg and Yohalem, p. 87.

66. Margaret Hennig and Anne Jardim, *The Managerial Woman* (Garden City N.Y.: Doubleday, 1977).

67. Many recent works discuss the professional and familial problems and conflicts faced by professional women who are also wives and mothers. The following are useful introductions to the subject: Margaret M. Polema, "Role Conflict and the Married Professional Woman," in *Toward a Sociology of Women*, ed. Constantia Safilos-Rothchild (Lexington, Mass.: Xerox College Publishing, 1972), pp. 187-98; Rhona Rapoport and Robert N. Rapoport, "The Dual-Career Family: A Variant Pattern and Social Change," in ibid., pp. 216-44; Athena Theodore, ed., *The Professional Woman* (Cambridge, Mass.: Schenkman Publishing Company, 1971), sec. 6; Alan Roland and Barbara J. Harris, *Career and Motherhood: Struggles for a New Identity* (New York: Human Sciences Press, 1978); Curtis, *Guide for Working Mothers;* Sara Ruddick and Pamela Daniels, eds., *Working It Out* (New York: Pantheon Books, 1977).

Bibliography

Abrams, Annie. "Women Traders in Medieval London." *Economic Journal* 26 (June 1916): 276-85.

Alaya, Flavia. "Victorian Science and the 'Genius' of Women." *Journal of the History of Ideas* 38 (April-June 1977): 261-80.

Alcott, Louisa May. *Little Women*. New York: Collier Books, 1962.

American Woman: Report of the President's Commission on the Status of Women. Washington, D.C.: Government Printing Office, 1963.

Ariès, Philippe. *Centuries of Childhood: A Social History of Family Life*. New York: Vintage Books, 1962.

Bainton, Roland H. *Women of the Reformation in France and England*. Boston: Beacon Press, 1973.

———. *Women of the Reformation in Germany and Italy*. Boston: Beacon Press, 1971.

Banks, J. A., and Banks, Olive. *Feminism and Family Planning in Victorian England*. New York: Schocken Books, 1964.

Beard, Mary R. *America Through Women's Eyes*. New York: Greenwood Press Reprint, 1969).

———. *Women as Force in History*. New York: Collier Books, 1962.

Beauvoir, Simone de. *The Second Sex*. New York: Bantam Books, 1961.

Benton, John F. "Clio and Venus: An Historical View of Medieval Love." In *The Meaning of Courtly Love*, edited by F. X. Newman, pp. 19-42. Albany: State University of New York Press, 1968.

Bernard, Richard M., and Vinovskis, Maria A. "The Female School Teacher in Ante-Bellum Massachusetts." *Journal of Social History* 10 (March 1977): 332-45.

Bird, Caroline. *Born Female: The High Cost of Keeping Women Down.* Rev. ed. New York: Pocket Books, 1971.

Blackwell, Elizabeth. *Opening the Medical Profession to Women.* New York: Schocken Books, 1977.

Blake, John B. "Women and Medicine in Ante-Bellum America." *Bulletin of the History of Medicine* 39 (March-April 1965): 99-123.

Bruni d'Arezzo, Leonardo. "De Studiis et Literis." In *Vittorino da Feltre and Other Humanist Educators,* edited by William Harrison Woodward. Classics in Education, no. 18. New York: Bureau of Publications, Teachers College, Columbia University, 1964.

Bunkle, Phillida. "Sentimental Womanhood and Domestic Education, 1830-1870." *History of Education Quarterly* 14 (Spring 1974): 13-30.

Castiglione, Baldesar. *The Book of the Courtier,* bk. 3. Garden City, N.Y.: Doubleday, 1959.

Chafe, William Henry. *The American Woman, Her Changing Social, Economic, and Political Roles, 1920-1970.* New York: Oxford University Press, 1972.

Chojnacki, Stanley. "Patrician Women in Early Renaissance Venice." *Studies in the Renaissance* 21 (1974): 176-203.

Clark, Alice. *Working Life of Women in the Seventeenth Century.* New York: Augustus M. Kelley, 1968.

Conable, Charlotte Williams. *Women at Cornell: The Myth of Equal Education.* Ithaca, N.Y.: Cornell University Press, 1977.

Conway, Jill K. "Perspectives on the History of Women's Education in the United States." *History of Education Quarterly* 14 (Spring 1974): 1-12.

———. "Stereotypes of Femininity in a Theory of Sexual Evolution." In *Suffer and Be Still: Women in the Victorian Age,* edited by Martha Vicinus, pp. 140-54. Bloomington: Indiana University Press, 1973.

———. "Women Reformers and American Culture, 1870-1930." In *Our American Sisters: Women in American Life and Thought,* 2d ed., edited by Jean E. Friedman and William G. Shade pp. 301-12. Boston: Allyn and Bacon, 1976.

Cott, Nancy F. *The Bonds of Womanhood: "Woman's Sphere" in New England, 1780-1835.* New Haven: Yale University Press, 1977.

———, ed. *Root of Bitterness: Documents of the Social History of American Women.* New York: E. P. Dutton, 1972.

Curtis, Jean. *A Guide for Working Mothers.* New York: Simon & Schuster, 1976.

Davis, Natalie Zemon. "City Women and Religious Change." In *Society and Culture in Early Modern France*, pp. 65-95. Stanford, Calif.: Stanford University Press, 1975.

————. "Ghosts, Kin, and Progeny: Some Features of Family Life in Early Modern France." *Daedalus* 106 (Spring 1977): 87-114.

Degler, Carl N. "What Ought to Be and What Was: Women's Sexuality in the Nineteenth Century." *American Historical Review* 79 (December 1974): 1467-90.

Demos, John. "The American Family in Past Time." *American Scholar* 43 (Summer 1974): 422-46.

————. *A Little Commonwealth: Family Life in Plymouth Colony.* New York: Oxford University Press, 1970.

Dexter, Elisabeth A. *Career Women of America, 1776-1840.* Francestown, N.H.: Marshall Jones Company, 1950.

————. *Colonial Women of Affairs: Women in Business and Professions in America Before 1776.* 2d. ed., rev. Clifton, N.J.: Augustus Kelley Publishers, 1972.

Douglas, Ann. *The Feminization of American Culture.* New York: Alfred A. Knopf, 1977.

Edwards, Lee R. and Diamond, Arlyn. *American Voices, American Women.* New York: Avon Books, 1973.

Epstein, Cynthia Fuchs. *Woman's Place: Options and Limits in Professional Careers.* Berkeley and Los Angeles: University of California Press, 1971.

Erickson, Carolly. *The Medieval Vision*, chap. 8, "The Vision of Women." New York: Oxford University Press, 1976.

Fee, Elizabeth, "Science and the Woman Problem: Historical Perspectives." In *Sex Differences: Social and Biological Perspectives*, edited by Michael S. Teitelbaum pp. 175-223. Garden City, N.Y.: Doubleday, 1976.

Ferrante, Joan. *Woman As Image in Medieval Literature, from the Twelfth Century to Dante.* New York: Columbia University Press, 1975.

Finch, Edith. *Carey Thomas of Bryn Mawr.* New York: Harper & Brothers, 1947.

Flexner, Eleanor. *Century of Struggle: The Woman's Rights Movement in the United States* New York: Atheneum, 1971.

Friedan, Betty. *The Feminine Mystique.* New York: Dell, 1963.

Friedman, Jean E., and Shade, William G. *Our American Sisters: Women in American Life and Thought.* 2d rev. ed. Boston: Allyn and Bacon, 1976.

Garrison, Dee. "The Tender Technicians: The Feminization of Public Librarianship, 1876-1905. In *Clio's Consciousness Raised*, edited by Mary S. Hartman and Lois Banner, pp. 158-78 (New York: Harper Torchbook, 1974).

George, Margaret, "From 'Goodwife' to 'Mistress': The Transformation of the Female in Bourgeois Culture." *Science and Society* 37 (Summer 1973): 152-77.

Ginzberg, Eli, and Yohalem, Alice M., eds. *Corporate Lib: Women's Challenge to Management*. Baltimore: Johns Hopkins University Press, 1973.

Goldthwaite, Richard. "The Florentine Palace as Domestic Architecture." *American Historical Review* 77 (October 1972): 977-1012.

Gordon, Linda. *Woman's Body, Woman's Right: A Social History of Birth Control in America*. New York: Grossman Publishers, 1976.

Gordon, Michael. "From an Unfortunate Necessity to a Cult of Mutual Orgasm: Sex in American Marital Education Literature, 1830-1940." In *Studies in the Sociology of Sex*, edited by James M. Henslin pp. 53-77. New York: Appleton-Century-Crofts, 1971.

Goulianos, Joan, ed. *By a Woman Writt: Literature from Six Centuries by and about Women*. Baltimore: Penguin Books, 1974.

Graham, Patricia Albjerg. "Women in Academe." In *The Professional Woman*, edited by Athena Theodore, pp. 720-40. (Cambridge, Mass.: Schenkman Publishing Company, 1971).

Haller, John, and Haller, Robin. *The Physician and Sexuality in Victorian America*. Urbana: University of Illinois Press, 1974.

Haller, William. "Hail Wedded Love." *ELH: A Journal of English Literary History* 13 (1946): 79-97.

Haller, William, and Haller, Malleville. "The Puritan Art of Love." *Huntingdon Library Quarterly* 5 (January 1942): 235-72.

Harris, Barbara J. "Recent Work on the History of the Family: A Review Article." *Feminist Studies* 3 (Spring-Summer 1976): 159-72.

Hartman, Mary, and Banner, Lois. *Clio's Consciousness Raised*. New York: Harper Torchbook, 1974.

Hennig, Margaret, and Jardim, Anne. *The Managerial Woman*. (Garden City, N.Y.: Doubleday, 1977).

Herlihy, David. "Women in Medieval Society." *Smith History Lecture*. Houston: University of St. Thomas, 1971.

Hill, Christopher. "Clarissa Harlowe and Her Times." In *Puritanism and Revolution*, chap. 14. London: Mercury Books, 1962.

Hole, Judith, and Levine, Ellen. *The Rebirth of Feminism*. New York: Quadrangle Books, 1971.

Horowitz, Maryanne Cline. "Aristotle and Women." *Journal of the History of Biology* 9 (Fall 1976): 183-213.

Houghton, Walter. *The Victorian Frame of Mind*, chap. 13. New Haven: Yale University Press, 1957.

Hughes, Diane. "Domestic Ideals and Social Behavior: Evidence from Medieval Genoa." In *The Family in History*, edited by Charles E. Rosenberg, pp. 115-43. Philadelphia: University of Pennsylvania Press, 1975.

Hunt, David. *Parents and Children in History: The Psychology of Family Life in Early Modern France*. New York: Harper Torchbooks, 1972.

Hunt, Harriot. *Glances and Glimpses*. New York: Sourcebook Press, 1970.

James, Edward T., ed. *Notable American Women, 1607-1950*. 3 vols. Cambridge, Mass.: Belknap Press, Harvard University Press, 1971.

Johnson, James. "The Covenant Idea and the Puritan View of Marriage." *Journal of the History of Ideas* 32 (January-March 1971): 107-18.

Kelly-Gadol, Joan. "Did Women Have a Renaissance?" In *Becoming Visible*, edited by Renate Bridenthal and Claudia Koonz, pp. 137-64. Boston: Houghton Mifflin, 1977.

Kerber, Linda K. "Daughters of Columbia: Educating Women for the Republic, 1787-1805." In *Our American Sisters: Women in American Life and Thought*, 2d ed., edited by Jean E. Friedman and William G. Shade, pp. 76-92. Boston: Allyn and Bacon, 1976.

―――. "The Republican Mother: Women and the Enlightenment—An American Perspective." *American Quarterly* 28 (Summer 1976): 187-205.

Kraditor, Aileen S. *The Ideas of the Woman Suffrage Movement, 1890-1920*. Garden City, N.Y.: Doubleday, 1971.

―――. *Up from the Pedestal*. Chicago: Quadrangle Books, 1968.

Lasch, Christopher, and Taylor, William R. "Two Kindred Spirits: Sorority and Family in New England, 1839-1848." *New England Quarterly* 36 (March 1963): 23-41.

Laslett, Peter. *The World We Have Lost*. New York: Charles Scribner's Sons, 1965.

Lerner, Gerda. *The Female Experience: An American Documentary*. Indianapolis: Bobbs-Merrill, 1977.

―――. *The Grimké Sisters from South Carolina*. New York: Schocken Books, 1971.

―――. "The Lady and the Mill Girl: Changes in the Status of Women in the Age of Jackson." In *Our American Sisters: Women in American Life and Thought*, 2d ed., edited by Jean E. Friedman and William G. Shade, pp. 120-32. Boston: Allyn and Bacon, 1976.

Lifton, Robert Jay, ed. *The Woman in America*. Boston: Beacon Press, 1965.

Lopate, Carol. *Women in Medicine*. Baltimore: Johns Hopkins University Press, 1968.

Lougee, Carolyn C. *Le Paradis des Femmes: Women, Salons, and Social Stratification in Seventeenth-Century France*. Princeton, N.J.: Princeton University Press, 1976.

————. "Modern European History." *Signs* 2 (Spring 1977): 628-50.

Lumpkin, Katharine Du Pre. *The Emancipation of Angelina Grimké*. Chapel Hill: University of North Carolina Press, 1974.

Macfarlane, Alan. *The Family Life of Ralph Josselin, a Seventeenth Century Clergyman*. Cambridge: Cambridge University Press, 1970.

McIntosh, Glenda Riley. *The Origins of the Feminist Movement in America*. Forums in History. St. Charles, Mo.: Forum Press, 1973.

McNamara, JoAnn, and Wemple, Suzanne F. "Sanctity and Power: The Dual Pursuit of Medieval Women." In *Becoming Visible*, edited by Renate Bridenthal and Claudia Koonz, pp. 90-118. Boston: Houghton Mifflin, 1977.

Martines, Lauro. "A Way of Looking at Women in Renaissance Florence." *Journal of Medieval and Renaissance Studies* 4 (Spring 1974): 15-28.

Massey, Mary Elizabeth. *Bonnet Brigades*. New York: Alfred A. Knopf, 1966.

Melder, Keith. *Beginnings of Sisterhood: The American Woman's Rights Movement 1800-1850*. New York: Schocken, 1977.

————. "Ladies Bountiful: Organized Women's Benevolence in Early Nineteenth-Century America." *New York History* 48 (July 1967): 231-54.

————. "Mask of Oppression: The Female Seminary Movement in the United States." *New York History* 55 (July 1974): 260-79.

Meyer, Annie Nathan, ed. *Woman's Work in America*. New York: Henry Holt and Co., 1891.

Moller, Herbert. "The Social Causation of the Courtly Love Complex." *Comparative Studies in Society and History* 1 (1958-1959): 137-63.

Monter, E. William. "The Pedestal and Stake: Courtly Love and Witchcraft." In *Becoming Visible*, edited by Renate Bridenthal and Claudia Koonz, pp. 119-36. Boston: Houghton Mifflin, 1977.

Morgan, Edmund S. *The Puritan Family: Religion and Domestic Relations in Seventeenth-Century New England*. New York: Harper & Row, 1966.

————. "The Puritans and Sex." In *American Family in Social-Historical Perspective*, edited by Michael Gordon, pp. 282-95. New York: St. Martin's Press, 1973.

Myrdal, Alva, and Klein, Viola. *Women's Two Roles: Home and Work*. London: Routledge and Kegan Paul, 1956.

Newcomer, Mabel. *A Century of Higher Education for American Women*. New York: Harper & Brothers, 1959.

Norton, Mary Beth. "Eighteenth-Century American Women in Peace and War: The Case of the Loyalists." *William and Mary Quarterly* 33 (July 1976): 386-409.

Notestein, Wallace. "The English Woman, 1580-1650." In *Studies in Social*

History, edited by J. H. Plumb, pp. 77-107. New York: Longmans, Green & Co., 1955.

O'Neill, William L. "Feminism As a Radical Ideology." In *Dissent: Explorations in the History of American Radicalism*, edited by Alfred F. Young, pp. 275-300. DeKalb: Northern Illinois University Press, 1968.

————. *The Woman Movement: Feminism in the United States and England*. Chicago: Quadrangle Books, 1971.

Parker, Gail, ed. *The Oven Birds: American Women on Womanhood, 1820-1920*. Garden City, N.Y.: Doubleday, 1972.

Pedersen, Joyce Senders. "Schoolmistresses and Headmistresses: Elitist Education in Nineteenth-Century England." *Journal of British Studies* 15 (Autumn 1975): 135-62.

Powell, Chilton Latham. *English Domestic Relations*. New York: Russell & Russell, 1962.

Power, Eileen. *Medieval Women*, edited by M. M. Postan. Cambridge: Cambridge University Press, 1975.

————. "The Position of Women." In *The Legacy of the Middle Ages*, edited by C. G. Crump and E. F. Jacob, pp. 401-33. Oxford: Clarendon Press, 1926.

Putnam, Emily James. *The Lady*. New York: G. P. Putnam's Sons, 1910.

Reed, James. *From Private Vice to Public Virtue: The Birth Control Movement and American Society Since 1830*. New York: Basic Books, 1978.

Robinson, Paul. *The Modernization of Sex: Havelock Ellis, Alfred Kinsey, William Masters and Virginia Johnson*. New York: Harper & Row, 1976.

Rogers, Katherine M. *The Troublesome Helpmate: A History of Misogyny in Literature*. Seattle: University of Washington Press, 1966.

Rosenberg, Charles E. "Sexuality, Class and Role in Nineteenth-Century America." *American Quarterly* 25 (May 1973): 131-53.

Rosenberg, Rosalind. "In Search of Woman's Nature, 1850-1920." *Feminist Studies* 3 (Fall 1975): 141-54.

Ross, James Bruce. "The Middle-Class Child in Urban Italy, Fourteenth to Early Sixteenth Century." In *The History of Childhood*, edited by Lloyd de Mause, pp. 183-228. New York: Harper Torchbooks, 1974.

Rossi, Alice, ed. *The Feminist Papers: From Adams to de Beauvoir*. New York: Bantam Books, 1974.

Rossiter, Margaret W. "Women Scientists in America Before 1920." *American Scientist* 62 (May-June 1974): 312-23.

Rousmaniere, J. "Cultural Hybrid in the Slums: The College Woman and the Settlement House, 1889-94." *American Quarterly* 22 (Spring 1970): 45-66.

Ruddick, Sara, and Daniels, Pamela, eds. *Working It Out*. New York: Pantheon Books, 1977.

Ryan, Mary P. *Womanhood in America, From Colonial Times to the Present*. New York: New Viewpoints, 1975.

Safilios-Rothchild, Constantina. *Toward a Sociology of Women*. Lexington, Mass.: Xerox College Publishing Co., 1972.

Schücking, Levin L. *The Puritan Family*. New York: Schocken Books, 1970.

Scott, Joan W., and Tilly, Louise A. "Women's Work and the Family in Nineteenth-Century Europe." In *The Family in History*, edited by Charles E. Rosenberg, pp. 145-78. Philadelphia: University of Pennsylvania Press, 1975.

Shaw, Anna Howard. *The Story of a Pioneer*. New York: Harper & Brothers, 1915.

Shorter, Edward. "Illegitimacy, Sexual Revolution and Social Change in Modern Europe." In *American Family in Social-Historical Perspective*, edited by Michael Gordon, pp. 296-320. New York: St. Martin's Press, 1973.

Shryock, Richard Harrison. "Women in American Medicine." In *Medicine in America: Historical Essays*, pp. 177-99. Baltimore: Johns Hopkins University Press, 1966.

Simmons, Adele. "Education and Ideology in Nineteenth-Century America: The Response of Educational Institutions to the Changing Role of Women." In *Liberating Women's History: Theoretical and Critical Essays*, edited by Bernice A. Carroll, pp. 115-26. Urbana: University of Illinois Press, 1976.

Sinclair, Andrew. *The Emancipation of the American Woman*. New York: Harper Colophon Books, 1965.

Sklar, Kathryn Kish. *Catharine Beecher: A Study in American Domesticity*. New Haven: Yale University Press, 1973.

Smith, Daniel Scott. "Family Limitation, Sexual Control, and Domestic Feminism in Victorian America." In *Clio's Consciousness Raised*, edited by Mary S. Hartman and Lois Banner, pp. 119-36. New York: Harper Torchbooks, 1974.

Smith, Daniel Scott, and Hindus, Michael S. "Premarital Pregnancy in America, 1640-1971: An Overview and Interpretation." *Journal of Interdisciplinary History* 5 (Spring 1975): 537-70.

Smith-Rosenberg, Carroll. "Beauty, the Beast and the Militant Woman: A Case Study in Sex Roles and Social Stress in Jacksonian America." *American Quarterly* 23 (October 1971): 562-84.

———. "The Female World of Love and Ritual: Relations Between Women in Nineteenth-Century America," *Signs* 1 (Autumn 1975): 1-30.

Smuts, Robert W. *Women and Work in America*. New York: Schocken Books, 1971.

Southern, R. W. *Western Society and the Church in the Middle Ages*. Baltimore: Penguin Books, 1970, pp. 309-31.

Spruill, Julia. *Women's Life and Work in the Southern Colonies*. New York: W. W. Norton, 1972.

Stanton, Elizabeth. *Eighty Years and More, Reminiscences 1815-1897*. New York: Schocken Books, 1971.

Stone, Lawrence. "The Rise of the Nuclear Family in Early Modern England: The Patriarchal Stage." In *The Family in History*, edited by Charles E. Rosenberg, pp. 13-57. Philadelphia: University of Pennsylvania Press, 1975.

Stricker, Frank. "Cookbooks and Law Books: The Hidden History of Career Women in Twentieth Century America." *Journal of Social History* 10 (Fall 1976): 1-19.

Stuard, Susan Mosher, ed. *Women in Medieval Society*. Philadelphia: University of Pennsylvania Press, 1976.

Theodore, Athena, ed. *The Professional Woman*. Cambridge, Mass.: Schenkman Publishing Company, 1971.

Thomas, Keith. "The Double Standard." *Journal of the History of Ideas* 20 (April 1959): 195-216.

Thompson, Roger. *Women in Stuart England and America: A Comparative Study*. Boston: Routledge and Kegan Paul, 1974.

Tilly, Louise A.; Scott, Joan W.; and Cohen, Miriam. "Women's Work and European Fertility Patterns." *Journal of Interdisciplinary History* 6 (Winter 1976): 447-76.

Trecker, Janice. "Sex, Science and Education." *American Quarterly* 26 (October 1974): 352-66.

Ulrich, Laurel Thatcher. "Vertuous Women Found: New England Ministerial Literature, 1668-1735," *American Quarterly* 28 (Spring 1976): 20-40.

Vicinus, Martha, ed. *Suffer and Be Still: Women in the Victorian Age*. Bloomington: University of Indiana Press, 1973.

Walsh, Mary Roth. *"Doctors Wanted: No Women Need Apply"*: *Sexual Barriers in the Medical Profession, 1835-1975*. New Haven: Yale University Press, 1977.

Walzer, Michael. *The Revolution of the Saints*. Cambridge, Mass.: Harvard University Press, 1965, pp. 183-98.

Watt, Ian. *Rise of the Novel*, chap. 5. Berkeley and Los Angeles: University of California Press, 1957.

Wein, Roberta. "Women's Colleges and Domesticity, 1875-1918." *History of*

Education Quarterly 14 (Spring 1974): 31-47.

Welter, Barbara. *Dimity Convictions: The American Woman in the Nineteenth Century.* Athens: Ohio University Press, 1976.

Wilson, Joan Hoff. "The Illusion of Change: Women and the American Revolution." In *The American Revolution: Explorations in the History of American Radicalism*, edited by Alfred F. Young, pp. 385-445. DeKalb: Northern Illinois University Press, 1976.

Winchester, Barbara. *Tudor Family Portrait.* London: Jonathan Cape, 1955.

Wyntjes, Sherrin Marshall. "Women in the Reformation Era." In *Becoming Visible*, edited by Renate Bridenthal and Claudia Koonz, pp. 165-91. Boston: Houghton Mifflin, 1977.

Index

About the Author

Barbara J. Harris, professor of history at Pace University in New York City, has had articles published in *American Journal of Legal History*, *Feminist Studies*, and R. H. Hilton's *Peasants, Knights, and Heretics*. She is currently working on a book about career and motherhood.